Appreciation for Sonny Burgess and the Pacers

The Pacers were good showmen who played damn good dance music with a lot of movement on stage. They left it all on the bandstand and on the dance floor with acrobatics as they played. Few groups could back that up musically.
—Roland Janes

Sonny Burgess and the Legendary Pacers are true pioneers in history of rock and roll. As one of the earliest members of the Sun Studio roster, they defined what would become rock and roll. They didn't just open the door to the future of popular music, they kicked it in.
—**Charlie Rich Jr.**, musician and son of Charlie Rich

When Sonny Burgess skipped across the stage, everyone rocked. They played some of that great old time rock and roll. Sonny Burgess was one of the best rock and roll entertainers in the South in all the '50s.
—Ronnie Hawkins

Sonny Burgess was one of my favorites, always willing to try to do something different. I loved working with him.
—Jack Clement

Sonny Burgess gives me chills every time I hear him. He is a person that deserves much more than I could give him. A distinctive voice.
—Sam Phillips

Sonny Burgess is a warrior. He's been at it for years and is still going strong.
—Travis Wammack

From the first time I heard the Pacers until today, they have had that driving beat I like so well of all the bands I've heard play. Their shows are absolutely amazing, have always been and still are today.
—W. S. Holland

My dad always said Sonny Burgess had the best band that recorded at Sun.
—**Stan Perkins**, musician and son of Carl Perkins

T0308803

The Pacers are precious icons representing the whole state of Arkansas.

—**Mike Looney**, *The Big Shootout* film producer

Sonny Burgess is a national treasure.

—**Dan Griffin**, music producer

No one represents rockabilly more than Sonny Burgess and the Pacers. They had a sound that no one else was bringing out of Memphis. It knocked everybody out of their seats.

—**Hayden Thompson**

Sonny Burgess is the working man's rock and roller. He gets up there and gets the job done. The most amazing thing about Sonny is that after more than sixty years of entertaining, he still has fun at every show, and his sense of fun is felt by and reflected back from every audience. He is one of the best entertainers I know.

—**Scotty Moore**

Sonny Burgess is one of the originals and his heart is still in it. He's the real thing. Sonny and the Pacers have stood the test of time.

—**Sleepy LaBeef**

We Wanna Boogie

Also by Marvin Schwartz

History:

Racing Starts: A History of Swimming in Central Arkansas

Central in Our Lives: Voices from Little Rock Central High School, 1957–1959 (with Ralph Brodie)

Learning from the Land: How the YEA Program is Developing a New Generation of Rural Leaders

People of the Land: A History of Arkansas Land and Farm Development Corporation

J. B. Hunt: The Long Haul to Success

Tyson: From Farm to Market

In Service to America: A History of VISTA in Arkansas

Poetry:

Passages

Poems for a Temporal Body

We Wanna Boogie
The Rockabilly Roots of
Sonny Burgess and the Pacers

Marvin Schwartz

BUTLER
CENTER
BOOKS

The Butler Center for Arkansas Studies
Central Arkansas Library System
200 Rock Street
Little Rock, Arkansas 72201
www.butlercenter.org

First edition: September 2014

ISBN 978-1-935106-71-5 (hardcover)
ISBN 978-1-935106-75-3 (paperback)

Copyeditor: Ali Welky
Design: H. K. Stewart
Front cover color photo: Taken by Mike Keckhaver at the Sonny Burgess
    and the Legendary Pacers show for Arkansas Sounds at the CALS
    Ron Robinson Theater in Little Rock, Arkansas; June 20, 2014.

Library of Congress Cataloging-in-Publication Data

Schwartz, Marvin, 1948-
We wanna boogie : the rockabilly roots of Sonny Burgess and the Pacers / Marvin
Schwartz. -- First edition.
    pages cm.
Includes bibliographical references and index.
ISBN 978-1-935106-71-5 (hardcover : alk. paper) -- ISBN 978-1-935106-75-3 (pbk.
: alk. paper)
1. Rockabilly music--Arkansas--Newport--History and criticism. 2. Burgess, Sonny.
3. Pacers (Musical group) 4. Rockabilly musicians--Arkansas. 5. Newport (Ark.)--
Social life and customs. I. Title.

ML3535S39 2014
791.6--dc23
                            2014021311

The publishing division of the Butler Center for Arkansas
Studies was made possible by the generosity of Dora Johnson
Ragsdale and John G. Ragsdale Jr.

Printed in the United States of America

This book is printed on archival-quality paper that meets requirements of
the American National Standard for Information Sciences, Permanence of
Paper, Printed Library Materials, ANSI Z39.48-1984.

Table of Contents

The original Pacers; 1956.

Foreword

The development of rockabilly in northeast Arkansas holds a special place in my heart, as I was coming of age there at the same time the music was. *We Wanna Boogie* shows just how interwoven the histories of Newport and rockabilly music truly are. It tells the history of individuals and a community during the emergence of a new genre of music in the late 1950s and early 1960s. It is captivating to read, even for someone like me who was there to witness it firsthand.

The spectrum of musical talent that came through northeast Arkansas is still difficult to fully fathom. You had larger-than-life personalities like Elvis and Jerry Lee Lewis. You had Al Bruno, who moved to Newport so he could play guitar with Conway Twitty and went on to have a legendary musical career. And then you had Sonny Burgess and the Pacers. They took the sound they helped craft—and have continued to use to capture the spirit of the time—to generation after generation, decade after decade.

It you want to feel what it was like back then in northeast Arkansas, the following is a must-read. It was a time that saw the creation of rockabilly and the infancy of rock and roll. And as someone who was lucky enough to live in Newport then, I got to see much of it happen before my own eyes.

Governor Mike Beebe
April 2014

Introduction
by Sonny Burgess

Newport was the best place in the world to grow up. It's still a great place to live.

I grew up on a farm five miles out of Newport in the Anderson community and farmed and thought it would be my life, too. But along the way, I discovered music, thanks to my uncles—Theodore Cheshire, Paul Davis, and Leib Davis. I had found a new world.

We listened to the *Grand Ole Opry* show on Saturday night. The radio station here played country music mostly. Once in a while we got WDIA out of Memphis or WLAC from Nashville late at night. So when I started my first band, we were the Drifting Cowboys, named after Hank Williams' band. Then Gerald Jackson, me, Bobby Stoner, and Johnny Ray Hubbard became the Rocky Road Ramblers. We were doing all country. But even back then we liked the fast country music. That was my soul. We jazzed them up. Everybody did that back then.

We'd practice out at the airbase when Newport was in a boom period. All those air force people lived out there. We had a theater on the base, and for us it was like performing at the Grand Ole Opry. No money, just get up and play. Isn't that strange? The money didn't matter. You just wanted someone to listen to you.

It was a different atmosphere for me. I didn't smoke or drink, but I loved the music.

About that same time, we had a little thirty-minute radio show at KNBY in Newport. Fred Waner was with us then. He could really sing and play. When I came back from the army in 1953, Fred had gone to California (changing his name to Freddie Hart), where he became a star. He was just as good when he was with us back then as when he had all his hits. How he got to Newport I don't know, but something here attracted him.

My family used to come to Newport once a week on Saturday, and Front Street was filled with people and all kinds of excitement. We had three theaters, three drugstores, three men's stores, two 5 & 10 cent stores (Sterling and Ben Franklin), hotels, grocery stores, barbershops, restaurants, and hamburger places. The railroad depot had a restaurant then that always had action.

Newport always had all kinds of music. I remember a lot of them that folks never heard of: the Swift Jewel Cowboys and the Slim Rhodes family band from Memphis, the Gene Ridgeway band, Jimmy Davidson's band. I remember the Wilburn Brothers out on Front Street playing for tips.[1] Later on, they were on the *Grand Ole Opry* show, but back then they were just kids. And all kinds of bands played at KNBY on Saturdays.

I was not much aware of the night clubs in Jackson County until I came back from the army in 1953. I believe my first visit to the Silver Moon was with Johnny Ray Hubbard, my sister Ann, T. J. Hembry, and a girl who was kin to George Langston, who owned it at that time. Ann and Johnny were super-good dancers. People came to see them dance. I couldn't dance then and still can't.

We never had any trouble or bad times at the Moon. It was great. When you played there you reached the top. I don't remember a dress code, but maybe there was one. Them gamblers in the back of the Moon, that was their business. That's how come they hired the big bands coming through. And with all the people coming out to see the bands, it gave them a crowd to cover the gamblers. No wonder those guys don't remember that stuff like a dress code.

We played the Oasis and the Wagon Wheel at Bald Knob, at Porky's Rooftop and Jarvis' in Newport, and the B&I and Mike's in Swifton. We played a lot at the Cotton Club in Trumann and across the street at the C&R Club, where a lot of college kids came out to drink and party. There were a lot of DWIs. It never had the chicken wire around the stage. The Texas clubs had that. But the college kids liked to fight. There was more than one a night.

Jackson County has always been good for music. All kinds of people came down the Rock 'n' Roll Highway 67—bands like Bob Wills and His Texas Playboys, Ernest Tubb, Louis Armstrong, and Fats Domino. Along the way, I've been privileged to meet and play with a ton of stars and wanna-be stars: Carl Perkins, Elvis, Jerry Lee, Ronnie Hawkins and the Hawks, Billy Riley, Travis Wammack, and the Rock and Roll Trio. It goes on and on. Northeast Arkansas was full of great musicians. And it didn't cost an arm or leg to see those stars on Highway 67; anywhere from $1 to $5. Thanks to Sam Phillips and his Sun Records, I'm able to keep playing to this day.

Newport changed like every small town in the U.S. People changed. I remember that Jacksonport flourished and then faltered as Newport came along. Now it's Jonesboro and some other towns that seem to be on the rise. Maybe if we had a college long before we did, it would have really helped us grow.

Jackson County has got lots of good stories from a lot of people that are still here. And there's my good friend Charlie Watson who's doing a lot to keep the history of Newport music alive in the new Silver Moon Club at Tupelo, Mississippi. I'm proud to be part of this history. Thanks to the Legendary Pacers and some other musicians still trying to play, it's still fun.

Sonny Burgess
March 2014

Chapter 1.
Midnight at the Moon

On a Saturday night in the dead of winter, 1955, the air rising from Arkansas' White River was damp and cold. Halfway through the 720-mile journey from its headwaters in the Ozark Mountains to its confluence with the Mississippi, the meandering river left the hill country and formed a wide bend as it entered the flatlands of the Arkansas Delta.

Newport's Front Street was dark at that hour. Through the day, its movie theaters and mercantile stores were bustling with local shoppers and country folk in town for their weekly purchases. Now, only scraps of paper blew in the mist along deserted sidewalks. Beyond the downtown railroad depot and the levee, the water washed over the sunken hulls of steamboats and paddle wheelers, eroding remnants of a bygone age lost to time and the river.

In the surrounding countryside of Jackson County, skeletal cotton stalks had been picked clean by tenant farmers and their children. To those who did not own the land, the rich Delta soil offered a sparse and exhausting life. But 1955 had brought a decent harvest. It had been a year when a man might pay off some debt, perhaps gain enough credit to buy a tractor to till his rented acres and yield a greater return.

Times were improving, and the lure of factory jobs in northern states had diminished. Farm homes were now connected to newly strung rural electrical lines. A single 40-watt bulb hanging from a ceiling cord in the family room cast a dull white-yellow glow. In small frame houses surrounded by darkness, country folk sat close to their wood stoves and fireplaces, listening to their radios for the weekend broadcast of the *Grand Ole Opry* show live from the Ryman Auditorium in Nashville, Tennessee.

At the Newport Country Club, ice cubes clinked in the cocktails of civic leaders and manufacturers who toasted their town's prosperity. From its origins less than a hundred years earlier, the frontier roadway and primitive river crossing had blossomed to a model of civic progress. In earlier days, natural resources—timber, cotton, freshwater pearls, and mussel shell buttons—had brought enormous wealth to a few fortunate families. In 1955, the *Newport Daily Independent* touted the city's rapid industrial growth. Hundreds of paychecks were cut each week at Victor Metal Company, the world's largest producer of aluminum toothpaste tubes, and at Southern Compress, one of the largest cotton gins in Arkansas. Newport now boasted seventeen churches and 250 stores. Even a new $160,000 elementary school for the town's African-American children was under construction.

On tree-lined streets in middle-class homes, Newport's white children had brushed their teeth and were snug in their beds, immersed in the deep waters of sleep. Their parents settled into their dens. Perhaps next summer, they might drive across country to the new amusement park Walt Disney had opened in California. The radio played Bing Crosby and Patti Page. It was December 24, Christmas Eve. Presents were wrapped and placed beneath the living room tree. All was still, all was quiet.

At the Silver Moon, which was the most popular of Jackson County's numerous honkytonks and bars, Francis "Fats" Callis poured himself a drink from the fifth of whiskey in the paper sack on his table. Over six feet tall and weighing more than 200 pounds, he settled his thick muscular body into his seat. He was feeling good that Christmas Eve. Several men came by and slapped him on the shoulder, poured him more drinks from their bottles.

Fats was nineteen when he joined the U.S. Navy during World War II. Now, he was a thirty-year-old chief petty officer stationed at the Millington Naval Air Station at Memphis. His home was in Batesville, a town thirty miles north of Newport on the White River. But alcohol sales had been denounced by Batesville church elders and prohibited by city fathers. The churches of Newport had not achieved that righteous restraint. Despite the entreaties of preachers and deacons, despite the rumors of depravity and death, of bodies buried in the fields behind the Silver Moon and other riotous dens of sex and gambling, Newport was wet.

The Silver Moon was the largest club in Arkansas at the time, capable of seating more than 800 people. Louis Armstrong, Bob Wills, and the Dorsey brothers had performed there, as had Sun Records stars such as Carl Perkins, Roy Orbison, and Johnny Cash. Elvis Presley had already played at the Silver Moon twice that year. With his sandy brown hair not yet dyed black, the twenty-year-old's live shows were just beginning to create pandemonium among screaming teenaged girls.

Fats and hundreds of others from dry, parochial counties across the Arkansas Delta came to Jackson County for their drink and dalliance. And their money was welcome in the profusion of clubs along Highway 67, in area juke joints from southernmost Possum Grape to Newport and Tuckerman, and to northernmost Swifton where dry Lawrence County returned a traveler to a world of temperance and decorum.

That Saturday night at the Silver Moon, Fats knocked back another drink. The whiskey worked steady and slow, adding to his sense of invulnerable power and dominance. He was a judo instructor in the navy and was the toughest man in town. His friends jokingly called him "Tiny" and "Pee Wee." He had never been whipped.

Fats' exploits were common talk in Newport bars. One story told of his cousin Jabbo smashing a beer bottle on the back of Fats' head and Fats slowly turning to say, "You'd better go sit down before you get me mad." Another told of his mother in Batesville warning the local police when he was due home on leave. Still another recounted his rage in a local club when he threw chairs, tables, and the bouncer into the front yard.

Fats came often to the Silver Moon. On some Sundays, owner Don Washam gave him the keys to the closed bar. Fats and his friends drank and listened to the jukebox. They left their money on the counter and locked up when they were through.

Now it was nearly midnight, and his pals were on stage. The Moonlighters were the Silver Moon's house band and Newport's most popular group, with local favorite Sonny Burgess on vocals and lead guitar. Soon to be renamed the Pacers, the band had recently auditioned in Memphis, but Sun Records owner Sam Phillips sent them home to create new material and hone a unique sound. Now Sonny knew he had it.

As always, the Moonlighters had the Silver Moon crowd on its feet and dancing. Johnny Ray Hubbard, clown prince of the band, had jumped from the stage with his double bass and was dancing with it among the crowd. Sonny, angular and lean, played his red electric guitar, leading the group in "We Wanna Boogie," the song he wrote that would soon gain the band national exposure.

Well I jumped in my flivver, took my baby to town
We wouldn't do nothing, just cattin' around
Just cattin' and a-boogyin' all over town

Headin' down Front Street baby, and all over town
Man you oughta see the lights when the sun goes down
Just a-poundin' and a-boogyin' and a-paintin' that town

Went out to the dance hall and cut a little rug
Oh we're runnin' like wildfire and hittin' that jug
Just a-poundin' and a-boogyin' all over town

Yeah we're gonna pound and we're gonna boogie
Yeah we're gonna pound and we're gonna boogie
Just a-poundin' and a-boogyin' all over town

The huge dance area of the Silver Moon was thick with cigarette smoke and shouting voices. Kern Kennedy was pumping out a raucous boogie woogie on the piano. The musicians were wild in their stage antics, climbing onto Hubbard's bass to form a human pyramid. They did the bug dance, a routine they had learned when Roy Orbison's band played at the Silver Moon earlier that year. Now, one of them reached down to the stage floor to pick up an imaginary cockroach and throw it on another musician, who squirmed and wriggled until he threw it onto someone else.

Amidst the clamor, Fats looked on with interest as two men began a confrontation at a nearby table. Fats saw his brother Tommy poke his fingers into the other man's chest. Chairs were pushed back. A small crowd had gathered.

When the music came to a crashing end, the dancers cheered and clapped. No one was ready to leave. And as many hoped, a fight was brewing, a brawling spectacle of fists and red faces, with inflated pride and swaggering men soon to be bruised and bleeding.

And now midnight had passed, and Washam let the party continue. That Christmas morning, the spirit of goodwill and drunken fun was just too rich to end. Local ordinances and Sunday blue laws, Washam knew, could be stretched a bit on a holiday night like this.

Fats rose and walked slowly to the table where Tommy and the other man continued their confrontation. He brushed people aside and faced the drunkard who challenged his brother. A quick thrust of Fats' arms and the man went stumbling backward, knocking over a chair as he fell.

Ben Lindsey, a Jackson County deputy sheriff who worked as the Silver Moon's bouncer, quickly stepped in. "Stay out of this, Fats," he warned.

Fats laughed and pressed on toward the fallen man, who scuttled away without fully rising to his feet. Fats laughed again, and he and Tommy had another drink. The band started an encore tune, and the dancers in front of the stage clapped and whistled in delight. The men drank more. By one o'clock, Fats had tossed to the ground a few more men who attempted a weak interruption of his evening's fun. He was getting drunk. Lindsey kept a cautious distance.

At the Silver Moon that cold Christmas morning, as men will do when the spirit moves them, when perfumed women laugh and lean close in dimly lit rooms, the men flexed their muscles and loudly stated their views. Fats told again the story of how he once fought another sailor for three days, and how they ended up shaking hands on the deck of their ship. The men at his table poured him more drinks.

"Fats was tougher than a nickel steak," Hubbard said. "He liked to party like the rest of us, but he liked to fight, too. He was stout as a bull and had a short neck. He could pull his shoulders up so that all you could see was his eyes and the top of his head."

More than fifty years later, Hubbard dabbed at his eyes as he recalled Fats and the disastrous events of that Christmas long ago. "Fats was a sweet guy, but he was meaner than a skunk when drunk. When the sheriff came up, I begged Fats to go with him to jail."

Jackson County Sheriff Jake Winningham, fifty-seven years old and near the end of a long career in law enforcement, arrived at the Silver Moon about two o'clock that morning. Lindsey had already told Fats he was under arrest. Winningham repeated the order and told Fats he was going to jail. Fats refused to submit.

"I ain't going to your dirty old jail," Fats told them. "I'll come by there tomorrow and we'll settle out."

Winningham could not let Fats deny his authority, and the confrontation had to be resolved. But like everyone at the Silver Moon that night, he knew that Fats was not someone you laid hands on.

Doyle "Doc" Hawk, a dealer at the Silver Moon gambling tables, knew that Winningham had tried to force Fats' cooperation earlier that year. The encounter was at Porky's Rooftop, a Newport club with a lower-class clientele and a more raucous atmosphere than the Silver Moon's.

"Months before the shooting, Fats threw Jake over a fence at Porky's and broke his finger," Doc said. "They called the State Police and put Fats in jail. The next day, Jake told him, 'You're not going to treat me like this again.' Fats cried like a baby. He was a different man when he was sober. Then he quit drinking for several months. But when he came back to the Silver Moon, all the guys would buy him drinks. He'd get stinking drunk and chase the club constable around."

Fats was also well known by John Harkey, a prosecuting attorney for Jackson County in the 1960s, and in 2007 the circuit judge for a five-county region of central Arkansas. A Batesville native, Harkey recalled his early days drinking and fist fighting at Newport clubs. He remembered how Fats put his beer on the inside of the door at the Silver Moon, waiting for the bottle to be knocked over by people entering. Fats then challenged them to fight or a buy him a new beer, Harkey said.

"My stepfather Burton Arnold Jr. was the Batesville sheriff in 1949," Harkey said. "He once told Fats, 'Don't start any problems in this county. One of us will get hurt, and it won't be me.'"

With a long career in the judicial system, Harkey also knew Winningham and the history of the Newport sheriff's encounters with Fats.

"Jake Winningham was a good man, but he was scared of Fats," Harkey said. "A scared man will kill you faster than a brave man."

Now the encounter and its crowd of onlookers had moved outside the Silver Moon. Fats spurned the officers and strutted around the gravel parking area. He went to Washam's house next door, but it was locked and all lights were off. Fats came back to the Silver Moon, defying the officers to stop him. The club doors were locked, and all external lights on the building were dark. The headlights of the police car cast a stark glare on the crowd.

"Get in the car, Fats," Winningham repeated, his breath forming ghost vapors in the air, his face shadowed by the white headlamps.

Fats ignored him and pushed his way through the surrounding crowd. He went to his parked car and looked for something in the glove compartment. He strode back toward the sheriff, shouting, "I'll kill everybody that tries to take me to jail!"

Fats had no need of a gun. But Winningham had no alternative as the big man stepped toward him. Winningham pulled his pistol from its belt holster and shot from the hip. The sound of the gunshot exploded in the blackness of the night. The bullet struck Fats "squarely between the eyes," reported the *Newport Daily Independent*. He recoiled from the impact and staggered, then stood upright and still. The crowd stared in shocked silence.

Fats fell forward, landing on his face in the gravel. Blood poured out through the hole in his brow. He pushed up, trying to stand, but kept falling back to the gravel. An ambulance was called, and Fats was taken to a Newport hospital. He died at five o'clock Christmas morning, the bullet still in his cranium.

A coroner's jury was convened the next day, "attended by a capacity crowd of witnesses, naval officials, peace officers, and curious spectators," according to the *Newport Daily Independent*. The county newspaper, the *Jackson County Democrat*, reported that "Prosecuting Attorney W. J. Arnold directed the examination of the witnesses in the presence of attorney Fred M. Pickens, who had been employed by Sheriff Winningham. Former Circuit Judge S. M. Bone sat in at the hearing at the request of the veteran's mother."

The *Tuckerman Record*, "Jackson County's Family Newspaper," also reported on the shooting and the investigation, which included testimony from more than a dozen witnesses. The jury returned a unanimous verdict of justifiable self defense, clearing Winningham of any wrongdoing. Funeral services with a military burial were held on Wednesday. "Callis is survived," the paper stated, "by his wife Virginia, his mother, Mrs. Robbie Callis, and one brother Tommy, all of Batesville."

In the days and years that followed, the story of Fats Callis was often retold at the Silver Moon and elsewhere. As men paused in reflection on quiet afternoons and sought insight in the depths of their whiskey glasses, as vinyl discs spinning inside jukeboxes sang out mournful honky-tonk ballads of longing and loss, Fats' life became the stuff of legend. He was frozen in his power and drunken pride, forever tossing chairs and tables through doors, forever tearing up bar fixtures from the floor, like Samson carrying off the gates of Gaza.

One man's death became a harbinger of what was to follow. Newport in the 1950s was for many a place and time of excess and brash self-assertion, with adolescent pleasure unwilling to restrain its wild indulgence. In the end, order had to prevail.

But who could know that time was turning for Newport? Even as it ascended in its last heyday of power and privilege, Newport's decade would pass. Farms would fail and communities fade, factories would close and populations depart, and a ruined agricultural economy would incessantly creep west across the flatlands until it reached and consumed Newport as it had other Delta communities on both sides of the big muddy river. Today, the empty store fronts along once-thriving Front Street bear hollow witness to that long decline.

But in the ceaseless movement of the river, there is no stopping point. Lives dissolve in the mist, and truth turns to legend, eventually sinking below the flowing waters. The remnants persist. Flint spear points of early hunters rise through the earth of plowed cotton fields.

Rusted iron boiler plates of nineteenth-century paddle wheelers wash up on muddy banks from the darkness of the river channel.

And memories survive only as long as those who share them. In Newport today, a few white-haired men still retell the old tales of their fallen hero, the Arkansas sailor Fats Callis.

Francis "Fats" Callis (1925–1955), U.S. Navy Petty Officer 3rd Class. The winged insignia on his shoulder identifies him as an aircraft machinist's mate. In 1944, his first year of military service, a nineteen-year old Callis was aboard the USS Honolulu *when the light cruiser was torpedoed and seventy of his shipmates were killed.*

Chapter 2.
High-Water Marks

The rails are washed out north of town
We gotta head for higher ground
We can't come back till the water comes down,
It's five feet high and risin'.
                    —Johnny Cash, "Five Feet High and Rising"

On the western edge of Jackson County, the White and Black Rivers converge, forming the main channel that flows past Newport. Here, surface eddies hide the deeper current of the widening river, and the navigable channel is bordered by sandy shoals and shallow wetlands. Here, as well, the river is more prone to flooding than in the upstream hills. For a river must now and again overflow its banks, or it becomes predictable and tame, drained of its vitality and spark, no more than an irrigation channel, no longer a living force of nature. And similar to the people who live along its banks, whose history is defined as much by truth as by legend, as much by fact as by self-promotion, the river must be allowed its breadth and scope, its inherent need for expansion.

In the winter of 1958, the White River rose eleven feet in one night. Local historian Elizabeth Luker, whose Newport newspaper articles frequently portray the river as symbolic of Delta life, speculated on the submerged landscape and the tenacity of the few objects rooted deeply enough to persevere.

> Looking at the river from the bridge, notice if the loading tracks of the Mobley Construction Company are under water, if only the big trees on the opposite bank are showing…an old barn just across the

bridge, with advertisement on its side *Jefferson Island Salt*…sometimes surrounded by muddy flow, an island in the eddies.

—"The River, the Town, the Well-Beloved,"
Newport Daily Independent, December 5, 1958

Arkansas troubadour Johnny Cash sang of a more personal experience in "Five Feet High and Rising," recounting the flooded fields and homes of his childhood at Dyess, where sharecropper families with little to lose clung to a fundamental belief of overcoming adversity if their faith endured.

The river floods and recedes, changing the land in its passing. As the muddy water dries, the land is renewed as rich, black dirt settles on the fields. In the next cycle of planting and harvest, the cotton grows thicker. Additional dollars received at the local gin strengthen a family's hope for better times.

In the residue of the flood, high-water marks define the excess—how far the water spread, how fast the river was moving, what was washed away. But high-water marks are not limited to the river. In Newport and Jackson County, they were found along the streets and highways, the high-water marks of roadhouses and juke joints where music was played, where people danced and drank, where gamblers in backroom dice games shouted their desires and threw dollars on a table.

As the White River rose and fell with the seasons, numerous roadhouses and clubs in Jackson County evidenced a deluge of celebration. And it was in those clubs, and most prominently at the Silver Moon, that a portrait can be drawn of an Arkansas Delta river town at midcentury. The story of Newport can be told on the stage of its clubs. And standing center stage with his shining red electric guitar is Sonny Burgess, his rural heritage rooted deep in the American heartland, his athletic grace and musical talent products of the fertile land and the flowing river.

In the passion of Sonny's songs and the spirited antics of the Pacers' stage shows, two stories of Newport can be told. One details the history of a distinctive Delta town, the remarkable events that occurred there, and a regional heritage that continues to influence the nation. The other story is an American musical journey featuring a showcase of talented performers and an irresistible new artistic genre. "We Wanna Boogie" is the anthem of a town and its music. Sonny Burgess is at the heart of both tales, his life and achievements shaped by the larger forces of history.

All this occurred in the brief setting that was Newport in the 1950s. While other towns in the Arkansas Delta were failing and people were moving away, Newport celebrated its good fortune. Its displays of power and privilege were similar to Hot Springs' in the 1920s, when that central Arkansas resort town was favored by gamblers and gangsters from New York and Chicago. But unlike Hot Springs, where Al Capone and Babe Ruth took their baths, Newport offered no natural springs of hot water to restore the corporeal frames of the debauched and indulgent. When the celebrations ended, the river town provided no such cleansing baptism to purify the soul or a compromised liver, and Newport's gamblers and entertainers took their pleasures elsewhere.

Newport's high-water marks, its clandestine betting rooms and boisterous night clubs, have become the detritus of bygone days. The clubs have shut down, becoming abandoned sites along the rural highway. Weeds have reclaimed gravel parking lots littered with broken bottles and trash. Fires are common. Newport's original Silver Moon burned in 1987. A 2010 fire destroyed the King of Clubs at Swifton, the last of the area's storied roadhouses.

Fires and floods establish archetypal patterns, a mythos and landscape with pilgrims who follow the historical routes. In recent years, the pilgrims have been Asian tourists searching for Elvis, such as Japan's prime minister Junichiro Koizumi who visited Graceland in 2006 as a guest of President George W. Bush. Flying in on Air Force One, the heads of state were served grilled peanut-butter-and-banana sandwiches and watched in-flight Elvis movies. At the Memphis shrine, Koizumi donned gold-rimmed glasses and sang a few Elvis songs for the press. He hugged Lisa Marie and Priscilla Presley and told them the visit was his "dream come true." His departure gift from Bush was a jukebox loaded with Elvis hits.

Other Asian visitors, having exhausted their urban journey in Memphis and Graceland, seek out the rural sites where Elvis once performed. Their destination in Newport is an open lot along Highway 67. Here they find a concrete foundation where the Silver Moon once stood and a rubble-filled ditch into which the remains of the burned club were bulldozed. Climbing on the debris, the pilgrims seek a shred of carpet among the stones, some strand of memory of the place where the King once danced and sang.

Sonny, with a lifetime in the entertainment industry, understands the adoration of the devotees. His dry country humor is balanced by the stoic realism of the lowland sharecropper.

"One of these days, Elvis really is going to die," Sonny said.

Lessons from the River

Elvis Presley first performed in Newport on March 2, 1955. He played two shows that evening—one at the Newport Armory and one at Porky's Rooftop.

Porky's was a small drive-in restaurant on Highway 67. A stairway in the rear of the building led to an upstairs venue that held a few tables and chairs. Newport musician Jug Wallace remembered it as a "spartan place, not very big." He added, "If you got a hundred people there, you had a crowd." Sonny said Porky's attracted a different class of people than the Silver Moon. "At Porky's," Sonny said, "there was a fight every thirty minutes."

Presley had released his debut single "That's All Right" just months earlier, and it was gaining immense national attention. The nineteen-year-old rising star was still a sandy-haired newcomer who had only recently been driving a truck in Memphis. Sonny was on hand for the second show. Today, he stills finds it amusing that stories told about the evening differ from what he witnessed.

"People tell the story of Elvis at Porky's, that he was at the piano and knocked over his beer bottle, and that he lapped it up with his tongue," Sonny said. "At that time, Elvis didn't drink."

The lines between memory and imagination are blurred by time. Elizabeth Luker suggested that only the river can provide understanding of the American microcosm that is Newport, Arkansas.

"It is the thread that ties us all together, the past, the present, and the future. Our children and grandchildren will stand in its banks and dream—the story of the river is the story of this country."[2]

Look to the river for answers, Luker proposes. Look as well to Newport's bygone juke joints and roadhouses upon whose stages the story of the town was performed.

Phyllis Holmes, a member of a prominent Newport merchant family, suggested the character of Newport at this time could be revealed by comparing the townspeople's bank statements to those of residents of Batesville, the prosperous upriver hill town and Newport rival since the pioneer era.

"The difference between hill and bottoms people is that they save their money and we spend," Holmes said. "We get paid Saturday morning and it's gone by Saturday night."

Front Street today faces the railroad tracks, with rows of empty storefronts and open lots of brick and rubble. Some of the old structures show the residue of past fires and floods. Boom times and bust: these extremes form repeated patterns in Newport's history. Did a series of bad choices by city leaders, of options not taken over time, produce these dire consequences? Is the history of Newport more than gambling, bootlegging, prostitution, and rock and roll?

Yet it was once a vibrant world, reflective of the American character and enterprise. For Newport, the 1950s was a time when all was achievable; all was youthful and energetic. When you came in from the land thirsty for the cold slide of beer into your gullet, the cool wave of air conditioning dried the damp collar of your shirt. And the new music was in the air. Sonny and the boys were at the Silver Moon. And the people were drinking it in and dancing.

The Music

Chapter 3.
Ramblers and
Moonlighters

Sonny Burgess:
Son of the Delta, 1929 to 1955

He came from "The Sand," a local name for the Anderson community, five miles out of Newport, where the Black River loam was ideal for family farming. Grandfather Chock Burgess owned enough land to establish his son Albert and his son's wife Esta with a small farm of their own. They had a Ford tractor. They grew melons, peanuts, soybeans, and cotton. Their children swam in the river bottoms.

The Burgesses had weathered the fires and floods of the 1920s. Like other rural families, their survival and prosperity were based in the hard work that the small farms demanded. Never far from the Black and White Rivers that shaped their lives, the Burgesses were part of the larger Delta landscape, a confluence of water and music.

Sonny Burgess was born Albert Austin Burgess on May 31, 1929, but the family called him "Son."[3] His uncles played harmonica and fiddle at country dances. Sonny accompanied them on his Gene Autry flat-top guitar, bought for $3.25 from the Sears Roebuck Company. Before electric lines reached their home, the family listened to a battery-powered radio, enjoying the *Grand Ole Opry* show and country music shows from Memphis and KNBY in Newport. The family also went to traveling shows that played the rural circuit of farm communities. The act of Curly Fox and Texas Ruby was the first "name act" Sonny recalled seeing.

Albert Burgess and a six-year-old Sonny ride to church on a Sunday morning; 1935.

Texas Ruby was a husky-voiced, radio cowgirl who had a popular stage and recording career. Her husband Curly Fox was a skilled showman on the fiddle and one of country music's top performers at the time.

"They came to the Anderson School before they had microphones, just got up there with flat-top guitars and sang," Sonny said. "That was some great sounds."

The scene of the Burgess family and other country folk attending the show offers a moment in time from a bygone rural life. In the crowded school as folks waited for the show, one would see barefoot children in bib overalls and cotton dresses sitting on the wooden floor between the front bench seats and the stage, sharing bottles of Coca-Cola. Their mothers are the young farm women sitting behind them in calico and print dresses. The men are standing to the sides, smoking cigarettes. Outside in the summer night, mules and wagons stand among the cars and farm trucks parked under the trees.

Another Grand Ole Opry star would more directly inspire Sonny's later stage act with the Pacers. William Toliver Carlisle, better known as "Jumpin' Bill," would become a Country Music Hall of Fame singer, songwriter, and guitarist—the same triple skills Sonny would develop.

"Bill Carlisle and his brother Cliff on fiddle came to Jim Grubbs' little theater alongside the grocery store. It had a dirt floor," Sonny said.

"Sunshine Slim Sweet was the singer. They all came from Nashville. I thought it was greatest thing I ever heard. Bill jumped off that little stage and said, 'Ooh, this dirt feels good between my toes.' Later on, he became a big star."

Carlisle's clowning and high-energy leaps on stage had audiences screaming with delight in those early shows. Years later, Sonny would describe the Pacers' stage choreography thusly: "It's a three-ring circus. We just go wild."

Baseball and Farming

A 1948 graduate of Newport High School, Sonny had grown into a lean, broad-shouldered young man with an athletic build. Baseball was his game. He was an infielder, playing shortstop or third base, all quickness and reflex, skillful enough to be offered an athletic scholarship to Louisiana State University.

"I didn't have the sense to take it," Sonny said. "I thought I didn't need to go to college just to sit out there on that farm the rest of my life. My folks weren't upset. I had gotten out of high school. None of them had done that."

Sonny had choices unavailable to most of his peers. Because the Burgess family owned land, he could continue to work on the farm. But teenaged years picking cotton had already soured him on that lifestyle. Or he could play baseball on one of the minor league teams common in the Delta towns. He was already making a little weekend money playing ball at Tuckerman. Baseball was the most popular sport of the era, and Sunday games drew large crowds and big bets among affluent farmers.

The Newport Dodgers, a Class D minor league affiliate of the Brooklyn Dodgers, sent several players to the major leagues during Sonny's youth. Professional ball players who played in Newport included Pete Reiser, who played for Brooklyn and held the National League batting title in 1941; Danny Gardella, who played for the Detroit Tigers; and Chuck Connors, who played for the Dodgers in Newport in 1949 and later gained fame as star of the television show *The Rifleman*.

The Jackson County town of Swifton produced several major league players and coaches. Two of them—Bobby Winkles and Everett

Lee "Skeeter" Kell—were the same age as Sonny, and the boys competed through their school and town teams. Skeeter's older brother George, who would be inducted into the Baseball Hall of Fame in 1983, was already a star player for the Detroit Tigers, narrowly beating out Ted Williams for the American League batting title in 1949.

Sonny Burgess and manager Johnny Brown in spring training with the Orlando Senators; 1950.

Sonny signed with a farm team of the Washington Senators and spent the 1950 season in Orlando, Florida. He could hit the fast, straight pitches, but the curve balls got past him. By the end of spring training, he was back in Newport working alongside his high school friends at a local factory.

"Between baseball, farming, and music, I gave up baseball and farming," Sonny said, adding, "We were all a bunch of country guys out of a little area in the South. Most all of us picked cotton. One day picking cotton really makes you want to play music."

Rocky Road Ramblers

His first band was called the Drifting Cowboys, named after Hank Williams' group, but it was soon changed to the Rocky Road Ramblers, a name created from "Rocky Road Blues," a Bill Monroe song they performed. The band included Johnny Ray Hubbard on bass, Gerald Jackson on guitar, A. L. Wilson on pedal steel guitar, and Bob Stoner on vocals. Stoner worked at a Newport department store, and he got them discounts on their band outfits: bow ties, large belt buckles, and western shirts.

As a teenager in the Rocky Road Ramblers, Sonny made more money and had more fun than most guys his age. He sometimes played just for the exposure of standing up before the hometown folks at the Newport airbase movie theater. When the band did get paid, it was rarely enough. Their first show was at the school gym in Cord, twenty-five miles north of Newport. Total payment for the five-member band was $2.50. They also had to cross the Black River at Elgin and pay the ferryman fifty cents each way.

"A quarter apiece was what we was making," Sonny recalled, laughing.

The most memorable event of the evening came when Hubbard drove them home in the rain. The wet tires could not keep the car from slipping. Hubbard, easily excited, screamed, "We're going in the river!" and jumped out of the moving car. Sonny said the driver-less car and its four remaining passengers were saved from veering into the river only by some wire fencing.

The band once played for the Mexican farm workers housed on the Hubbard farm. These were braceros, trucked-in workers who picked cotton. The workers gave the band ten dollars for the music. When the boys later bragged to Mr. Hubbard about it, they were surprised when he showed compassion for the farm workers. They were more surprised when he made them return the money, saying the cotton pickers couldn't afford to spend that much.

The first band, the Drifting Cowboys: Bob Stoner (left), Gerald Jackson (center), and Sonny Burgess (right); 1949.

In 1949, the young men had a popular early morning radio show on Newport's KNBY. They played country music, mostly songs heard on the *Grand Ole Opry* show. Afterward, they went to work at an airbase factory making wooden ammunition boxes and Pepsi crates. For recent high school graduates, a factory job paying seventy-five to ninety cents an hour was fortunate. Almost all employment in the area was low-paying farm work. On Saturdays, the KNBY lobby filled with friends who watched through the interior studio windows. A period photo shows Newport teenagers lined up outside the radio station doors. In the photo, Porky's Rooftop Drive In—where adult musicians such as Ernest Tubb and Bob Wills performed to weekend crowds—is visible across an open field.

The Ramblers also played in rural schools and churches. As new electric lines were strung across the landscape, the Rural Electric Administration (REA) and Jackson County's Farmers Electric Cooperative hired local musicians for the community meetings where rural families were introduced to the new power system.[4] In a period Gerald Jackson called "an industrial revolution for rural Arkansas," traveling salesmen came to rural areas, pitching lifestyle-changing electric appliances such as washing machines, refrigerators, lamps, and pumps for home water systems. The music heard over the radios was also changing.

"Growing up, all we got on the radio stations was country music, so that was really the big influence," Sonny said. "We got into R&B a little later when we were playing dances and started looking for stuff to play. There was a good supply of R&B records at the KNBY record library. Big Joe Turner was one of my favorites. Jimmy Reed was another black artist I liked."

The Rocky Road Ramblers: (from left) Sonny Burgess, Charles Middlestat, Bob Armstrong, Gerald Jackson, and Jay Armstrong; 1954.

Freddie Waner, Freddie Hart

The band's radio show introduced them to future country music star Freddie Hart, whom the Ramblers backed up at several shows. In Newport in 1949, he called himself "Freddie Waner, the Georgia Balladeer," but he was actually from Alabama, born as Frederick Segrest, one of fifteen children of sharecropper parents. Sonny remembered Waner showing papers that documented his release from prison. As a twenty-three-year-old musician, he was trying to build a new life. Each radio show, he dedicated a song for a young Newport woman, Wilma Posey, whom he married.

Newport teenagers line up for a Saturday morning music show at KNBY, 1955.

Waner moved to California when Sonny was in the army. The next time Sonny heard him sing was five years later. He was now Freddie Hart, appearing on *Town Hall Party*, a country music radio show (and later a live television program) from Pasadena, California. As a cast member with Tex Ritter, Merle Travis, and others, Hart went on to great success as a songwriter and performer, earning several number-one ratings in the 1970s and awards over a lifetime career.

In 1949, Waner's singing gave Sonny and the Ramblers a talent advantage. The Ramblers, at this time including Forest Miller on violin and Bob Armstrong on accordion, were selected to play in a Hadacol show at the Strand Theater that featured Arkansans Wayne Raney and Lonnie Glosson. The Ramblers played the "Hadacol Boogie," and they wore shirts that promoted the popular patent medicine (which had a twelve percent alcohol content).

Sonny was a teenager when the Silver Moon was established in the 1940s. He saw national artists such as Bob Wills and Hank Snow perform there. Ernest Tubb's Texas Troubadour band was a favorite, and Sonny was impressed by the guitar skills of band members Jerry Byrd and Tommy "Butterball" Paige. He also took note of Tubb's interaction with the audience.

"He was the best I'd ever seen about mingling with the crowd," Sonny recalled. "Tubb would get off that stage and go around and shake hands, make people feel they was an old time buddy. I learned how to treat your fans good and they'll come back to you."

Sonny had frequent opportunities to learn from popular musicians. At the Silver Moon, he watched crowds dance to big bands such as the Dorsey Brothers and the Glenn Miller Orchestra. In downtown Newport, he saw country music stars the Delmore Brothers and Wayne Raney, whom the newspaper called a "hillbilly singer," perform at the opening of the Heard Music Store. And he had seen Arkansans his age form successful local groups, dance bands such as the Townsmen and country bands such as Glynn Hipp and his Sunny Slope Boys.

Hipp's band also played on KNBY six days a week. The popular group featured the talented Scroggins brothers—Hal on fiddle and Johnny on bass. The teenaged twins came from a farm in Cleveland, Arkansas, but with their parents' approval, they rented rooms and attended high school in Newport. Johnny, who continues to live in central Arkansas, recalled that he and his brother made more money from their part-time music work than their father did farming. Like Sonny, he remembered the KNBY lobby crowded with Newport teenagers who gathered to listen to the band's live radio shows.[5]

Glynn Hipp and the Sunny Slope Boys were among the numerous bands that performed at Newport radio station KNBY. (From left: Hal Scroggins, Johnny Scroggins, Hipp, Jerry Stevens, and W.T. Bittle); 1950.

Sonny's development as a professional musician was interrupted when he was drafted into the U.S. Army in 1951. Scoring high on aptitude tests, he was sent to Military Counterintelligence School in Maryland. Even in the service, Sonny's fate steered him toward music. He was assigned duty in the military police at a base in Germany, where he met other aspiring musicians, mostly Texans. They formed a country music band and were chosen to entertain American troops at Frankfurt at a military version of the Grand Ole Opry.

"It was a country club set-up," Sonny said.[5] "They had a stage and the whole big deal. They picked eight bands out of everybody in Europe to be on this every Saturday night. Well, we were one of the bands. We had a guy who looked like Hawkshaw Hawkins singing for us and I just played guitar for 'em."[6]

In Germany, Sonny formed a country band and performed in the army's version of the Grand Ole Opry at Frankfurt; 1951.

Show Business Wages

Back in Newport in 1953, Sonny again found work at the "box factory," one of the last remaining businesses from the region's timber boom. He regrouped the Ramblers and arranged for weekend shows at local clubs. The group had regular gigs in Swifton—Friday nights at Bob King's B & I Club and Saturday nights at Mike Hulen's 67 Club. As always, show business wages were far better than factory pay.

"On Fridays and Saturdays, we played at Bob's and at Mike's for $10 each," Sonny recalled. "That was $20 a week we'd pick up playing music, plus a lot of fun. I was working for $45 a week at the box factory. You take $5 out of that for the government, which left me $40. I was making half as much money for two nights."

About this time, Sonny paid $225 for his first electric guitar, a 1952 Fender Telecaster, bought on credit at Heard Music Store, and he took over as the group's lead singer. Gerald Jackson also bought a new guitar, an electric Kay, purchased on Beale Street in Memphis for $55, "big money" at the time, he said. One winter night, the boys played a show at the old airbase theater. Packing up afterward, Jackson's new guitar was left unnoticed on the ground. Sonny, who had borrowed his father's 1948 Jeep, put the vehicle in reverse and crushed the guitar.

"I didn't have any money to pay Gerald for it," Sonny said. "We just laughed and threw it aside."

By 1954, Jackson was twenty years old, newly married, and still working at the airbase box factory. Farm jobs were available, but none paid a decent wage. "I could find work, but I couldn't make any money," he said. And he was increasingly put off by the beer, smoke, and smell of the taverns where the Ramblers performed. "I liked the people but not the lifestyle," Jackson said.

Like many young men of his generation, Jackson left Arkansas seeking a life better than tenant farming or factory work could provide. But out-of-state employment, he quickly discovered, only repeated the scenario of limited jobs and low quality of life. Within a few years, he returned to Tuckerman to find things changed.

"I went to California, and the band went to rock and roll," Jackson said.

The Moonlighters

By 1954, the Rocky Road Ramblers, renamed as the Moonlighters, were the house band at the Silver Moon. Kern Kennedy, a boogie-woogie piano player from Tuckerman, joined the group. For a while, the boys played behind Paul Whaley, a guitar player and singer from Griffithville, Arkansas, whom Sonny called a "Hank Thompson sound-alike." Whaley had played with local bands at the Silver Moon since the late 1940s. After a brief time with the Ramblers, Whaley moved to

California, where he had a long career as a country-and-western singer. Characteristic of a life in the entertainment industry, Whaley's 2011 obituary stated that the musician "enjoyed bingo, horse racing, playing cards, and the ladies loved him."[7]

When Whaley left, Sonny became the lead singer. "I was so bashful," he said. "When I first started singing at Bob King's, I turned my back to the audience until I finally got up the nerve and faced them."

Drummer Russ Smith joined the group at this time, as did saxophonist Davy Hooks, whose horn added to the big band sound still popular in Jackson County. They played country music, jazzed up and fast, and one of their popular numbers was "The Prisoner's Song," an old folk tune also known as "Wings of an Angel."

"Even back then, we liked the fast country music," Sonny said. "We did a lot of other stuff that way, too. We did a lot of country and pop stuff like 'Stardust.' That's why we had the horn. Country club folks would come out to see us because we drew the kids. We drew a young crowd at the time."

Playing the same clubs on alternate nights was the Punky Caldwell Band from Searcy. Walter Garnett "Punky" Caldwell played clarinet and saxophone in a band that included two black musicians, a rarity in the rural South at this time. A photo of Caldwell's quartet from the period identifies the black drummer as Coot Brown and the piano player as Bishop Hooten. The white man playing bass was L. C. Coyle. The photo shows Caldwell, an extremely overweight man, blowing the saxophone—supporting Sonny's memory of him as weighing more than 300 pounds. But the rotund Caldwell was an extraordinary performer whose music brought people to the dance floor. "He could blow that sax and clarinet," Sonny said. "He had 'em turning flips."

The Moonlighters often hired Caldwell to join them for shows, and he was sitting in with the band at the B&I Club on December 9, 1955, when they opened for Elvis. Caldwell's wailing clarinet and Kennedy's pumping piano so impressed Elvis that he offered them a job in his band. Kennedy declined, aware that band sidemen rarely shared in a star's fortune. Caldwell as well had career plans of his own. By 1960, he had formed the Punky Caldwell Trio, a jazz group based in Yakima, Washington, that toured in northern states and Asia in the 1960s and 1970s. Caldwell died in 1978, four months after his forty-eighth birthday.

Walter Garnett "Punky" Caldwell, a talented saxophone player from Searcy, performed in many Jackson County music clubs and frequently joined the Pacers in 1955 when the band was called the Moonlighters. Caldwell's own group was integrated, a rarity at the time. The band included L. C. Coyle, bass; Coot Brown, drums; and Bishop Hooten, piano.

In 1955, the Moonlighters had been the opening act for Elvis shows at the Silver Moon in July and October. By that December evening at the B&I Club at Swifton, the musicians were friends and familiar with each other's style. Elvis liked the rocking sound of the Newport band, particularly their cover version of Smiley Lewis' "One Night of Sin," which he recorded in 1958 as "One Night." Sonny too liked what he heard from the Blue Moon Boys, Elvis' original touring band of Scotty Moore and Bill Black.

"Scotty had that great sound on his guitar and Elvis could really sing," Sonny said. "He was just the best we had ever seen. We knew he'd be big."

When the show ended in Swifton that night, Elvis suggested that Sonny and the band audition for Sam Phillips and Sun Records. The Moonlighters took his advice and quickly scheduled a session at the Memphis recording studio.

"We wanted to be on Sun Records after that. That's all we could think about," Sonny said. "All we wanted was to get that little yellow record in our hands. That was big time to us."

A Visit with Gerald Jackson

On a December morning in 2007, Sonny stopped in at the Tuckerman City Hall. Behind a counter in the front office, four women sat at desks, their work stations cluttered with stacks of papers and ledgers, framed photos of children, and decorated coffee mugs. The women smiled as Sonny walked through. They knew the lean, white-haired man was a local celebrity. They laughed as he asked if the mayor was in his office or "out in the deer woods." One tried to be extra help-ful, rising from her desk to show him the open hallway just past the office door.

Mayor Gerald Jackson was delighted to see his old friend, and the men shook hands warmly. Jackson had an easy smile and the relaxed comportment of a small-town politician. Sonny gave him a gift, a lam-inated 2008 Pacers wall calendar with a photo of the two of them from sixty years before.

In the photo, two teenagers are playing guitars. They are standing in a club or some type of performance space, surrounded by people sit-ting at small tables. A drummer with a basic snare set accompanies them. The young musicians are very intent on their playing, both look-ing down at their hands. Neither is smiling. Both have short hair and wear short-sleeved white shirts. They are very thin, almost stick figures of wiry youth—farm boys with Depression-era childhoods.

Jackson was thrilled to see the photo, and he began telling stories of their high school years in the 1940s and the Rocky Road Ramblers.

"Our first jobs were on Saturday evenings playing the bars along the main streets of Newport," he said. "They'd put us in a corner, and we'd play thirty minutes, then pass the hat. At the time, REA was putting in rural lines, and they talked to us about playing music for little rural meetings in country schools and local churches. They always had soda pop and candy, and they'd tell folks about the electricity. They would explain what it would cost and how to prepare."

Sonny Burgess (left) and Gerald Jackson perform for an REA community program; 1949.

Jackson said his older brother wired their house, a skill learned at Newport High School. "Our house had a ten-foot ceiling with a single cord hanging from the center of the room with a little switch and a light bulb," he said. "Then we got a refrigerator. Before that, the ice man had been delivering three days a week in the summer. We'd be out in the field working and see him coming. We knew we'd have iced tea that day."

Jackson spoke of the shows he and Sonny played in nearby Swifton and Bald Knob, the "governor" in the Burgess family Jeep set to thirty-five miles per hour by Sonny's father. They played dances at the airbase theater and on stage at the Strand Theater. Farmers Day, a Newport festival sponsored by the Farmers Electric Co-op, was the biggest show of the year, and Jackson recalled the event parade, with the band playing to people who lined the streets as they rode on a flatbed trailer pulled by a tractor.

"Any time there was a band in Newport, there was a crowd," Jackson said.

The men talked for a while longer, and then Sonny stood to leave. They joked about their age and the passing years. They shook hands again. Jackson held the photo calendar and wished his old friend a happy holiday season. On the way out, Sonny paused for a moment at the front office. When the clerks looked up from their desks, he gestured down the hall to the mayor's office.

"He says y'all are fired," Sonny said, a sly smile on his face.

Chapter 4.
Rockabilly and Razorbacks

Sonny Burgess:
The Sun Years, 1956 to 1959

I never heard the term "rockabilly" back then. Nobody did. We never really pinned it down, where that term came from. When people asked what music we played, we were rock 'n' rollers.

—Sonny Burgess[8]

By 1955, the Moonlighters were the house band at the Silver Moon, as well as playing weekend shows at the B&I and Mike's clubs in Swifton. Their sets now included more rock and roll than country music. Sonny composed the tunes that would become their first Sun recordings: "We Wanna Boogie," drawing on the wild nights at Newport clubs, and "Red Headed Woman," loosely based on his wife Jo Ann Adams, a Newport High School basketball star and a Miss Newport beauty pageant winner.

The Sun releases in 1956 gave the band, by then known as the Pacers, new prestige in Newport, and they continued to draw capacity crowds at the Silver Moon. Payment from the first Sun single, however, was far less than expected. A $1,500 check was split among six band members and their manager.

"We only got that one check out of Sam Phillips, and it was the last time we ever got paid for the song," Sonny said. "Years later, Jack Nance told me 'We Wanna Boogie' was a big hit in Boston, selling more than 300,000 copies. The last estimate I had, those songs had been released on so many compilations they have sold between 750,000 and a million records. Every time I go to Europe, I see some new version that somebody has put out."

The wild musical arrangement and intensity of "Red Headed Woman" prompted false stories that the Pacers were drunk at the recording session. "We weren't even drinking. We were scared," Sonny said. "We could have cut better records, but nobody ever told us what to do. All Sam went for was feel—if it felt good. And even as bad as it was, it felt good to us."

Sonny and Jo Ann, their first Christmas; 1955.

Music writer Colin Escott believes those early recordings are the Pacers' best work. He described Sonny's sound at the time: "He had a passion for rhythm and blues, and he had a true R&B voice, like a tenor sax in full cry, a magnificent rock and roll instrument."[9]

Much like Jerry Lee Lewis, Sonny left a large amount of prime material unreleased in the Sun vaults. Fortunately, many of the original tapes have been issued in recent years, yielding a more diverse portrait of his artistic range and talent.

For Sonny, the sound was as natural as a flowing river. "You can't rehearse good rock and roll," he said. "If it ever gets in that groove and feels good, then you don't have to have the whiskey, you don't have to have the drugs. It's the music that provides the high."

In the Studio

We were all there trying to impress Sam Phillips. His liking what you did meant everything. Sam's secret was to get you to play like you'd play live. He'd just turn you loose.

—Sonny Burgess

The small, one-level building at 706 Union Avenue in Memphis was not impressive. Located in a district of auto dealerships and repair shops, the original Sun Studios occupied a former auto parts store. On one side was a used car lot. On the other was Taylor's café. Upstairs were a few apartments Mrs. Taylor rented out as a rooming house.

Today, some visitors approach the National Historic Landmark site of the original Sun Studios with reverence. Entry is through the café building, still arranged like a coffee shop. Inside the former studio, the acoustic wall and ceiling tiles are still where Phillips placed them in 1950. Much of the original equipment has been returned, such as the microphone used by Elvis and the basic recorders operated by Jack Clement. The display recreates the minimally equipped recording room in Phillips' small start-up business.

"There wasn't anything special about Sun when you stop and think about it, but it was the first recording studio we were in," Sonny said. "A lot of people still believe that place, that studio, was magic."

The Moonlighters scheduled an audition at Sun in early 1956. By this time, the business was a launching pad for the nation's hottest young talent. Following in the path of Elvis and Jerry Lee Lewis, southern rockers eager to be heard were contacting Sun or walking in unannounced. The studio was open to new talent, but most lacked originality. Phillips could afford to be choosy. The Moonlighters—Burgess, Kennedy, Hubbard, and Smith—were told they needed a fuller sound and sent away.

"Sam expected you to show great enthusiasm," Kennedy recalled. "You were jumping with a single-track recorder and had to get it right. I remember being terrified and exhilarated. Sam didn't want us to play good; he wanted us to play authentic. He wanted that rough edge. We weren't quite ready."

Back in Newport, the Moonlighters recruited drummer Jack Nance and guitar player Joe Lewis, who came up with the band's new name. With Smith already on drums, Nance switched to trumpet. Sonny wanted a saxophone player who could wail like Punky Caldwell, but Nance's trumpet added a shrill urgency, a unique voice that blended coarse boogie woogie and fluid rhythm and blues.

On May 2, 1956, the band, renamed the Pacers, returned to Memphis and recorded five tunes. Jack Clement would be the engineer on later recordings, but that first day, Phillips worked the recording board himself, no doubt adding to the nervous tension the Arkansas musicians were feeling at their debut session.

"Sam just sat there and rolled tape," Sonny recalled. "He let us set up our equipment wherever we wanted, just like we were on stage. He had one good microphone in the middle of the room, and we'd all stand around that mike and play like he was the audience, playing like he was 10,000 people out there. And he'd say, 'Well, go through it again.' When he got one he felt was right, that's what he put out. He had a talent for putting out stuff that was different, that felt good."

The session produced the band's first single, "We Wanna Boogie" / "Red Headed Woman," widely regarded as a landmark recording, one of the wildest and rawest records from the rockabilly era. Opening with a rush of piano and drums, "We Wanna Boogie" takes off with an urgent rhythm, propelled by Sonny's background shout of "Yeah, piano pound!" Amid howls and distorted guitar riffs, the song quickly reaches its cruising speed. Sonny's lyrics capture the southern vernacular, the idioms of the rural dialect—*"out to the dance hall, cut a little rug, running like wildfire, hittin' that jug"*—much like Hank Williams had done. Nance's bleating trumpet, with its bursts of screaming hillbilly bop, adds a taunting, guttural hint of tent show carnival dancers.

The Pacers at the Jackson County fair; 1956.

Over the next two years, the Pacers had three additional sessions at Sun. At the 1957 session for "My Bucket's Got a Hole in It," Kennedy decided to enhance the sound of the studio piano. He bought thumb-tacks from a nearby hardware store and inserted them into the piano hammers, a technique he had used on the piano at the Silver Moon.

"Everything that came out of Sun had that tick-tack sound," Sonny said. Years later when he was traveling in the Sun Rhythm Section,

Sonny learned that the tacks remained in the Sun piano for six months. Marcus Van Story told him that it took half a day to take them out.

Sonny and Jo Ann at the Silver Moon; 1958.

Sonny had an additional session in 1959, producing "Sadie's Back in Town" / "A Kiss Goodnight" for Phillips International. The alternate label, with a new studio at 639 Madison, had been established to engage additional distributors for Sun Records and to gain more air time for recordings.

The Pacers' reputation was established on the five records despite the band's name never appearing on the disc labels. All five labels were identified only with the name "Sonny Burgess."

- "Red Headed Woman" / "We Wanna Boogie"
- "Ain't Got a Thing" / "Restless"
- "My Bucket's Got a Hole in It" / "Sweet Misery"
- "Thunderbird" / "Itchy"
- "Sadie's Back in Town" / "A Kiss Goodnight"

Sonny dismisses the work on these five records as that of inexperienced young musicians with limited equipment. He believes an additional guitar player would have balanced his role as lead singer.

"In those days, we didn't even know how to record," Sonny said. "We were just poor boys, so playing music was fun for us. We just played as if we were playing for a crowd. That's how come there's all the mistakes. It wasn't super good music, but it felt good to us. Getting paid, that was icing on the cake."[10]

The Songs

We never did cut a good record, never did anything that was great, but we were really better musicians than that. We just thought "the wilder the better," and we were pretty wild.

—Sonny Burgess

Sun Releases First Record by "Pacers"; Burgess Stars
"Newport's popular rock and roll musicians, Sonny Burgess and the Pacers, were on their way to possible fame and fortune today with the release of their first commercial record. Sun Records Co. in Memphis… announced that the Pacers' first record will be released officially tomorrow to record shops, jukebox operators, and radio stations."

—*Newport Daily Independent*, July 24, 1956

Pacers Platter Crosses Counter
"Newport got a fresh shot of rhythm and blues today with its own rock-and-roll performers, the Pacers. The record went on sale at the Sterling Store and Heard Music Co. There was a brisk demand.…Both tunes bear the general jubilant characteristics of the current musical craze."

—*Newport Daily Independent*, July 25, 1956

The Pacers' first Sun single was repeatedly played on radio station KNBY. The record sold for eighty-nine cents at Newport's Sterling Store and Heard Music Company. Band manager Gerald Grojean, also the assistant manager at KNBY, had arranged a contract with Sun Records for the recording of sixteen "sides" over a period of two years. The band's optimism was high, but keeping a six-member group employed full time was more of a challenge than had been anticipated.

Though band membership had changed by the end of 1957, Sonny was still able to call his friends together as needed. At a 1959 recording session, Kennedy, Hubbard, and Crafford joined him at Wayne Raney's studio in Drasco, Arkansas. With Raney's son Zendall on harmonica, the group recorded seven songs. Somehow the tapes got lost. They were found twenty-four years later among stored items at the Jacksonport home of Sonny's mother. Six of the songs were later released on the British Stomper Time label as *Arkansas Rock 'n' Roll*. The Swedish SunJay label released all seven, calling the album *The Flood Tapes* because of the 1983 White River overflow that forced Mrs. Burgess to temporarily leave her home. The unedited tapes were found upon her return when she sorted through her belongings.

The original Pacers; 1956.

In 1960, Kern Kennedy and Joe Lewis joined Sonny at Conway Twitty's Newborn Studio in Marianna, Arkansas. Twitty produced the songs that day, which were also released years later on European labels.

Kennedy views those early recordings as the work of eager but undisciplined beginners. Sonny agreed that the original Pacers were overly influenced by the excitement of being in a studio and their own eagerness to try new things.

"We didn't spend the time working up these songs," Sonny said. "Most times, we did maybe three cuts. It wasn't as if we were working in a time limit. We'd spend a whole day or two in the studio just trying different things. But we were impatient, and we'd want to get on to something else."

Many artists become dissatisfied with their early work, but the flaws in the Pacers' Sun recordings do not reduce the records' jubilant energy and unrestrained expression. Between 1956 and 1959, the Pacers recorded about 150 songs at Sun Records. Most of them were erased and taped over, but much of the unreleased material was later published on compilation and solo CDs by Charly, Bear Family, and Rounder Records.

Sonny commented on the Pacers' early recordings in a 1991 issue of *Now Dig This* magazine.[11] Following are some of his remarks on the individual songs.

Ain't Got a Thing

Jack Clement wrote the words for this. He had a great gift of being able to put together words. With him being the engineer at Sun, he'd give us songs to record. We'd take anything he could give us.

Clement's short, rhyming lyrics were in the tradition of Louis Jordan's rapid-fire goofiness, low on meaning, but easy and fun to sing.

"I got a piano, ain't got no keys

I got crackers, ain't got no cheese

I got a woman, but she climbs trees"

The song was modeled on "Ain't Got No Home," Clarence "Frogman" Henry's debut rhythm and blues hit, recorded at the legendary Cosimo Matassa's New Orleans studio in 1956. Sonny originally hoped the record would be the Pacers' second hit. In retrospect, he thought the record failed because it was too fast for dancing.

Fannie Brown

We got that off the old scat tune "Caldonia." It's close to a lot of the old rhythm and blues things from back then.

Find My Baby for Me

This is one of the best songs we ever recorded at Sun. It might have been a little too fast, like "Ain't Got a Thing" and "Sadie's Back in Town." You couldn't really jitterbug to it.

Roy Orbison joined in the backing vocals, but his participation had not been planned. The Pacers were in Memphis to record some new tunes before joining a Grand Ole Opry tour that would leave for Kansas City the next day. The 1957 tour was to include Roy Orbison and the Teen Kings, but the Teen Kings had abandoned their lead singer and returned to Texas. The Pacers filled in as Orbison's band on the tour, a role they repeated at many shows over the next two years.

The song's tempo makes its Chuck Berry-style lyrics (rhyming "radio stations" with "United Nations") somewhat difficult to hear.

Itchy / Thunderbird

After "Itchy," we decided to write a fast tune right. We'd been in the studio all morning, now afternoon. We bought the cheap wine and got to drinking a whole mess of the stuff. It was a great song. I loved the thing. After we listened to it, we realized we'd got really pepped up and it got too fast.

Both tunes were composed at the Sun studio, with Billy Lee Riley and Jack Clement collaborating. Because Kennedy could not get off work to attend the session, Clement suggested adding Charlie Rich on piano and Riley on harmonica. Riley's outstanding harmonica lead kicks off "Itchy" and keeps it jumping. "Thunderbird" is a slower tune that follows a standard blues progression. The song title identifies the low-cost wine that was popular with the musicians. The instrumental tunes were released with the labels on the wrong sides of the record. The title "Thunderbird" was originally intended for the faster tune.

Little Town Baby

I wrote this about Newport. There's always a sweet thing in all those little towns.

Mr. Blues

We just worked this one up out of an idea we had, but we really didn't get a good cut on it. We did things the wrong way back then. We should have worked out the songs before we went into the studio. But we waited until we got in there and then worked on them. All these are just demo or rehearsal things we should have spent more time on. But we had nobody to tell us. We were out there stumbling around in the dark. We didn't know very much about the music business and how things worked.

My Bucket's Got a Hole in It

We did it first with an electric guitar. Then Jack Clement wanted to put on an acoustic guitar. He had that big Gibson Hummingbird, which turned out real well. We did that about 6-7 different ways. In one session, Kern put thumb tacks on the piano felt heads and created that tick-tack sound.

The popular song has had several recordings and modifications of its lyrics. Originally a turn-of-the-century message of hard luck, moonshine, and reefer from a New Orleans street hustler, the song was revived by Clarence Williams in the 1930s. Hank Williams and T. Texas Tyler recorded it in 1949. The Pacers' version came out in 1957. It included sixteen bars of Jack Clement's overdubbed guitar solo.

And in January 1958, Ricky Nelson's version made Top 10 listings. Nelson performed a note-for-note copy of the Pacers' except for this sanitized lyric, "My bucket's got a hole in it, won't work no more." Sonny often jokes that Nelson's version turned the song's "beer" into "milk."

One Night of Sin

It was most popular number we did on stage. We'd have to do it six or seven times a night. Women in the night clubs really went for that song. You would not believe the response we got. Elvis heard us doing it at Kings and the Silver Moon, and he saw the response we were getting. Elvis copied us to a "T."

The song was created by New Orleans rhythm and blues singer Smiley Lewis, a talented black artist whose career was marked by hardship and bad luck. His songs were covered by Fats Domino and Elvis with an enormous success that Lewis never shared. Elvis recorded the song in its original style in January 1957. Today, the chorus seems tame: "One night of sin is what I'm now paying for. The things I did and saw, would make the world stand still." But Elvis' manager and RCA record producers believed the lyrics were too suggestive for the national audiences. Within a month, Elvis cut a new recording with reworked lyrics: "One night with you is what I'm now praying for." Elvis' single was a No. 1 hit in England and peaked at No. 4 on Billboard's U.S. singles chart.

Please Listen to Me

This was a Fats Domino song we adapted. His writers sent stuff to Sam for Elvis to hear, and it just lay around the studio. We'd pick out the ones we liked. I'm sure the rest of the guys did the same thing.

Restless

It was a good record, one of the best we did. Jack Clement gave me the lyrics and said, "See what you can do with this." We put music to it, and the whistling. We thought it was gonna be a biggie. Sam thought it would be bigger than "Blue Suede Shoes." But it all comes down to air play and promotion. It got so far and that was that. When Conway Twitty recorded it exactly the way we did, that was a compliment.

Sadie's Back in Town

The song was loosely based on Jimmie Rodgers' "My Little Lady," recorded in 1928. In 1954, a movie *Sadie's Back in Town* starring Rita Hayworth played at Newport's Strand Theater, but Sonny said there was no link between the film and the song, recorded on the Phillips International label in late 1959. By this time, several of the original Newport musicians had left the band. J. C. Caughron, the Swifton guitar player who joined the Pacers in 1958, was the only other Arkansan on the recording. Sonny's high-energy rendition had drummer Raymond Thompson providing the voices for the woodpecker and chipmunk parts. Like much of the studio work that preceded it, the song had a thin and poorly balanced sound. Some consider it the last true rockabilly record ever made. But "Sadie's Back in Town," with its manic giggles, romping electric guitar, and wacky cartoon animal voices, was just too weird for the times.

We Wanna Boogie
This was inspired by what we did in Newport with the Saturday night crowds. Back then, people were really into the music. They went to have a good time.

Showtime with the Pacers

When we were live, we were like a three-ring circus. You can't see that on the record.

—Sonny Burgess

They were always well dressed, six guys in Lansky suits, with brightly colored jackets and ties.

"Sonny wanted his band to sound right and look right, all dressed alike," J. M. Van Eaton said. "He wanted them to look different than the guy in the front row in blue jeans and tee shirt. They needed to look professional, and Sonny kept that going."

On the road, each of them carried five or six outfits, Hubbard recalled, because their clothes would be soaked with sweat after a show. On any given night, they would do the bug dance and the human pyramid. They would drag each other across the stage by their guitar necks. Their fifty-foot cables gave them plenty of room to jump into the audience, drawing the crowd into the frenzied hilarity created by their high-energy music.

"I'd get out and dance with them with my bass," Hubbard said. "On the floor, I'd show out, stick my fingers in my ears and keep them laughing, but never stopped playing."

Sonny shouts to Johnny Ray Hubbard, while Joe Lewis and Jack Nance form a human pyramid; 1956.

On Tour

Pacers to Go on Tour of Midwest
"We just sort of get carried away."
               —*Newport Daily Independent*, August 20, 1956

They played for young crowds and energetic dancers. They would drive the music faster, pushing the dancers to exhaustion. Some of the songs lasted thirty minutes without stopping. Sometimes they played one song full blast for an hour at the end of the night. They became more confident and daring. Leaping off the stage at a Robinson Auditorium show at Little Rock in 1956, Sonny and Johnny Ray fell nearly ten feet into the orchestra pit.

"I waved to the others not to follow, but it was too late," Hubbard said.

"It was like we fell forever," Sonny said. "We dropped out of sight and the people were jumping up in their seats, wondering what was happening to us."

Hubbard broke the tail piece and the bridge on his bass, but he and Sonny were resilient enough to climb out and continue the song. The next night, Ray Price and Marty Robbins, not wishing to be upstaged again by the brash young band, had the Pacers perform last. This time, they kept their jumping on stage.

Sonny, a man not given to exaggeration, said the Pacers were the hottest working band in the mid-South, their shows rivaling those by Perkins and Lewis. Saxophone player Martin Willis, who first saw the Pacers at the Silver Moon in 1956 and briefly toured with them in 1958, agreed.

"Unless you'd seen the Pacers, you had no idea they were such a hard-playing group," Willis said. "They were different than others because of their stage presence. Sonny always put out that energy. We'd all tire out, but he'd keep going. If you had seen them once, you'd never forget them."

Bobby Crafford said Danny Rapp, lead singer of the doo-wop quartet Danny and the Juniors, called the Pacers the best show band he had ever seen. The Pacers toured with the Philadelphia-based group in 1958 when the singers had a hit single "At the Hop." When the two bands first met, Rapp gave the sheet music of the song to Kennedy.

"Kern said, 'I can't read this,' and gave the page back to Danny," Bobby said. "We listened to the record and played the show that night."

As a new act on the Sun label, the Pacers were booked with top southern artists Perkins and Cash while also filling in as a dance band back-up for performers such as Warren Smith, Eddie Bond, Billy Lee Riley, Johnny Burnette and the Rock 'n' Roll Trio, Bobby Lord, Brenda Lee, and others. Performing with the teenaged brother-sister act the Collins Kids affirmed an old show business truth.

"You can't upstage kids," Sonny said. "That's tougher than appearing with dogs."

*Two-to-a-bed was normal travel for Pacers Hubbard (left) and Crafford (right).
Memphis saxophonist Martin Willis (center) joined the trip; 1958.*

In addition to group tours and shows, the Pacers traveled on their own, booking weeks on the road in the United States and Canada. They also performed on television dance party shows, appearing several times on *Steve's Show* in Little Rock and on Memphis television shows hosted by Dewey Phillips and Wink Martindale.

Their reputation as a dance band with a fabulous stage show brought some odd engagements, such as the time they played at a debutant ball in Louisville, Kentucky. The booking came through a wealthy Batesville family whose granddaughter often came to the Silver Moon.

"We kind of felt out of place wearing all the tails on the tuxedos and that type of thing," Sonny said. "They had an orchestra out of Chicago that played the formal dancing. Then we set up and did about forty-five minutes. You've never seen so much carrying on. I think they gave us $5,000. Now that's a lot of money."

The Pacers' success was linked to the exposure gained from shows at elegant venues, such as the Peabody Hotel in Memphis and the country club in Jackson, Mississippi. But there were many late night shows at roadhouses and dance clubs across the South.

"We played these clubs, and then the kids would go off to college, and they'd call us to play a lot of fraternity parties," Crafford said.

"Mississippi in the 1950s may have been a poor state, but the whites had a lot of money to pay for their kids' parties."

The Pacers knew that teenaged crowds were ready for wild dancing. At the "Heaven and Hell Dance" in Memphis, the large dance floor had two stages, one for each band, facing each other across the open room. In 1958, the Pacers shared the bill with Clarence "Frogman" Henry. At the time, the New Orleans rhythm and blues singer had a fast-paced hit with "Ain't Got No Home." The Pacers later changed it to "Ain't Got a Thing." In Memphis that night, the high school dancers got excited and mobbed the stage.

"We had to get the police there to keep the crowds off us," Crafford said. "The kids came up on the stage trying to take over. They broke the bridge on Johnny Ray's bass. They didn't mean any harm, but they were drunk or crazy."

The Pacers were twice banned from the campus Boogie Fest at Arkansas State University in Jonesboro. In that dry county, their shows were judged to have incited excessive drinking among the audience. This was not the case when they played at fraternity houses on the University of Arkansas campus. In that wet county in the western Ozarks, raucous fraternity parties and student drinking were more tolerated.

The band working hard at a University of Arkansas party; 1956.

The other element of success for the Pacers at this time was their willingness to go anywhere to perform. A green Cadillac limousine with a steel box mounted on the roof to carry the drums and base was the band's main ride. On April 4, 1958, while playing at a country club in Jackson, Mississippi, a phone call came from booking agent Bob Neal. Sonny shared the news with the band during intermission. Instead of returning to Newport, they were to drive to Birmingham immediately after the show to perform the next night with Johnny Cash. There was no interstate highway in rural Mississippi in 1958. The drive was 250 miles of two-lane highway with no street lights outside the small towns.

"We drove all night and got to Birmingham at eight in the morning, then played the show that night," Crafford said. "Cash was hot at that time. People grabbed at us when we came off stage, wanting us to sign their hands and clothes."

Earlier that year, Sonny had gotten a job offer that tested his professional ethics. The band was playing the clubs in Hamilton, Ontario, familiar territory to other wild Arkansas rockers Ronnie Hawkins and Will Pop Jones. The booking agent Harold Kudlets called Sonny into his office and asked him to break up the Pacers.

"I knew what they wanted," Sonny recalled, adding that he never told the Pacers about the offer. "Me and Johnny Ray did our own little show. Kudlets said, 'We like you and the bass player. Send piano and drummer back home. We'll get you others.' I said, 'No thanks. We're going back to Arkansas.'"

Steve Stephens

The Pacers were the first band to appear on *Steve's Show*, a television dance party broadcast from KTHV Little Rock. Created in 1957 by Newport native Steve Stephens, the live show with its teenaged dancers began broadcasting six months before Dick Clark's *American*

Bandstand. Stephens was extremely popular with Arkansas teenagers, who voted him the state's top television personality every year from 1957 to 1961. In 1960, he came within a single vote of beating Clark for the national popularity title from *TV and Movie Screen Magazine.*

Steve Stephens at Newport radio station KNBY, 1956.

Stephens is the son of Newport merchants. As a boy, he sold the newspaper *Grit* to the Saturday crowds on Front Street, and he worked as an usher at the Strand Theater. His friendship with Sonny began at Newport High School. Both were 1948 graduates, both declined college scholarships (Steve's was for music from Ouachita Baptist University), and both returned to Newport following their military service in the early 1950s.

Stephens began working in his family's furniture store, but radio broadcast had greater appeal. Despite a winning smile and outgoing personality, Stephens said he failed his first KNBY job interview for having a "terrible southern accent." The setback encouraged him to develop a professional radio voice by reading the newspaper aloud each day. He was soon hired at the Newport station.

Steve Stephens interviewing Pacers Russ Smith (left) and Sonny Burgess (right); 1956.

Stephens frequented the Silver Moon, a club whose original foundation was built by his uncle Rufus Stephens in the 1940s. His booth in the bar section of the club was a social gathering place. But his parents wouldn't go there because of the drinking and gambling.

"The Silver Moon was the center of nighttime activity for anyone who wanted to get out of their rut," Stephens said. "You felt like you were in a real night club, and you went there hoping something good would happen. It would have been scandalous to see a respectable family at the Silver Moon."

Through his work at KNBY and his friendships at Newport's clubs, Stephens met Conway Twitty, Charlie Rich, and others who later appeared on his television show. In 1957, Stephens' friendship with the Pacers led to his breakthrough opportunity in television.

"Sonny invited me to travel with him to Little Rock in the Pacers' green limo," Stephens said. "I got a white coat just like the band members and went with them to the television station where they were rehearsing."

The Pacers stopped several times to buy drinks along the way, Stephens said, and he was in good spirits when they arrived at KTHV. He was wandering through the station when he ran into Program Manager Jack Bomar.

"In my infinite smoothness, I asked, 'You guys need an announcer?'" Stephens said. "It turned out they had just fired a guy, and Bomar asked me to send a tape."

Steve's Show began three months after Stephens was hired, and the show's wholesome approach to rock and roll rapidly attracted a large following of teenagers who showed up each afternoon at the Little Rock television station. At one time, counterfeit tickets were discovered among the eager attendees. Student groups from across the state reserved space for their dancers and drove to Little Rock on school buses. One group from Hot Springs High School included a teenaged Bill Clinton, who recalled his rite of passage as a young and awkward dancer. "I remember when I went and how old I was. I still remember the girl I danced with and how grateful I was that she was a better dancer," Clinton said.[12]

After seven years on air, Stephens left television to join the staff of Senator John McClellan in 1965. In the decades that followed, he became a leading public relations and communications strategist for business and nonprofit organizations. He is another high achiever shaped by Newport origins, a product of his time and place, just like Sonny Burgess.

Stephens praised the rock and roll musician and his lifelong friend. "Sonny always seemed to be just on the cusp of being discovered," he said.

Changes in the Band

We wanted to get on with Bob Neal, a promoter in Memphis. He had managed Perkins and Cash. He even managed Elvis for a while. He knew how to make money.

—Kern Kennedy

Despite the extensive touring and the exuberance of their stage shows, the original Pacers stayed together less than two years. Even as the first Sun recordings were being released and additional road shows were being booked, there were signs of hard times ahead. Perhaps the most dramatic of these was the realization that the band's manager had deceived them and lost them their opportunity to travel as Elvis' opening act and back-up band.

In 1956, Bob Neal, a partner with Sam Phillips in the booking agency Stars Incorporated, promised the Pacers that he would put them on the road with Elvis. As they waited for that to be arranged, the Pacers were booked on tours with big-name acts. These road shows featured older country stars such as Bob Wills and Merle Travis matched with younger talent such as Lewis, Orbison, and the Pacers.

By the end of the year, Neal gave the band the bad news. He had been contacted by their manager, Gerald Grojean, who had pleaded with him not to take the Pacers away. Neal said he complied as a professional favor and did not tell the band.

With his full-time job as assistant director at Newport radio station KNBY, Grojean was able to provide rehearsal space at the station and access to new records. But Grojean was unfamiliar with the music industry beyond radio, and he was inexperienced in finding work for the band outside Jackson County.

"Grojean had a good job with a steady salary at KNBY," Sonny said. "He managed us and made more money than ever. Why would he want us to leave Newport? Our mistake was to stay with him. We should have quit playing in Arkansas sooner."

The news of their manager's deception was coupled with disappointing record sales. Despite their success on tours and enthusiastic shows in local clubs, the Pacers realized their Sun contract would not be renewed.

Joe Lewis, Jack Nance, and Russ Smith left the band shortly after the Pacers' second record was released in early 1957. Later in the year, Kern Kennedy returned to his full-time job at Zenith Seed Company at the Newport airbase. Thinking his musical efforts had achieved little of value, the discouraged piano player stood in the back door of his home in Tuckerman and threw away copies of the Pacers' recently pressed Sun singles, sailing the seemingly worthless discs into the weeds like miniature Frisbees.

In August 1957, with new drummer Bobby Crafford on board, the Pacers were booked on a West Coast tour. Seeking a new label, they used connections by Neal and Cash to audition at Challenge Records, a Los Angeles label started that year by Gene Autry. They spent a day at the record studio with the western singer and Challenge recording star Johnny Bond producing the demos.[13] The Pacers also made demo tapes at the home studio of country music singer Wynn Stewart, another Challenge artist.[14]

Bond was from Oklahoma, Stewart from Missouri. He had been discovered by Arkansan Skeets McDonald, a star at this time, who arranged for Stewart's debut recording.[15] All from the mid-South, the musicians were leading West Coast artists who shaped county music at the time. The Pacers had the same background as the West Coast performers, but the Arkansas band had found its voice in rock and roll.

Nothing came of the auditions. Sonny believes the Pacers didn't fit common radio play lists of country or rhythm and blues. Without a niche, record companies found the Pacers' music difficult to market.

Crafford recalled Bond telling the band that "we'll see what we can do" if they stayed in California. With neither contract salaries nor housing provided, that was not possible. The Pacers returned to Arkansas, and Sonny worked for a time with his brothers-in-law Sam and Harry Adams in a Newport sporting goods store. The Pacers eventually found talented replacements for the original band members, but Sonny conceded that by late 1957, "we'd lost the show."

With the addition of J. C. Caughron on guitar in early 1958, the Pacers resumed road trips and their show-stopping performances. On another western tour with Cash, the Pacers played on the *Town Hall Party*, a Los Angeles television program hosted by Tex Ritter, who also hosted the similarly named radio program that once featured former Moonlighter Freddie Hart. The July 1958 live television broadcast ran from 10 p.m. until 1 a.m., and the Pacers played four sets, backing up Cash and others. The tour later took them up the coast to Seaside, Oregon. Following the concert show and Cash's departure for other bookings, the band picked up a three-night gig at a local venue, the Bungalow Skating Rink. Never too proud to refuse a paying job, the Pacers played in a large, low-ceilinged room where the roller skaters' oval track surrounded the central dance floor. Returning to Los Angeles, another introduction by Cash led to a two-week gig at the Hillbilly Ranch, a club operated by Gene Davis. The band got paid, but Sonny grew cautious of potential problems.

Town Hall Party, Los Angeles. Johnny Ray Hubbard, bass, and Bobby Crafford, drums. Sonny's dyed red hair matched his red jacket; 1958.

"I could see Davis was having trouble collecting the money because he paid us in $5 and $10 bills," Sonny said. "That's when I realized again it was time to go back to Arkansas."

After "Thunderbird / Itchy" was released in August 1958, the Pacers toured with Cash, Merle Travis, and others on another western circuit. The band at the time included Sonny, Caughron, Bobby Brown on bass, and Johnny Welker on drums. Brown, another Newport musician, was the first artist to record on Vaden Records. His band, Bobby Brown and the Curios, included the St. Louis drummer Welker.

Three of the original Pacers—Crafford, Kennedy, and Hubbard—were willing to rejoin the band, and an agreement had been reached that the change would occur following a November 1958 show in Memphis. In October, Carl Perkins' brother Jay died from cancer. Cash arranged a November 14 benefit concert and recruited some of the biggest stars in country music at the time. The Memphis benefit would be the final performance for Brown and Welker as Pacers. At the end of the concert, Cash's manager, Stew Carnall, gave Sonny $100 and made a remarkable offer to the band.

"Cash wanted us to come out to California where he had a television show," Sonny said. "We would back up whoever he had on the show and get to do a song once or twice a week. I sat around here at home and decided I didn't want to go, so I sent him the $100 back."

It was another road not taken. The opportunity must have seemed promising, if only for the exposure of a national television show. But the Pacers needed more than exposure at this point. They had already made several forays to the West Coast, never securing lasting work. In Newport, hometown loyalties were strong, and though the guys were willing to make another try, the original problem had not been solved.

"We weren't going anywhere," Sonny said. "We were playing six nights a week, but all in Arkansas, making peanuts playing the little joints. We didn't use our heads. We didn't want to leave Arkansas."

Crafford was called into military reserve training for six months from March to September 1959. When his training ended and he returned to Newport, Crafford found the Pacers had again broken up.

"When I got back, there was no band," Crafford said. "Sonny was playing with Bobby Brown, Kern was with someone in Blytheville, and Johnny Ray was hanging out the Silver Moon.[16] I went back to Cotton

Plant and worked with my dad at a service station. When I moved back to Newport, we got together again."

By 1960, Sam Phillips began pursuing other business interests and became less interested in producing records. Sun Records was no longer booking tours. The message became clearer that success for the Pacers required more booking outside of Arkansas. Ronnie Hawkins and Conway Twitty were examples, and Hawkins told them that to succeed in Canada, they would have to stay in Canada.

Sonny made the move in early 1960, joining Twitty and former Pacers Nance and Lewis. But the Canada connection was poorly timed, and Sonny was back in Newport again in 1961 starting a new band. Both he and Crafford would struggle through the decade, facing unproductive time between shows and the increasing difficulty of securing well-paid bookings. By 1970, neither musician could maintain the effort.

Sonny in Canada while a member of the Conway Twitty band; 1960.

Much has been written about the end of the rockabilly era and the changes that followed in rock and roll. "The Day the Music Died," as Don McLean sang in his hit "American Pie," refers to the aviation accident that occurred on February 3, 1959, near Clear Lake, Iowa, killing rock and roll musicians Buddy Holly, Ritchie Valens, and J. P. "The Big Bopper" Richardson. At the same time, rock pioneers of even greater status were temporarily out of the spotlight. In the army from 1958 to 1960, Elvis resumed his career as a balladeer with a more commercial sound. Jerry Lee Lewis and Chuck Berry had fallen from grace as a result of scandals, and Little Richard had joined the ministry. Audiences now were less attracted to the raw energy of the bad boy early performers. The teen idols of the early 1960s were well-groomed and smooth-voiced crooners such as Fabian, Frankie Avalon, Paul Anka, and a host of guys named Bobby— Rydell, Vinton, Dee, and Darin. Many of the early rockabilly stars were now in their late twenties and had retired from the music business.

The early Pacers experienced frustrations and disappointment common to recording artists of the time. Their bad luck, their missed timing, and their manager's deceptions would have convinced most bands to quit. Ironically, the Pacers' most successful trait—their vibrant sound and galvanizing stage show—also contributed to their demise.

The Pacers excelled as a dance band for parties and roadhouse shows. They were a dependable back-up group for name acts. And they added to the collective talent as an opening act on tours. But the exuberance of the Pacers' stage act—the wild antics of the bug dance, their spontaneous leaps into the audience, and their hour-long closing numbers—could not be successfully translated to a recording. In the late 1950s, screaming fans and high-spirited dancers might reflect a band's popularity, but it was record sales that made money. And sales resulted from disc jockeys playing the records. Radio air time was arranged by recording studio promoters who convinced disc jockeys to put artists on a station's play list.

"The talent at Sun was unbelievable, but not everyone got the same breaks," Memphis guitar player Travis Wammack said. "Sonny Burgess and Billy Lee Riley were some of the best singers Sun ever had, but Sam chose to push Elvis and Jerry Lee."

Jack Clement suggested that Phillips was challenged by keeping up with more than one hit at a time in his small business. Phillips, who rarely conceded his own limitations, put it another way. "Sonny Burgess has a distinctive voice that gives me chills every time I hear him," Phillips said. "He is a person that deserves much more than I could give him."

Looking back, Sonny recalls the Sun years with neither animosity nor regret.

"Nothing lasts forever, especially bands." Sonny said. "Sam always said he didn't know what to do with us. We didn't fit any category. The only thing I would have done different is me and the Pacers would have hit the road early on. We might not have become superstars, but we would have made a good living."

Sonny Burgess: After the Pacers, 1960 to 1996

Chicken Today, Feathers Tomorrow

By the end of 1959, Sonny had experienced the highs and lows of a rock and roll life: wild stage shows, tours with top stars, exhausting road trips, and a series of professional disappointments that would have convinced many performers to seek a career change. Sonny's acceptance of these challenges was rooted in the Sand community and the steadfast farm families of his youth. He quotes Kern Kennedy on the insecurity of his chosen career. "That's the music business," he said. "It's chicken today and feathers tomorrow."

Sonny left the Pacers in early 1960 to join Conway Twitty's band in Canada, but the timing was not right, as Twitty's career placed him in several Hollywood movies that year, and he frequently performed without his band. Joe Lewis assumed leadership of the group he renamed "Friday Nights" when they played in Hamilton, Ontario, without Twitty. Not finding the exposure or opportunity he desired, Sonny returned to Newport in 1961 to re-evaluate his options.

"I came back and went to work for my brother-in-law at a filling station," Sonny said. "One day, Bobby, Kern, and Johnny Ray drove up in the green Cadillac. I began playing some jobs with them here and there, but a few weeks later, they hired Paulman. That's when I hooked up with Larry Donn."

Donn was another Arkansas original. Born as Larry Donn Gillihan in the tiny farm community of Bono, he first saw Sonny when the Pacers played a show at his high school in 1955. When Elvis Presley also played at the Bono school that year, Donn decided his future was not in farming. He slicked back his hair, flipped up his shirt collar in the defiant teen style, and began to rock as a piano player and singer. Donn's partner at the time was drummer Sammy Creason, and both men would go on to extensive careers in music—Creason as a drummer with Kris Kristofferson, and Donn as a lead performer with a 1959 hit "Honey Bun" and in his later years as a music historian who wrote "Rockabilly Days," a series of articles in the British magazine *Now Dig This*.

For the next three years, Burgess, Donn, and Creason performed with the same brash energy that had characterized the early Pacers. The trio played at Jackson County clubs and other Arkansas venues. And there was an occasional show with Jerry Lee Lewis, who was playing small venues as he regained popularity following the scandalous exposure of his marriage to his thirteen-year-old cousin. Now in his thirties, Sonny had extensive experience as a performer and a band leader. He was known and respected by Jackson County club owners. And a new generation of local musicians was on hand, willing and able to give show business a try.

A new band, the Kings IV, was created, named for Bob King's club at Swifton, where the Newport musicians—Sonny, Gene Grant, Tommy Tims, and Skeeter Grady (later replaced by Doug Greeno)—began performing. Some of the band members were still learning to play, Sonny admits, and Bobby Nelson made up for his limited talent by providing the van to haul equipment. But among a changing roster of musicians, the Kings IV also featured the skilled piano playing of Kern Kennedy and the professional fiddle playing of Buck Odie, who had worked on *The Louisiana Hayride* show. By 1965, the Kings IV had become the house band at Jarvis', a small club located in the riverfront area of old Newport.

Sonny Burgess, Sun Records publicity photo; 1950s.

"We packed that thing for seven years, four nights a week," Sonny said. "I had all these young guys playing around here. We did some college shows and stuff like that, but nothing to take us out of here."

Sonny balanced music with his new day job as a salesman for St. Louis Trimming, selling lace and trim for women's clothing in three states. At first, the work allowed him to travel the regional territory and return to Newport to play music several nights a week. By 1974, the company asked him to expand his territory to eight states, offering a steady salary far better than what local music jobs provided. Sonny settled into this unplanned midlife role. Music became a sideline as he focused on providing for his family. From 1971 until he retired twenty-four years later, Sonny pursued a full-time sales career, traveling some but home enough to coach his sons John and Payton in American Legion baseball games.

Memphis Rhythm and Blues

As a changing economy further reduced the entertainment scene in Newport, Memphis remained a place to hear black rhythm and blues performers, among them Willie Mitchell, who played at the huge Paradise Club.

"That was the only chance we got to see real good rhythm and blues acts," Sonny said. "We were just listeners, but we picked up how they played."

The Memphis musicians welcomed the Newport guests, who were some of the few white patrons in the club. Rhythm and blues in the segregation era of the 1950s and 1960s was still a black musical style, but white fans were common. But as racial tensions increased, particularly in Memphis following the 1969 shooting of Martin Luther King Jr., Sonny stopped going.

In Memphis, Sonny met Travis Wammack, a local guitar player with impressive speed and style, a distinctive talent he has maintained through a lifetime career in music. "I brought Travis to Newport to play with us at Jarvis' a few times," Sonny said. "He was a good-looking kid, about sixteen years old then, and those Front Street gals about carried him home. The women were still pretty thick in the 1960s, a lot of good old gals just trying to make a living."

Sonny still played occasional weekend gigs and recorded with his Newport friends, now named the Kings V. A few times a year he joined others from Sun Records—Stan Kesler, Roland Janes, and Paul Burlison—for shows at the Memphis in May festival and other local jobs. Burlison had played in the Rock 'n' Roll Trio, a Memphis group that featured the legendary brothers Dorsey and Johnny Burnette, both former Golden Gloves boxers renowned for their willingness to start fights with audience members or each other.

Kings V band: Doug Greeno (left), Sonny Burgess (center), Gene Grant (right), Tommy Tims (front left), and Bobby Nelson (front right); 1965.

"We crossed paths with the Rock 'n' Roll Trio all the time," Sonny said. "Johnny Burnette used to come to the Silver Moon, and he always had three or four gals with him. The Trio didn't make much of an impression back then, but they liked to fight. We'd play Memphis three or four times a year, and Burlison would always play with us."

By the mid-1980s, as a rockabilly revival began in England, Sonny was invited to play at festivals in Weymouth and Birmingham. But for the most part, it seemed the high-spirited performance phase of his life was over.

"Sonny's forte was rock and roll," Sam Phillips said. "He could have been one of the greats, but he never got the right break. I believed in the guy. We gave him what exposure we could, but ultimately it was the DJs and the public who made the decision."[17]

Sonny might have gotten the national exposure for a hit if a disc jockey in a trend-setting market gave extensive air play to one of his Sun singles. But that didn't happen. "It doesn't mean he couldn't have been a star," J. M. Van Eaton said. "The stars just didn't line up for him."

One of the numerous reasons why Sonny didn't gain the highest success, Van Eaton suggested, was "the curse and the blessing" that came with being a Sun label artist. "At Sun, Sam was putting out a lot of records. He couldn't push them all. That's the curse," Van Eaton said. "The blessing is that many of the guys are still living off that label."

Sonny at The Powerhouse, a Birmingham, England, rockabilly club. Bob Fish (left) was guitar player with the band Johnny & Roccos; 1985.

The Sun Rhythm Section

In 1986, Sonny was fifty-seven years old, working as a salesman and settled into the familiar life of his hometown. Newport was far past its heyday of the 1950s. The gambling rooms were shut down, the music and night life were diminished, and the bustling retail activity of Front

Street was slowly giving way to blocks of vacant and boarded-up stores. But a phone call from Memphis would soon change Sonny's placid world into a ten-year run of international performances, setting the stage for the Pacers' reunion and the band's leading role in a world-wide celebration of American rockabilly music.

Jay Orr, a historian at the Country Music Hall of Fame and Museum in Nashville, had come to Memphis to recruit musicians from the Sun Records era. A two-week gig at the Smithsonian Institution's Festival of American Folklife in Washington DC was the draw. The annual festival, ongoing since 1967, focuses on U.S. and international folk culture and encompasses multiple performances on the National Mall. The 1986 festival featured the state of Tennessee, and Orr had convinced event organizers that rockabilly music was an art form rooted in a tradition that should be recognized.

At the time, the rockabilly group the Stray Cats had hit singles in the United States and Europe, but most of America associated the music with the early recordings of Elvis Presley and appreciated it only as nostalgia. The veteran musicians who came to Washington that year provided a jolt of creative energy that revitalized the medium, reminding fans and folklorists that the origins of rock and roll were still a contemporary American musical experience.

They were called the Sun Rhythm Section, a name created by Stan Kesler, a Sun staff musician and songwriter who played steel guitar and bass on sessions with Carl Perkins, Roy Orbison, Jerry Lee Lewis, and many others. Kesler also wrote five songs for Elvis Presley and produced "Wooly Bully" and "Lil Red Riding Hood" by Sam the Sham and the Pharaohs.

The Sun Rhythm Section featured Sonny, Kesler, and a roster of southern talent that included:

- **Marcus Van Story**—front man and road manager for Warren Smith, well known for creating the slap bass sound that was used on many rockabilly records in the 50s
- **J. M. Van Eaton**—drummer with Billy Lee Riley, Jerry Lee Lewis, and on most early Sun recording sessions
- **Paul Burlison**—guitar player with the Rock 'n' Roll Trio and co-writer of most of their songs

- **J. L. "Smoochy" Smith**—one of the first rockabilly piano players in Memphis, instrumental in creating the Memphis pumping piano sound
- **D. J. Fontana**—Elvis Presley's drummer for seventeen years (Fontana joined after Van Eaton, unable to travel, withdrew from the group.)

The Sun Rhythm Section: (from left) J. L. "Smoochy" Smith, Stan Kessler, Sonny Burgess, Marcus Van Story, Paul Burlison, and D. J. Fontana; 1990. Not pictured: J. M. Van Eaton.

The group was a stunning surprise hit at the festival, drawing the attention of Bob Dylan, who came to an afternoon show to hear them, Orr said. Arriving too late for the performance, Dylan and his limo-driven entourage appeared that evening at an American Legion hall in Maryland where the enterprising musicians had booked a gig. The music hall later became famous through its alternate "weekend" identity and the 1992 Grammy-winning song by Mary Chapin Carpenter, "Down at the Twist and Shout."

The group's deep well of talent and the attention of a music industry giant such as Dylan gave the Sun Rhythm Section a rarefied status, leading to later appearances at national folk festivals in Virginia and Massachusetts. These festivals, established in 1934, are some of the nation's most prestigious and longest-running celebrations of the arts. They are hosted by the National Council of Traditional Arts (NCTA), an organization charged with helping the U.S. State Department put on overseas tours. "We took Washington DC by storm and got more jobs than we knew what to do with," Sonny said.

The Sun Rhythm Section played at rockabilly revival shows around the country. With the NCTA endorsement, the group was recruited by State Department officials who recognized the goodwill potential of the music and sent the band on a three-month tour that included North Africa, England, Norway, Sweden, and Bangladesh. For the next ten years, Sonny and the Sun veterans played international festivals and traveled the world as ambassadors of American rock and roll. "The audiences were local folks, few Americans, but they loved us over there," Sonny said. "They knew about Elvis, but the only song they recognized was 'Tutti Frutti.' They called it the 'ice cream song.'"

By 1996, several members of the Sun Rhythm Section had passed away or were unable to continue performing. Over its ten-year run, the band was featured in countless media stories about "the old guys and our great show band," Sonny said.

An Ageless Vitality

When the group disbanded, Sonny, now in his sixties, continued with unflagging energy. For a brief period, he performed on local television. *The Sonny Burgess Show* was a thirty-minute, weekly program broadcast from KAIT in Jonesboro. Sonny had to provide the show's sponsors, so he recruited the Burton Farm Equipment Company, a Jackson County business with family roots dating back to the pioneer era. "I would get them up there to talk about tractors," Sonny said. "We'd sing and have commercials."

In the 1990s, the Kings V recorded at Roland Janes' Sonic Studio in Memphis. "For $300, you could get one hundred discs," Sonny said. "We sold a few records to local fans and gave the rest away."

The Sonny Burgess Show *on KAIT-TV Jonesboro. Kings V band members: Doug Greeno, bass; Bobby Nelson, keyboard; Gene Grant, drums; and Tommy Tims, vocals; 1965.*

In the early 1990s, Sonny toured with a group of contemporary and veteran musicians known as the Tennessee All Stars. He performed with roots rock musician Dave Alvin of the Blasters and recorded the album *Tennessee Border* with the group in 1992. That same year, Sonny played a show in Memphis for the fifteenth anniversary of Elvis' death and a two-night show in Woodstock, where he impressed music promoter Dan Griffin. He played a wireless red Fender Telecaster, Griffin said, as he ran and jumped though the audience and all over the stage. Sonny's stage presence and talent were equally striking at a 1995 benefit show in New York for the family of guitar player Danny Gatton.

"When Sonny played, he was like a man on fire," Griffin said. "Sonny brought the house down with his onstage antics and jumping into the audience, just like Springsteen used to do."[18]

Cover of 1996 album produced by Garry Tallent.

Upon retirement from St. Louis Trim, Sonny threw himself back into music full time, singing with a local gospel group Stranger's Home, touring overseas, and eventually reuniting in 1997 with the surviving Pacers.

In the mid-1990s, he recorded for Rounder and High Tone Records, and he completed the self-titled album *Sonny Burgess* produced by Bruce Springsteen bass player Garry Tallent. The album included "Tiger Rose," a song written by Springsteen that was unpublished at the time. "We were recording in Nashville when Tallent told me Springsteen had a really good song that would be right for me," Sonny said. "We called him up and he gave us the lyrics to the song right then over the phone."

"Tiger Rose" tells the story of a working-class husband discovering his wife's infidelity. It is far from the youthful rantings of Sonny's early rockabilly tunes, the pounding and the boogie of Newport night clubs. In 2001, Sonny was videotaped on stage with Bruce Springsteen at a 9/11 benefit show at the Count Basie Theater in Red Bank, New Jersey. Performing "Tiger Rose," Sonny's deep voice resonates with a betrayed love and the acceptance of loss. It is vibrant rock and roll, now showing its maturity and age, heartbreaking and slow.

The album *Sonny Burgess*, with its dramatic cover photo of Sonny, middle-aged and white haired, was called "a modern rockabilly classic" by Allmusic.com reviewer Cub Koda.[19]

> If trying to bring back an old artist from the '50s is an idea that seldom merits results that exceed "you can't go home again" or worse, here is an album that proves it can be done and done right. Producer Garry Tallent keeps Sonny Burgess focused with the lead vocal and blistering lead guitar duties squarely on his shoulders, gives him a pile of great songs…to interpret, then frames it all with a backing band that's the essence of drive and simplicity. The spotlight stays on Burgess throughout, just letting him do what he does best. While it all sounds simple enough, it seldom—if ever—happens on these kinds of affairs, making the achievement of this record all that more astounding….The tray card on this reads "Sonny Burgess has still got it." Believe it.

Also in 1996, Sonny appeared on the television program *Late Night with Conan O'Brien*, performing with Rosie Flores, a Texas-based rockabilly guitar player and singer, and kicking off a six-week duo tour across the South.

"Touring with Sonny was all about showmanship," Flores said. "He taught me you're allowed to get crazy as you play lead guitar. He taught me to have fun on stage. The shows were always amazing."

Sonny performing with Rosie Flores on the Conan O'Brien Show; *1996.*

Chapter 5.
Rockabilly Roots

Southern Rockers

Rockabilly has always been here in the South. We just didn't know what it was. It wasn't loud music because we didn't have anything loud to play it with. It wasn't the speed, even though people play it too fast. Rockabilly was the beat, a certain feeling when you get that drive that makes you want to dance. Wherever blue collar workers were, there was that hard rough sound, there was rockabilly.

—Teddy Riedel

Good southern players have a better feel for the music than others. We all grew up poor. We didn't go to music school. We play from the heart, not from the chart. It's the "feel" you put into the music.

—Travis Wammack

Rooted in the land and the cycles of agricultural life, southerners have accepted social change reluctantly. Although sharecroppers and tenant farmers replaced the slaves of pre-Civil War plantations, generations of working-class black and white southerners continued a labor-intensive lifestyle, the only way they knew to make a crop.

That world collapsed in the 1950s with the introduction of tractors, chemicals, government subsidies, and alternate crops. As agricultural wealth and farms consolidated, a new creative energy emerged. Drawing on the perseverance and strengths the land had instilled in them, what historian Pete Daniel calls "the hard gem of working-class spontaneity and genius," certain young men produced the South's greatest contributions to American culture in the twentieth century: stock car racing and rock and roll.[20]

Stock car racing began in the daring feats of moonshiners outrunning revenue agents. It has evolved into NASCAR. And rock and roll has its origins in the brash rockabilly music heard in the roadhouses of Newport, in the Sun Records studio at Memphis, and in juke joints and dance halls across the greater Mississippi Delta.

Rockabilly emerged and disappeared in a five-year window flung open in 1954 by Elvis Presley's first Sun Records single "That's Alright" and slammed shut in 1959 with Sonny Burgess' recording of "Sadie's Back in Town." The new music appeared during a region-wide transformation that eroded the holistic nature of small-town life and decimated rural populations. One Delta town after another saw its people and businesses depart, creating a landscape of abandoned schools, sharecropper shacks, and cotton gins. Weeds overran neglected rural cemeteries, and labor crews cut and uprooted the remaining trees, burning the waste wood in bulldozed piles as the new acreage was prepared for the expanding farms of select landowners.

The Last Generation of Sharecroppers

The people who left the land went to towns such as Newport that offered factory jobs, housing, schools, and commerce. Newport also offered what Pete Daniel described as dense, loud, and sexually charged dance halls where the explosive talent of the last generation of sharecroppers was released.[21]

"We wanna pound, we wanna boogie!" screamed Sonny Burgess as he leapt from the Silver Moon stage with his red Fender Stratocaster. His fifty-foot guitar cable provided the freedom to join Johnny Ray Hubbard on the dance floor, who spun his bass fiddle and climbed onto the instrument as he mugged for the crowd with women's bloomers on his head.

"Playing music beats the hell out of picking cotton," Roland Janes said. Janes was born in Brookings, Arkansas, a Delta town that no longer exists. The former logging and cotton community was about two hours from Memphis, where Janes became one of the top guitar players at Sun Records. Arkansas was full of rockabilly musicians, Janes suggested, because it was a crossroads for a mixture of blues and country artists.

Jerry Kattawar, a Pacers' piano player in the 1960s, agreed that the most successful musicians were raised with a rich regional heritage. For those with talent and ambition, Kattawar added, the easy money and the night life of a musician's world provided an attractive means of evading farm work and factory jobs.

"If you were not in sports or music, you would go to a small town factory or farm. And nobody wanted that," Kattawar said. "Most of us gravitated to music because that was all that went on. If you were within one hundred miles of Memphis, you heard about Sun."

Something in the Water

Arkansas and the mid-South produced a remarkable number of talented musicians in the post-war generation. "It was something in the water," the players jokingly say. Yet Sonny and other Delta musicians grew up listening to regional rhythm and blues and *Grand Ole Opry* radio programs. They heard country music at local dance halls and from musicians that traveled the rural circuits. They sat in tent shows and heard performers such as Ma Rainey and the Rabbit Foot Minstrels that toured the South.

The music created by the Pacers and other early southern rockers became the backdrop for a generation of young people who voiced their impatience with conformity. Rockabilly bragged of hedonistic intentions and personal capacity. Its lead instrument, the electric guitar, provided a raucous release of energy that initially gave a derogatory identity to its player, according to Larry Donn. "The term 'Rockabilly' was originally a putdown of the Sun artists," Donn said. "Rock 'n' roll was getting a big name, and northern people in the business wanted to keep the name for the tie-wearing, finger-snapping artists like Bobby Darin, Paul Anka, and the like. They started calling our rock 'n' roll 'Rockabilly' so it wouldn't be confused with their kind of rock 'n' roll. They couldn't stand it that these hoodlums and hillbilly hicks from the South were taking all their record sales."[22]

Sonny disagrees. "I never thought of it as a put down," he said. "There's nothing negative about it to me. They used to call us 'hillbilly,' same as they did with Hank [Williams] and Elvis. And that was alright with me."

But the new music caused fistfights and riots at shows, bringing out horseback police to control crowds. Associated with juvenile delinquency, the early rock and roll challenged family values and the mainstream music of the 1950s, which brought soothing romantic ballads by crooners Bing Crosby and Perry Como. The music was also perceived as a threat to segregation. It opened new markets for black performers, and it encouraged white musicians, particularly those from Arkansas and Tennessee, to sing and dance in a manner associated with African Americans. Many white politicians and religious conservatives found the new music alarming. For them, the federal imposition of civil rights was a form of communism, and they believed the Bible forbade racial mixing.

The wild new sound was heard across the country in regional genres. In the North, it became the energetic syncopation of Bill Haley and the Comets. From New Orleans came the rhythmic, flowing dance blues of Fats Domino, and from Macon, Georgia, the loopy falsetto of Little Richard. From Chicago came an urban rock and blues, the driving beat of Chuck Berry and Bo Diddley. From New York and Philadelphia came doo wop, the urbane hipster's streetcorner a cappella sound.

In the South, the new sound was a marriage of country music with rhythm and blues, two genres that were themselves evolving even as they influenced change. The balance of those sounds could be heard in the early music of Elvis Presley, whom the Newport newspaper called "the king of western bop." Presley, the paper stated, benefited from his childhood surroundings "in which country music and Negro blues were everyday music to him."[23]

As rural African American music became urbanized and electrified, it evolved into rhythm and blues and up-tempo gospel. At the same time, traditional country music accelerated its rhythm and became hillbilly bop. Both genres had rural roots. And both were natural to the mid-South region of the Delta. Whites from the mid-South mixed their music with black styles. They played country music sped up, or as Carl Perkins suggested, a country man's song with a black man's rhythm.

Rockabilly Roots
in Rhythm and Blues

Black bands play rock a little differently. They've got a little more gospel in their blues. But we're all sons of the delta. We all play rockabilly, a three-chord rock and roll.

—C. W. Gatlin

In the era of abundance and prosperity of the 1950s, Americans were encouraged to conform to standards of decorum. The expectation was that young adults would get a job, marry, and raise a family.

But another pattern emerged within the culture of the displaced rural southerner, particularly among white young men. This group was more attracted to the provocative energy of early rock and roll than the promised compensations of a factory job. Fast cars, "loose" women, and frenzied dancing to electrified guitar licks and a pumping piano filled their need for immediate gratification.

Through the early phases of the civil rights movement, rockabilly pioneers found a model for their yearnings in the social group denied access to the 1950s patterns of conformity and reward. As African Americans began to confront the confining traditions of segregation, black artists sang of their sexual prowess and desires in an up-tempo dance rhythm propelled by saxophone solos.

The term *rock and roll* had been black vernacular for sex since at least 1922 when Trixie Smith sang, "My Daddy Rocks Me (With a Steady Roll)." By the 1950s, sexual double entendres and salacious lyrics were widely used. In "Shake, Rattle, and Roll," one of the decade's biggest hits, the singer proclaims "I've been holdin' it in, way down underneath / You make me roll my eyes, baby, make me grit my teeth." He describes himself as "a one-eyed cat peepin' in a seafood store."

The music industry gave the sound a new name. *Billboard* magazine in 1945 had changed its "Harlem Hit Parade" listing to "Race Records," a term which had been in use since the 1920s to describe African American recordings of jazz, blues, and gospel. In 1949, the magazine renamed the genre "Rhythm and Blues." The emerging new music, well documented in Preston Lauterbach's *The Chitlin' Circuit and the Road to Rock 'n' Roll*, had its origins in cities with sizeable black populations such as New Orleans, Houston, Memphis, Macon, and Indianapolis.[24]

Memphis Radio

Television was the new mass media of the post-war period, capturing a large percentage of the white radio audience. Many radio stations responded by cultivating a new black audience through popular music and black disc jockeys. WDIA in Memphis was a prime example.

Established in 1947 with a country and western format, the station struggled to survive its first year. In 1948, WDIA's popularity surged when it began broadcasting *Tan Town Jubilee*, the first radio program in the nation to specifically target black listeners. After switching to all-black programming, WDIA became the city's top station. By 1954, WDIA's increased broadcasting power of 50,000 watts reached listeners from Missouri to the Gulf Coast, a region that included ten percent of the African American population in United States.

WDIA disc jockeys included Memphis musicians Rufus Thomas and B. B. King, his show titled *Bee Bee's Jeebies*, as well as local personalities with catchy on-air names such as Honeyboy, Hot Rod, and Princess Premium Stuff. They played records by popular rhythm and blues artists, such as:

- **Joe Turner**—a "blues shouter" and a personal favorite of Sonny Burgess. Turner had a string of hits in the 1940s and more than fifty singles on the market by 1951. His recording of "Shake, Rattle, and Roll" held the No. 1 spot for three weeks on the Billboard R&B chart in 1954. Commenting in the mid-1950s on the music that had become known as rock and roll, Turner said, "It wasn't but a different name for the same music I been singing all my life."[25]
- **Louis Jordan**—an Arkansas native whose style of "jump blues" featured an up-tempo and strongly syncopated beat. His records were cross-over hits to the pop charts. A gifted lyricist, Jordan wrote songs about fish fries, clattering railroad journeys, and brash women. His songs were vivacious and fun, with rapid-sequence rhymes and bold rhythmic stops. Music writer Nick

Tosches called Jordan the "king of postwar hep," whose style of party music "did more to prepare whiter folks for the coming of rock and roll than any other man of the era."[26]

- **Wynonie Harris**—often cited as a direct influence on Elvis Presley. Harris' "Good Rockin' Tonight," one of the biggest R&B hits of 1948, became Presley's second single in 1954. Presley also repeated Harris' stage moves of pelvic thrusts, lip curling, and evangelical waving of arms and hands. Presley's penchant for making spontaneous gifts of Cadillac cars may have been influenced by Harris, who was also noted for his excess in cars, romance, and spending. At one time, Harris kept two chauffeured Cadillacs at a Harlem club waiting for him to pick one to take him home.

In 1949, WHBQ hired Dewey Phillips, a white "rhyming DJ" who delivered a rapid verbal patter in a thick southern drawl. He played a mix of country, rhythm and blues, gospel, and rock and roll on his *Red Hot and Blue* late night show. The music was popular with white listeners, who began buying records by black artists, affirming a statement by Ahmet Ertegun, founder of Atlantic Records, who said, "You can't segregate the radio dial."[27]

In the last years of segregation, whites' enthusiasm for black music gave it added respectability and created a more lucrative market. White teenagers from Memphis drove across the Mississippi River bridge to the Plantation Inn of West Memphis where blacks performed. Girls came from their high school proms with corsages, white gloves, and formal dresses. They came back, as Glenn Altschuler wrote, "carrying their shoes and hose, having danced and sweated the night away."[28]

Paths of Influence

In the city, and particularly in black working-class neighborhoods, night clubs and bars were the breeding grounds for rhythm and blues and its feisty young sibling, rock and roll. Though Preston Lauterbach contends that Roy Brown's "Good Rockin' Tonight" is the true rock and roll predecessor, the original 1947 release of the jump blues placed it a bit early for prime influence. As a cover hit by Wynonie Harris and as Elvis' selection for his second Sun recording, "Good Rockin' Tonight" does provide the rhythm patterns and sexual messages that define an early rock classic. Yet Jackie Brenston's "Rocket 88," first recorded in March 1951, offers more explicit examples of the path of influence from rhythm and blues to rock and roll.

Brenston's record became a rock and roll milestone because of its fast pace, its raw style, and its distorted tone, created by a torn amplifier speaker cone stuffed with newspapers. The makeshift repair, legend has it, was an attempt to minimize damages after the amp fell from a vehicle on the way to Sam Phillips' Memphis Recording Service, the predecessor to Sun Records.

"Rocket 88" had the good fortune of being in the right place at the right time. Phillips brought the song to disc jockey Dewey Phillips, who chose it as the theme song for his *Red Hot and Blue* show. A Memphis Oldsmobile dealer played the song on loudspeakers at its car lot, and the *Memphis Commercial Appeal* picked up the story. The song's promotional exposure by white businesses, as well as its more fortuitous timing, arriving at a time when more black artists were achieving crossover hits, gave it an advantage that Roy Brown's earlier efforts lacked.

Brenston was a saxophone player in Ike Turner's band, the Kings of Rhythm, from Clarksdale, Mississippi. "Rocket 88" was derived from a song in the band's repertoire, "Cadillac Boogie" by Jimmy Liggins, who was a successful bandleader in the jump blues period of the late 1940s and early 1950s. Liggins was noted for a stage presence and hyper performance style that influenced black and white early rockers. Brenston's song was also influenced by Los Angeles-based Pete Johnson with his instrumental "Rocket 88 Boogie."

Produced by Turner, "Rocket 88" was released by Chess/Checker Records and maintained an R&B No. 1 position for five weeks that year. Brenston and the Kings of Rhythm moved on in the wake of the record's success, but Turner remained in Memphis for a time, working as an arranger and talent scout of blues artists for Sun and other record labels. He was instrumental in bringing numerous blues artists— Howlin' Wolf, Bobby Bland, and others—into the studios.

"Rocket 88" is an urban anthem of personal freedom for those bound by asphalt streets and a working-class life. The car was a light-weight Oldsmobile whose aerodynamic features, wrap-around windshield, and V8 engine set a pattern for 1950s automotive design. Brenston sings of cruising in a fast and stylish new car while sharing a bottle among the riders, celebrating movement, release, and camaraderie. The car, as always, is a metaphor for the singer's sexual prowess.

Sonny Burgess continued the motif of cars, romance, and freedom in 1956, celebrating Newport nightlife and the town's most prominent street in "We Wanna' Boogie": "Headin' down Front Street baby, and all over town / Man you oughta see the lights when the sun goes down / Just a-poundin' and a boogyin' and a-paintin' that town."

A Battlefield for Segregation

Rock and roll became a battlefield for segregationists who believed it prompted depraved behavior among blacks and encouraged racial mixing. In the early years of the civil rights movement, many southern school boards and state legislators issued bans on social functions that promoted racial mixing. Membership increased in local chapters of the Ku Klux Klan and white citizens' councils, where racist ideology considered rock and roll a black device for the sexual conquest of white women.

A riot broke out in Cleveland on March 21, 1954, when an all-black rock and roll show drew a racially mixed crowd of 25,000 teenagers to a facility that could accommodate only 10,000. On April 10, 1956, three members of the anti-black, anti-rock and roll North Alabama White Citizens Council attacked Nat King Cole on stage at the Birmingham Municipal Auditorium. Cole was no rocker, but his jazzy, crooning style was popular enough to enrage white racists. At the time, Cole was the first African American to host a national television music program. *The Nat King Cole Show* ended in 1957 when sponsors, fearing a white boycott of their products, refused to underwrite it.

Among rural, low-income people, many blacks and whites regularly crossed the color line. They sometimes worked for the same landowners and lived in the same neighborhoods. White musicians heard black music in juke joints and honky tonks. For Arkansan Billy Lee Riley, exposure to black music was among his earliest childhood memories. "When I was four or five years old," he said, "we lived in a house on Red Row in Osceola that had black families of either side.... There was no color barrier. There were two little black boys I played with, and we used to go downtown on Saturdays. They would take me round to the black section of town, and we would sit for hours and listen to the music coming out of the juke joints and maybe watch guitar players sitting on the side of the street. That was my first introduction to the blues."[29]

Riley was influenced by Jericho Leon "Lightning" Carter, a black bluesman and family friend honored in a 1960 album when Riley recorded under the name "Lightning Leon." Two other rockabilly pioneers, both sons of rural cotton farmers, credited older black men with influencing their musical tastes. For Carl Perkins, it was John Westbrook, a field hand who worked alongside the Perkins family in Tiptonville, Tennessee. For piano player Charlie Rich, who grew up in Colt, Arkansas, it was a black man named C. J. Allen.[30]

An early exposure to rural black music and the common lifestyle of black and white farmers was also the heritage of Sam Phillips. Born to poor tenant farmers near Florence, Alabama, Phillips worked with his parents alongside black laborers, and he heard them singing blues, field hollers, and work songs. When Phillips opened the Memphis Recording Service in 1950 and Sun Records in 1952, he began each business by recording black blues artists whose rural southern backgrounds matched his own.

Rufus Thomas, born in rural Mississippi and raised in Memphis, was among the profusion of black performers in the area at the time. "It is no accident that so much talent came from the Memphis area," Thomas said. "From Beale Street and the Blues comes every kind of music you can think of. The Blues is the mother of them all."[31]

Phillips sold his recordings of black musicians to larger record companies, where many of the songs generated impressive sales. White performers freely covered the songs, and many versions were listed on the Billboard pop charts. A few black artists signed contracts that gave them copyright protection, but full compensation rarely came to the black originators.

Arthur Crudup, whose song "That's Alright" became the smash debut hit for Elvis Presley, offers a dramatic example of a black artist struggling for equity. Over a nearly forty-year career as a songwriter and performer, Crudup jumped from label to label and worked day jobs to support a family of four children and nine stepchildren. When Elvis made his milestone recording for Sun Records in 1954, Crudup was a forty-nine-year-old migrant laborer en route to Florida.

As black rhythm and blues evolved into rock and roll, the field was rapidly overtaken by white rockabilly artists and record producers. Rockabilly, critic Greil Marcus wrote, proved that "white boys could be as strange, as exciting, as scary, and as free as the black men who were suddenly walking America's airwaves as if they owned them."[32]

Rockabilly Roots in Country Music

"Blue Moon of Kentucky" was the B-side tune on Elvis Presley's debut recording for Sun Records. The country song was chosen even though fans were already screaming for more rhythm and blues interpretations from the nineteen-year-old Memphis sensation. But like rhythm and blues, country music was changing, and country audiences were ready for a modern style.

The change was not immediately welcomed at the Grand Ole Opry. At Elvis' debut in 1954, Opry Manager Jim Denny limited the newcomer to one song. Afterward, an unimpressed Denny supposedly recommended that the Memphis teenager continue driving a truck.

Elvis huffed and puffed his way through a fast version of Bill Monroe's tale of loneliness and infidelity. It was an old story that country music shared with the blues. Out in the country somewhere, somebody had done somebody wrong. If it featured black people, the song became blues. If it featured white people—Jimmie Rodgers singing about loneliness and tragedy, Hank Williams singing about fear and failure—it was country. Elvis turned it into rock and roll.

Traditional country music appealed to middle- and lower-class whites. The music was often about family and marriage, mothers or sweethearts, and memories of rural life. Starting in the 1940s, songs reflected the social tensions emerging from a changing landscape. The new themes were of resignation and rural fundamentalism. Beer-drinking torch songs told of men lost to the bottle or temptress women, bad farm years, and the price paid for succumbing to human weakness: alcoholism, divorce, and loneliness.

But the new sound of country music also expressed a lively happiness, adding a distinctive rock beat as country singers moaned, yelped, and whined about dancing and having good times with their gal. They added electric guitars and drums, and they played louder and with a more danceable rhythm and blues style than previous country bands. In 1947, Hank Williams cut "Rootie Tootie," his third MGM release, with its nonsense lyrics about getting married, its bouncy call-and-response slang expressions, and its hot, western swing fiddle licks. In "Setting the Woods on Fire," Williams sang of America's favorite new pastime—riding around with a sweetheart in the car.

Origins of the Terms

In a radio interview with Hank Williams in 1950, an Alabama disc jockey called him "the Number One Hillbilly artist today."[33] By this time, *Billboard* magazine had already changed the name of Hillbilly charts to Country and Western charts. Accompanying the name change, several musical styles were rapidly becoming popular.

Boogie woogie originated in Texas and Louisiana at the turn of the century as a piano-based blues. The music was well suited to ensembles and small bands, and the piano was played as a lead instrument or to accompany a singer. Early piano players Jimmy Yancey and Meade Lux Lewis featured a steady rhythmic pattern in the left hand mixed with free rhythm and melody highlights in the right. The style became extremely popular following the 1938 Spirituals to Swing concert at Carnegie Hall, setting off a national boogie-woogie craze.

Black, white, and country music audiences each had distinctive boogie-woogie styles. For black audiences, the ensembles evolved into rhythm and blues bands. Pioneers included Lionel Hampton and Louis Jordan, whose small groups combined light blues and novelty songs and played popular boogie-woogie rhythms. Jordan's "Choo Choo Ch'boogie" is a classic in the genre. For white audiences of jazz and pop music, the boogie-woogie fad peaked in the 1940s with pop hits by the Tommy Dorsey and Woody Herman bands and with songs such as "Boogie Woogie Bugle Boy of Company B" by the Andrews Sisters. And in country music, the Delmore Brothers introduced the term "Hillbilly Boogie" as the title of their 1945 recording. Grand Ole Opry star Red Foley had many boogie-woogie hits, including "Chattanooga Shoe Shine Boy."

Honky tonk music celebrates the working class. Its lyrics emphasize more drinking and night life than those of boogie woogie. Before World War II, honky tonk was called "hillbilly music." Influenced by western swing, it often included a fiddle or a steel guitar, and it was popular in barrooms from Texas and Oklahoma to the West Coast.

Honky tonk music is synonymous with the rough drinking establishment often called a roadhouse, many of which had a back room for gambling. Ernest Tubb had the first honky-tonk hit, "Walking the Floor Over You," in 1941, but Hank Williams had the best sound and range for the genre. Songs such as "I Saw the Light" radiated happiness, "Jambalaya" told of the joy of life in the bayous of south Louisiana, and "Calijah" offered a charming fairy tale of the wooden Indian that fell in love.

Similar to rockabilly pioneers of the 1950s, Williams was influenced early in his life by a black musician. This was Rufus "Tee Tot" Payne, a Greenville, Alabama, street performer who mentored the young Williams and taught him a New Orleans standard, "My Bucket's Got a Hole in It." Williams recorded the song in 1949. The Pacers covered it at Sun Records in 1957.

Western swing is an additional country music influence on rockabilly. From Texas, Bob Wills created a popular, danceable sound blending ragtime fiddle tunes and jazz and blues licks with Mexican music, waltzes, and polkas. Family bands such as the Maddox Brothers and Rose added vibrant western costumes, whoops, and yelps to enliven their shows.

Barrelhouse came from the lumber and turpentine camps of Texas and Louisiana. This was a boisterous piano style with a driving two-beat rhythm originally played to raucous crowds in shacks where liquor was sold from barrels. Barrelhouse musicians such as Sunnyland Slim and Pinetop Perkins were also innovators of boogie woogie, which developed from the barrelhouse style.

Bluegrass came from the Appalachian Mountains of eastern Tennessee and Kentucky, where jigs, reels, and mournful ballads were rooted in the traditional fiddle music of the British Isles. The term *bluegrass* was first used in 1948, when it became a subcategory under Country and Western for radio airplay charting. The name was derived from the Bluegrass Boys, the band Bill Monroe established in 1938, whose "high, lonesome sound" included fast-paced solos on the banjo, mandolin, and acoustic guitar. Sonny's inclusion of the Monroe tune "Rocky Road Blues" in the Rocky Road Ramblers performance list reflects the bluegrass influence during his formative years.

Rockabilly Style and Its Stars

Rockabilly is a couple of guitars, bass, and drums. That's it. That's the rockabilly. When you started adding piano and horns, that's when you got into rhythm and blues or rock and roll.

—Sonny Burgess

To some, the music was loud, threatening, and hedonistic. Performers wore pink and black clothes, sporting sideburns and slicked-back long hair. They played their music with an assertive confidence, then came driving home at dawn, sweaty and weary from a night of full exertion, their equipment crowded with them in the car.

The typical rockabilly performer was born between 1930 and 1935 into a low-to-middle-class home. Because he was not educated beyond high school, he worked in a trade, at a blue collar job, or on a farm. He served in the armed forces; Germany and Korea were the most common assignments. The performer had a country music background mostly gained by listening to the radio, but he was also interested in music by black performers.

By 1955, his guitar and bass had become electric. Drums and piano were added to the band. Band members played aggressive, energetic solos and sang at their upper range, a rasping or shouting voice adding to the impression of strain, of a performer's giving his all. All was presented with an acrobatic showmanship. Movement was essential, be it strutting the stage or dancing in place with a long-neck electric guitar or pounding a keyboard with elbows and feet.

They sang of women and dancing, no devotional or romantic love, fast living, cars, booze, and parties. Lyrics were direct statements, often simplistic clichés or even ludicrous babble, such as Roy Orbison's "Ooby Dooby," a song of few words beyond its title, repeated with enough verve and rhythm as to somehow suggest meaning.

The figures profiled in this chapter—Sam Phillips/Sun Records, Elvis Presley, Carl Perkins, Roy Orbison, and Jerry Lee Lewis—all meet some criteria of the rockabilly demographic. Most of them made their first recordings at Sun Records, which puts them among the core group of southern pioneers who have influenced rock and roll. All have worked with the Pacers, on stage together or on tour. Many became lifetime friends of the band.

Sam Phillips and Sun Records

Everybody in the world wanted to record for that little old label. It didn't last but a few years, but it was magic.

—Sonny Burgess[34]

Memphis in the 1950s was the center of the musical universe, attracting black bluesmen from the cotton-rich counties of Mississippi, barrelhouse piano players from the Louisiana wetlands, and country bands and rock and rollers from the hills of Arkansas and Tennessee. Their pilgrimages to Memphis originated in their common rural heritage. Their destination was a start-up recording studio whose label featured a rooster crowing at the rising sun.

"Sun" recording companies had been established in numerous locations worldwide—Canada, England, India, and several U.S. cities—well before Sam Phillips created its most famous incarnation. The Sun logo as well had an earlier existence, having been created in 1946 for a New York-based Sun Record Company that billed itself as "The Brightest Thing on Records." The New York company, which recorded Jewish musicians and singers, was closed by 1952 when Phillips transformed his Memphis Recording Service into Sun Records. Despite its design being credited to John Gale Parker Jr., an Alabama high school classmate of Phillips, the logo was copied directly from the short-lived New York business.[35]

Phillips was more interested in style than in labels. He was looking for new and original recording artists whose confidence and talent surpassed their social status or the quality of their equipment. When Ike Turner's band arrived at the Memphis studio in 1951, it was Phillips who performed the makeshift repair on the torn speaker cone of Willie Kizart's guitar amp. The result was a new sound, raw and buzzing with energy, a tone that characterized nearly all early rock and roll music.

"I didn't want to lead them astray from what they had been doing," Phillips said. "If they had broken down equipment or their instruments were ragged, I didn't want them to feel ashamed. I wanted them to play what they were used to playing. Because expression was the thing. I never listened to the sound of one instrument. I listened for the total effect."[36]

Sonny said Phillips had artists perform as if they were in a live show rather than a recording studio. "He'd just turn you loose, and you'd play like you had a crowd watching," Sonny said. "That's how come there are all the mistakes. It wasn't super good music, but it felt good to us."

Sonny mentioned Jerry Lee Lewis' "Whole Lotta Shakin'," a 1957 Sun record he said contains an audible error, an authentic small stumble that often happens in recording studios. But in this case, the error was not corrected.

"If you listen real closely in the middle of the song just after a drum roll, J. M. [Van Eaton] gets out of time," Sonny said. "There is a momentary loss of rhythm, then he gets back in it real quickly. But the record sold over twelve million copies. That was Sam's talent, capturing that."

The mistake did not slip by unnoticed. Van Eaton said two cuts of "Whole Lotta Shakin'" were recorded, but Sam Phillips chose the flawed one for release. In comparison, Van Eaton said Sun engineer Jack Clement was not satisfied until Lewis and the band recorded twenty cuts of "It'll Be Me," a song Clement had written.[37]

Phillips' intuitive sense for music was enhanced by Sun Records' distinctive "slapback" echo, an effect that defined rockabilly music and many early rock and roll recordings. The echo or delay effect was achieved when a magnetic recording tape passed through a recording head, then made a small loop before passing through a second playback head milliseconds later. The distance between the recording head and the playback head determined the depth of the echo.

A good example of this can be heard on Scotty Moore's guitar work on "That's All Right." The echo effect gave depth to the raw music and the gritty sound of the country musicians and bar singers who recorded at Sun. Outside the studio, some rockabilly guitar players used a special portable amplifier with a built-in tape loop system. This was the Echosonic Amp built by Illinois sound engineer Ray Butts. Only sixty-eight of the guitar amp and speaker cabinet combos were ever built.

"It was a real good amp that cost about $600," Sonny said. "Scotty Moore had one. Carl Perkins did, too. Roy Orbison had one, and we used it all the time when he traveled with us."

Phillips was seeking a sound he called "imperfectly perfect," a sound he knew was right when he heard it. "Honey Don't," the 1956 Carl Perkins hit, was an example of the "feel good" music he was after. Drawing on his southern Christian heritage, Phillips said, "'Feel' is my John 3:16."[38]

In the years before his death in 2003, Phillips offered profound statements about his involvement in the birth of rock and roll. Having been questioned for nearly forty years about his influence on American culture, Phillips responded with deep gravitas about his search for the breakthrough white artist who could sing with the same feeling black people brought to their music. Phillips spoke of his work as an evangelical mission. He suggested that Sun Records freed black and white people to express their complex personalities and their shared rural heritage.

Sonny affirmed the near-religious status Phillips created at Sun. "That little studio was the biggest cathedral in the world to me," he said.[39] The musicians who came to record at Sun Records certainly had faith. The African American bluesmen who made the first recordings in 1950–1952 had faith in Phillips' business skills and integrity. The white musicians who came to Sun in the later 1950s had faith that the records they cut and the bookings and tours arranged by Bob Neal would change their lives. Memphis teenagers like Elvis Presley, who walked in off the street and paid $3.98 to record two songs (the sound tracks going straight from the microphone to the acetate with no mixing), they, too, had faith in the music and the magic that might happen once their music was heard.

And their faith was rewarded by the child of Alabama sharecroppers, a former radio announcer and part-time recording engineer, whose rural background matched their own, a man who said he "heard the innate rhythms of people that had absolutely no formal training in music, didn't know one note from another."[40]

Elvis Presley

In 1955, the "Hillbilly Hep Cat" played 265 shows across the nation, thirty-five of them in Arkansas. Many of the Arkansas shows were in small Delta clubs, armories, and high school auditoriums, in towns close enough to get home to Memphis afterward. The Catholic Club in Helena was a repeated site, and there were several shows in Little Rock and Texarkana on the way to Shreveport and performances on the *Louisiana Hayride* radio program.

Elvis played six shows in Jackson County that year, and the Moonlighters opened for him at two of those.[41] Elvis' first shows in Newport were a double bill on March 2—an early show at the Newport Armory, followed by a performance at Porky's Rooftop. The newspaper described Elvis as a "twenty-year-old fireball from the LA Hayride who combined country music with bop in the fastest selling style available."[42]

The front-page article stated that the performer was "remarkably pleasant and friendly, and always enjoys chatting with his many fans. He's single and has no serious interests of the heart, devoting what time he has to spare from his busy schedule of personal appearances to working on his car and indulging in his hobby of collecting pink and black clothes."

Shelby Smith, a local farmer, saw both shows in Newport that night. He didn't like either of them. "I came out of the service in 1954," Smith said. "Back home, I had a date one night. She wanted to go to the Armory show. I never heard of Elvis. He was on a low platform stage with his small group. He played thirty or forty minutes. I didn't like the show. I told my girl I was going out. We went to Porky's Rooftop. Here he comes again. Porky said to me, "That Elvis." I said, "I know. I already left one show with him."

Elvis, sporting the iconic footwear of the time, poses with Arkansas State Trooper Ken McKee, who lent the performer his service revolver for the photo. Back-up band members Scotty Moore and Bill Black are also at the table. The photo was taken at a south Arkansas diner as the singer was en route to Shreveport to perform on the Louisiana Hayride *radio program; 1955.*

The Newport Armory and Porky's shows were on a Wednesday night. Even at midweek, Newport had no shortage of live music venues.

The Moonlighters performed at the Silver Moon that night. Afterward, Sonny went to Porky's to see the Memphis rising star. "Elvis had a great sound, and his act was entirely different than anybody else. Just he and Scotty and Bill. I hadn't seen anything like that," Sonny said. "He wasn't handsome; he was 'purty.' Elvis didn't do anything vulgar. He was just shaking; he was just feeling good."

Sonny recalled a small crowd at Porky's when Elvis began. "But the women there, I guess, started calling everybody they knew," he said. "The next thing you knew, every one of the streetwalkers off Front Street was there. There were a lot of them, and they were going crazy."

Elvis' first appearance at the Silver Moon on July 21, 1955, featured two opening acts and the back-up band of Porky Sellers & the White River Playboys. One of the acts was Arkansan Bud Deckelman, born thirty miles east of Newport in Harrisburg. At the time, Deckelman was a Memphis-based country singer with a regional hit, "Daydreamin'" on Meteor Records.

The other opening act was the attractive eighteen-year-old Wanda Jackson, performing country music at the time but gaining attention and encouragement from Elvis to sing rockabilly. Jackson would soon achieve immense popularity as one of the first female rockabilly stars, her raw and rough-edged vocal style delighting fans and shocking critics. That night in Newport, Sonny recalled, it was her good looks and her stage outfit, designed by her mother, that got the most attention.

"She had a white dress with fringes all over. She started shaking that fringe. That's when Elvis started chasing her; everybody was after her. But her Daddy traveled with her," Sonny said. "At that time, she didn't have a guitar. She just got up there and sung. But Porky had a pretty good size western band to back her up."

Twenty-year-old Elvis was the star of the show, drawing a fee of about $150. Sonny recalled his Lansky-designed suit had a "Mr. B" collar, a black velvet collar with blue and white pinstripes named for Billy Eckstine, the performer who created the fashion. Sonny's memories of performers' clothing was likely heightened by his twenty-five years in the garment industry, working for St. Louis Trimming, a store that sold cloth and bridal wear.

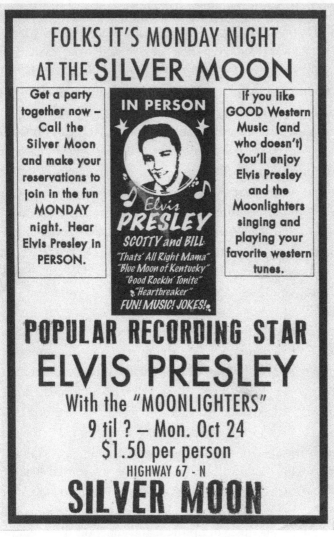

Elvis' October 1955 show at the Silver Moon was with the Moonlighters (soon to become the Pacers), who opened for him and joined his back-up musicians.

"Elvis was a really nice guy, real shy. He didn't drink, and he still had blond hair," Sonny recalled. "Scotty was a good-looking guy back then, too. D. J. looked like the mafia. You could tell he was Italian. And Bill Black, you could dress him up in a tuxedo and it looked like he'd slept in it."

During intermission at the Silver Moon show, Elvis sat in the audience with Newport teenagers, some of the boys wearing their school football jackets, and he invited the girls to visit him in Memphis. Kaneaster Hodges, a high school student at the time, said, "Elvis liked to talk with Joe Lewis," Hodges recalled, referring to the tall, handsome football player who was the Pacers' rhythm guitarist. Hodges said the night of Elvis' show was also distinctive because it did not include one of the club's frequent fights, the "big punch outs" that were common at the Silver Moon.

Through 1955, Elvis received nearly constant media coverage, and reporters searched for any shred of information about the new national sensation. On June 5, Gladys Presley, Elvis' mother, awoke in a fright in her Memphis home. She had dreamed her boy was in danger. At that moment, Elvis was heading home from a show in Hope, Arkansas, in his first pink Cadillac. The car caught on fire. Elvis was unharmed, but to many fans, their adoration already at near-hysterical levels, the incident served as an affirmation of their idol's rarefied stature.

On August 6, Elvis left the stage after playing only four songs at the White River Carnival at Batesville. According to Jimmy Davidson, who handled stage logistics and lighting at the Carnival, Elvis was booed off the stage after sliding on his knees and wiggling too much. Davidson was a former Tuckerman radio repairman and Silver Moon band leader who had moved to Batesville and established a cable television company. Davidson was aware of Batesville's strong religious heritage and large number of churches. He said he cautioned Elvis to restrain his on-stage dancing.

Another account of the walk-off has Elvis and the band acting too loose and cracking risqué jokes. The Carnival promoter Ed Lynn wrote to Elvis' manager Col. Tom Parker, demanding a refund of the $100 fee. Parker sent $50. He also sent an admonishing letter about professionalism to Bob Neal, the booking agent who traveled with Elvis that year.

At a show at Bono High School on September 6, Elvis fans crowded the high school gym and damaged the floor. Word quickly spread among other Arkansas school principals of the need for crowd control.

Elvis' last two appearances in Arkansas in 1955 were at Swifton on December 9. The first show was a fundraiser arranged by the high school senior class. Johnny Cash, who had signed on with Sun Records earlier that year, was the opening act. Elvis introduced the song "Heartbreak Hotel" at the Swifton shows, a record that would become a huge hit for him. As a precaution, the Swifton school principal had the performers stand off the gym floor under the basketball goal.

In the audience that night was a thirteen-year-old Swifton boy, Joel Anderson. More than fifty years later, Anderson, having become the chancellor of the University of Arkansas at Little Rock, gave this nostalgic account of the evening while speaking to the Little Rock Rotary Club:

> That night at the gym in Swifton was quite an experience. When in one of his songs Elvis started gyrating, my buddies and I were convinced he was drunk. And the shrieking and squealing by the girls was simply ridiculous. We'd never seen or heard anything like it.…
> When the show was over and the crowd was gone—that was when I saw and heard the King up close…my dad, and Elvis, and I stood over in the corner by the door. Elvis stood there with us…incredibly handsome…leaning against the wall…in his yellow blazer and purple pants…with his hair combed into a ducktail in the back.
> He was not very talkative as I recall. But I do have vivid memory of something Elvis said. As he was standing there…looked up and around in the gym…and here are the King's immortal words: "You just can't get any sound out of a gym!"

After the high school show, Elvis and Cash performed at Bob King's roadhouse, at that time called the "B&I Club." The Moonlighters were the opening act that night, and Searcy saxophonist Punky Caldwell was sitting in with the band

Johnny Cash and his group, the Tennessee Two, came to the B&I first.[43] Cash had already played his opening set at the sold-out school gym, and he came to the B&I rather than endure another hour of teenaged girls shrieking for Elvis. After the Moonlighters' opening set, Cash's band went on stage about ten p.m. The band played for an hour and Cash sang "Rock and Roll Ruby," a song he wrote that had already been recorded by Warren Smith. Sonny recalled that Cash was preparing to leave when Elvis and Bob Neal arrived.

"I'm back there talking to Bob Neal and Cash came up and said, 'We're going back to Memphis, these people don't want to hear us,'" Sonny said. "He was right. 'Rock and Roll Ruby' was his only fast song. He was good, like he always was, but that crowd wanted to hear Elvis. And it was jam packed."

After Cash left for Memphis, Elvis did his set with the Blue Moon Boys: Moore, Black, and Fontana. About midnight, the Moonlighters went back on stage.

"At 12:30, we were knocking them out," Sonny said. "Elvis was still there, hanging out with the kids. I was on stage when I felt something behind me and looked back. It was Scotty. He said, 'Just keep playing.' I felt Scotty reach around me from the back. We were both playing the same guitar. It was my gold Gibson. Then Elvis decided he would come back up and sing. So we got the rest of them up there, too. We wound up with two bands on stage. We played till about two o'clock."

It was a jam session and a classic roadhouse night. Along a rural highway, a low-ceilinged cinderblock building was crowded with dancers and drinkers, the whole place pounding with the energy of the music. It was also the night Elvis offered Kennedy and Caldwell jobs as sidemen in his traveling band—an offer both declined.

Sonny later learned that Elvis' interest in a larger band stemmed from a Memphis show earlier that year when he shared the bill with Carl Smith and Hank Thompson, both top country music artists who performed with a ten-piece orchestra. Backstage, Elvis threw down his guitar and kicked it across the room, vowing never again to go on stage with a small band.

The Swifton jam session that night was a turning point in the lives of the Newport musicians. Within a short time, the Moonlighters added new musicians, changed the band's name, and recorded their first song at Sun Records. Years later, Sonny still identified the talented young performers on stage that night as formative influences on his career.

"I always wanted to play like Scotty Moore," Sonny said. "I couldn't do it because he did a thumb picking style. But he was the guy that influenced me the most. I always wanted to sing like Elvis and play guitar like Scotty."

And Elvis' fans, as well, especially the women in Newport, never lost interest. The remarks of speaker at a 1957 Rotary Club meeting reflected the public fascination with the entertainer, whose image had become far more wholesome than three years earlier, when he had been seen as a rebel.

Mrs. Ila Huff of Memphis, a nationally known girls club director and youth advisor, said, "Elvis is a boy who doesn't cuss, doesn't drink, and honors his father and mother." Huff praised his church involvement and dismissed charges that rock and roll was too promiscuous. After a session of rock and roll, she stated, "almost anyone would be too tired for sex."[44]

By 1958, the closest Elvis would get to Newport was on the marquee of the movie theater. He starred in the title role of *King Creole*, which played at the Strand Theater on July 4 that year.

Sonny said his last meeting with Elvis was in 1959 as the Pacers were preparing for a western tour with Johnny Cash. The Newport musicians were in Lansky Brothers clothing store on Beale Street, and Elvis was home on leave from the army. He came into the store with his bodyguards and his old friend Red West, a key member of Elvis' inner circle sometimes called the Memphis Mafia. Elvis selected a shirt, took off the one he was wearing and threw it into the trash, then put on the new one as he stood in the store.

"He bought us all Pepsi Colas, and we were standing around talking about Porky's Rooftop and the Silver Moon," Sonny said. "All of the sudden, the word got out that Elvis was there. Just like magic, the place was full of people wanting autographs. That's when he left. They went outside to a red Lincoln Continental convertible. They just stepped over the seats and off they went. That was last time I talked to him."

Carl Perkins

The most famous refrain in rock and roll history—"Don't step on my blue suede shoes"—continues to raise questions. Was it the young man who warned his girlfriend to tread carefully, or did the young woman caution her excited dance partner to watch his step? And where were the words actually spoken?

The search for answers begins in Arkansas on March 21, 1955, when Carl Perkins and Johnny Cash opened for Elvis Presley at a show at Parkin High School. During a backstage conversation, Cash reminisced about a friend from his days in the air force who wore colorful shoes, and he suggested to Perkins that a song could be written about them. Driving home later that night, two and half hours from Parkin to Jackson, Tennessee, Perkins crossed the dark expanse of the Arkansas Delta and the rumbling roadway of the high bridge at Memphis. And perhaps a song germinated in Perkins' mind as he felt the droning thrum of worn tires and heard a syncopated rhythm in recurring clicks and bumps of his car on the highway.

But it was not until October, when Perkins performed at Union University in Jackson, that the song came into being. At a student dance at the school, Perkins supposedly heard a well-dressed dancer telling his date to be careful about his shoes.[45] Yet another version has the event at a club near Jackson where local high school students went dancing.[46] When Perkins' son Stan tells the story, it is the girl dancer who warns her partner with the much quoted line.[47]

Followers of fashion will assert that well-dressed girls in the 1950s wore saddle oxford shoes and that shoes made of blue suede would have been part of a man's wardrobe. But the enigmatic mythology of rock and roll has never been overly concerned with such details. What is true is that an inspired Perkins sat at the kitchen table of his housing project apartment late that night. The lyrics of the new song were scrawled on a brown paper sack emptied of potatoes, and written in the former sharecropper's rough hand, "suede" was spelled "swade."

Perkins recorded "Blue Suede Shoes" in December 1955, taking suggestions from Sam Phillips to shorten the original phrase and to revise the verse, "drink my corn from an old fruit jar." The song was released January 1, 1956, on the Sun label and rapidly rose to the top of all Billboard charts, reaching No. 1 on Country, No. 2 on Pop, and No. 3 on R&B. The song became the first record by a Sun label artist to sell a million copies, and it was covered by Elvis and a multitude of other performers. Sonny considers it a definitive rockabilly record because of the purity and balance of its four-man structure.

On March 22, 1956, Perkins and his band—brothers Jay and Clayton with drummer W. S. Holland—were in a catastrophic vehicle accident while traveling to New York for their television debut on the *Perry Como Show*. The car crash killed their driver and severely injured the band members. Perkins recovered and returned to performing. Sonny said he first met him later that year when Perkins had made the iconic shoes a part of his stage wardrobe.

"We opened for Carl at the Jackson Auditorium where they were honoring him," Sonny recalled. "At the end, he did 'Blue Suede Shoes' with us. Then he took off them big shoes and threw them out to the audience. He was a big man. I said, 'You will kill somebody with one of them shoes.'"

Perkins often played at the Silver Moon and at the B&I Club, but he more frequently performed at Porky's Rooftop. With its rougher crowd and more country style music, Porky's may have been the more comfortable venue for Perkins. The band also had a friend in Porky's owner Hershell Sellers, who, like other Jackson County club owners, ran a back-room dice game.

Holland recalled Sellers' generosity in returning the Perkins brothers' gambling losses. He also remembered the long rides home from Arkansas performances, particularly shows played in the northeast corner of the state.

"We'd cross the Mississippi River north of Memphis at Dyersburg," Holland said. "There was no bridge then, and you had to wait for the ferry. If it was on the other side at night, you'd raise a lantern and they would come get you. Carl and his brothers were bad about drinking, and they would fight there as we waited."

Reflecting on his stature as a rockabilly trailblazer, Perkins has said, "We were just taking country music and putting that black rhythm in it. It was a marriage of the white man's lyrics and a black man's soul."[48] Sonny agreed, offering a rockabilly compliment. "Carl had a good black sound the way he sang and played his guitar," Sonny said. "I always thought he sounded more black than Elvis did."

Despite his core talent, Perkins was upstaged by the top names of his era. Elvis, Johnny Cash, and Jerry Lee Lewis became huge stars while Perkins' career diminished in his middle years. Stan Perkins, an accomplished musician who played drums for many years in his father's band, sees a similarity between Sonny in Newport and his father in Jackson. Both men recognized the value of everyday living, and both remained grounded in their communities. Stan said, quoting his father, "After the party was over, I went home and found it wasn't a bad place to be."

Roy Orbison

The Pacers began touring with Roy Orbison at a low point in the singer's career. The crooner from Wink, Texas, had been deserted by his band, the Teen Kings, who had packed up their instruments and walked out of a recording session at Sun Records. The mutiny occurred just as their single "Ooby Dooby," originally recorded in early 1956 on the Odessa, Texas, Je-Wel label and re-recorded at Sun Records later that year, was selling well.

"Ooby Dooby" had been written by two friends of Orbison at North Texas State College as the students sat on the roof of a campus fraternity house. The song was a lively dance number, its nonsense lyrics meant to encourage hilarity and wild partying. The Teen Kings' version captured that feeling, but the single's success only increased the tension between Orbison and the band members. Frustrations were high about money, name recognition, and the grueling life of one-night shows. At

Sun Records, Sam Phillips recognized Orbison as the core talent of the group. Phillips suggested the band change its name to Roy Orbison and the Teen Kings. Though payment to each musician was to remain unchanged, arguments continued and the rift widened.

"The Teen Kings quit him when they got paid for 'Ooby Dooby,'" Sonny said. "It was a big seller, about 400,000 copies, and that was pretty big back then. They got their money and went back to Texas to become stars on their own. They never did."

In late 1957, the Pacers came to Memphis to record some new songs. They were to leave the next day for Kansas City and the start of a three-week tour. At Sun Records, they found Orbison, also scheduled for the tour but now without a backup band. The Pacers' session that day included "Find My Baby for Me," a song Sonny believes is one of the best his group recorded.

"Orbison is in the backing vocals," Sonny said. "That wasn't planned. He's on there because he was hanging around the studio waiting for us to get through. That's when Orbison started traveling with us."

Orbison was no stranger to the Arkansas band. Riding the wave of success of "Ooby Dooby," the Teen Kings performed in Newport several times in 1956 and 1957 at the Silver Moon, Porky's, and the Farmers Day concert. In Newport, the Pacers copied the Teen Kings' stage antics of the "bug dance." In addition to the established friendship, the Pacers' versatility as a backup band made them an ideal support for the now solo Orbison.

Orbison made several tours with the Pacers over the next two years. Memphis booking agent Bob Neal put them with Johnny Cash, whose "Folsom Prison Blues" was popular at the time. But working on a package tour did not always guarantee getting paid, Sonny learned.

"Some of those tours we went on, we'd get shafted," Sonny said. "We were country boys that didn't know any better. But Orbison was smarter than we were. He'd get his money every night after we'd play."

Life on the road included compromising sleeping arrangements.

"We'd get a room in a cheap motel and there'd be two of us to each bed," Sonny recalled. "Orbison was tight with a dollar, but I guess he wasn't making all that much. He wouldn't get his own room. He paid $5 for a rollaway bed and rolled it in there with us to save money."

On all their travels, Orbison never bought a nickel's worth of gas, Sonny said. Hubbard, the band's high-spirited jokester, got even by stealing the $100 bill Orbison kept in his wallet, returning the money at the end of the tour. The same $100 bill was part of an elaborate hoax played out on another tour, Sonny recalled.

"We were traveling with Orbison and Riley's band in Florida," Sonny said. "Riley's guys told us they were going home because the tour was canceled and we weren't getting paid. So we loaded up and headed back to Newport. But Riley and them talked Orbison into riding with them." Once the Pacers were gone, Orbison learned there was one last show still scheduled and that Riley's band was planning to make more money as the single act. That show also got canceled at the last moment, and the band spent the night in a local hotel. Now the plan changed again. Riley's band members knew that Orbison had the $100. They had to find a way to make him use it.

"Orbison was supposed to fly out the next day, and they were to take him to the airport," Sonny continued. "They turned his clock back so he wouldn't wake up in time to catch the plane. So he missed his plane. Then he had to take the $100 and buy the gas to get them back to Memphis because none of them had enough money to get home."

Biographies of Orbison describe him as a shy man who wore dark glasses on stage to hide what he thought were his small, beady eyes. In an age of wild showmanship, Orbison stood nearly motion-less as he sang.

"As an entertainer, he didn't do much, but he did shake that leg," Sonny said. "A lot of people don't realize he was a great guitar player and a good singer. But he had to wear thick eyeglass, them Coke bottle things. He thought the girls wouldn't go for a guy with glasses, so he'd take them off and wear the dark glasses. He'd tell us, 'Don't let me get too close to the edge of the stage. I'll fall off.'"

Sonny recalled Orbison's sense of humor following a show in Grand Rapids, Michigan.

"We were in the car with the windows rolled down and kids were all around trying to get an autograph. Someone gave him a piece of notebook paper with a swatch of jacket. Roy had been up there earlier, and they'd charged the stage and tore that coat off of him. Then some DJ got a piece of that coat, cut it into one-inch squares, and was selling them. Orbison said, 'The fans were on that stage and pulling my hair. That hurt.'"

In his later years, Orbison became famous for his soaring voice and for his carefully crafted ballads of loneliness and heartache. His image was of a man in dark clothing and dark glasses tormented by introspection and sadness. That stage persona was shaped by the tragedies of his real life: the loss of his first wife in a vehicle accident and the death of two young sons in a house fire. Orbison was fifty-two years old when he died of a heart attack in 1988.

The Pacers' drummer Bobby Crafford recalled their friendship when Orbison played a 1961 show in Jonesboro, Arkansas. The Pacers were playing twenty miles away at the Cotton Club in Trumann. Late that night, Orbison showed up at the club and joined the Pacers on stage with his harmonica.

For Sonny, a show in Albuquerque stands out from the years when he and Orbison were energetic young rockers. On tour with Cash in 1957, Orbison dyed his hair black, as Elvis had done. Sonny decided he would try a hair color, as well.

"I read about a detective in a pulp magazine that had white hair and black eyebrows. I thought that would be cool," he said. "I decided to use peroxide to bleach my hair white, but it turned orangey-red. I already had red suede shoes, red socks, and a red tux jacket. And I had a candy-apple red Stratocaster. When my hair came out red, I was stuck with it for a time. That image of me has somehow stuck over time, too. Orbison liked to tell people that they'll always remember us in Albuquerque as the 'Wink Wildcat and the Red Clown.'"

Jerry Lee Lewis

I love Jerry Lee's piano playing. He is so good. He's a little bit crazy, but he's alright crazy.

—Sonny Burgess

The Pacers opened several shows for Jerry Lee Lewis in the late 1950s when the piano-playing fireball from Ferriday, Louisiana, was just beginning to gain notoriety. An exuberant performer with a scandalous personal life, Lewis has generated decades of musical acclaim and moral rebuke.

Like the Pacers' piano player Kern Kennedy, Lewis was influenced by Aubrey Wilson "Moon" Mullican, a Texas singer, songwriter, and pianist who played country and western, as well as hillbilly boogie. Mullican's energetic style was reflected in his statement, "We gotta play music that'll make them goddamn beer bottles bounce on the table."[49]

Lewis' piano style bounced more than a few beer bottles in his time, using an innovative technique that Sonny believes established the piano as a lead rock and roll instrument. "Jerry Lee on that piano invented stuff that nobody else was playing, nobody was even thinking about," Sonny said. "His secret was his strong left hand. He could keep that boogie rhythm going with his left hand, and do all this stuff with his other hand. Most piano payers can't do that. He was a country singer singing rock and roll. He just blew us away."

For Lewis, the piano was a stage prop to be climbed on and slammed with elbows and feet. In true rockabilly style, Lewis acted as wild as necessary on stage to convince audiences he was holding nothing back. Writer Craig Morrison has called him "one of the most fascinating of rockabilly stars...complex, charismatic, talented and tormented...tortured by religious beliefs and love of music, women, and whiskey."[50] Sonny, however, views Lewis as "not nearly as wild as you'd thought," adding that "he had a lot of energy, and he was always a little cocky, but most of those guys are."

Lewis came to Sun Records in 1956, where his talent and ambition soon placed him among the label's top stars. Sonny recalled a show that year at the Catholic Club in Helena, Arkansas, just before Lewis' first hit "Crazy Arms" was released. At the time, the piano player was accompanied only by his cousin J. W. Brown on bass guitar. Brown was also the father of Myra Gale Brown, the thirteen-year-old girl Lewis married in 1957.

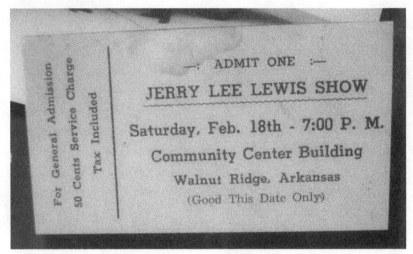

Jerry Lee Lewis show ticket; 1962.

"I thought they needed drums, and I suggested to Russ Smith that he go up with him," Sonny said. Smith took the advice one step farther, leaving the Pacers in 1957 to work as Lewis' drummer. At this time, Lewis also hired J. M. Van Eaton, the Memphis drummer who was a member of Billy Lee Riley's group, the Little Green Men.

Van Eaton recalled the small clubs in the Arkansas Delta where he and Lewis played. "We were on the road playing in redneck roadhouses like the Twin Gables in Blytheville Arkansas," Van Eaton said. "We played four-hour dance gigs. I don't think we even knew enough songs for four hours. But when Jerry Lee played 'Whole Lotta Shakin','' people went crazy. We played it four times some nights."[51]

Jerry Lee Lewis' early success crashed in May 1958 while on tour in England. British media discovered his marriage to the young Myra Brown and targeted him with sensationalized moral condemnation. The scandal continued in the United States, where Lewis was blacklisted from radio and rejected by fans and the music industry. But he was still invited to the benefit concert for Jay Perkins' family that Johnny Cash organized in Memphis late that year.

"Jerry Lee had just come back from Europe, and he was mad at the world," said Sonny, who was one of the many stars who performed at the benefit. "He put on a good show and got wild, but he couldn't get a reaction from the crowd. They didn't really get into him after the deal about his wife. That's when he got up on top of the baby grand piano and started taking his clothes off. A couple of security guards came out and took him off stage."

Nearly a decade passed before Lewis' unstoppable talent and drive brought him renewed stardom. But in the early 1960s, with his performance fees reduced from $10,000 per night to $250 or less, he once again played in Newport clubs and other small venues. Bobby Crafford recalled a show in the early 1960s when Lewis arrived at the Silver Moon with only J. W. Brown. The Pacers were scheduled to open the show that night, and Lewis paid Crafford and guitar player J. C. Caughron an additional $50 each to back him up during the main set.

Booked at the upscale Silver Moon for another show about this time, Lewis performed in jeans, tennis shoes, and a tee shirt, as George Eldridge, a successful music promoter and businessman, recalled. At the time, Eldridge was a teenaged musician from Augusta, Arkansas, who often hung out at the Newport club. "Where can I get some whiskey?" Lewis demanded of Eldridge, giving him $20 to get some Old Charter, which Lewis then drank out of the bottle while he played.

Silver Moon owner Don Washam had temporarily moved the club's notorious backroom gambling to a more discreet location in the building's attic, accessible only through a drop-down ceiling ladder in the office. Washam's son Donny recalled Lewis asking to be admitted to the gambling room. His father refused Lewis entry, Washam said, because of the performer's volatile reputation.

Sonny, as well, tells stories of Lewis' drinking, such as the night at another Newport club, Jarvis' Bamboo Room, when he, Lewis, Smith, and others crowded into a backstage storeroom to share a whiskey bottle. The backstage gathering was an attempt to hide the drinking from the musicians' mothers, who were out front in the audience.

Unfazed by wild show business behavior, Sonny remains deeply impressed by Lewis' talent and originality. "We never heard nothing like that. Nobody had," he said. "Jerry Lee was different than anyone else who ever came along, and he could sing, too. Every piano player in the world copies him."

Arkansas Talent

The Arkansas sound is not as lazy as Mississippi, all blues and slow pokey stuff. There was a different stream of music coming from Arkansas. It was younger. It was from the west with a little bit of Texas mixed in. I used to say, "Thank God for Arkansas." Those Arkansas boys could rock.
—Jack Clement

Sam Phillips called them "hillbilly cats." They were Arkansas' pioneer rockers, country boys who came down from the hills or out of the cotton fields. They listened to radio stations from West Memphis and Helena where songs by Howlin' Wolf and Muddy Waters reshaped acoustic country blues with the urgent power of the city. They heard the new music of country radio shows, Nashville's *Grand Ole Opry* and Little Rock's *Barnyard Frolics*, where Arkansans Wayne Raney and Skeets McDonald played an infectious hillbilly boogie. And they could no longer be still.

"Once Elvis, Scotty, and Bill played 'Mystery Train,' us country guys laid down our hoes, hitched up our mules, and went to town," J. T. Rhodes, a bass player from Coy, Arkansas, said. "We played a lot of rockabilly stuff. Everyone did at the time."

Numerous Arkansans were inspired by the infectious new music of the 1950s. Some came from isolated rural locations, like Sleepy LaBeef from Smackover and Narvel Felts of Keiser. Others were born in neighboring states—Floyd Cramer in Louisiana and Lefty Frizzell in Texas—but they were raised in Arkansas and their musical careers began with rockabilly.

In towns and regions across the state—Helena and Phillips County in the east, Fayetteville and Washington County in the northwest, and Little Rock and Pulaski County in the center—numerous Arkansans performed in honky tonks and roadhouses much like the clubs found in Jackson County. They were influenced by similar experiences—late nights of loud, raucous music; long road trips in crowded old cars; and low pay and the easy temptation of alcohol and drugs. Not surprisingly, most of the young, eager rock and rollers were having the time of their lives.

The central Arkansas music scene shaped the career of J. T. Rhodes, who began playing in local clubs in 1954 when he was fourteen years old. At Arkansas State Teachers College (now the University of Central Arkansas in Conway), Rhodes began playing bass with Alabama-born rocker Jimmy Ford. The men became lifelong friends and bandmates.

Ford grew up on an Alabama farm, then moved to Arkansas after his military service and "got me a little rockabilly band," as he put it. Ford and Rhodes recorded on the Stylo label for Little Rock's music entrepreneur Foster Johnson, and they opened shows for Johnny Cash and Jerry Lee Lewis. They played at the Silver Moon (Ford: "the most mosquitoes I've ever been in") and Club 70 (Rhodes: "They'd check you at the door for a gun. If you didn't have one, they'd give you one."). They worked on numerous road trips, performing on the Canadian circuit and dropping in at radio stations for impromptu interviews and record promotions.

"Foster Johnson and I toured through the mid-South and East Coast," Ford said. "Back then, several television stations had dance parties. We'd go in and lip sync. I didn't even stand with a guitar. I was on *Steve's Show* in Little Rock several times. He came up with corny stuff, like me on my knees, singing to a girl."

At the Beverly Gardens, a large dance hall in Little Rock, Rhodes and Ford met James Harvey "Mouse" Hockersmith, a skilled blues guitarist from Benton who, a few years later, played bass with Charlie Rich and with the Pacers.

"We wanted to play like Mouse," Ford said, "so we'd punch holes in our amp speaker with an ice pick to get a more guttural, rattle sound."

A Limited Future in Rock 'N' Roll

Most Arkansas early rockabilly performers realized their rock and roll careers offered a limited future. Ford used his veteran's benefits for a college education, earning a PhD from Ohio State University and eventually becoming chairman of the Department of Foreign Languages at the University of Arkansas.

The music program at Arkansas State Teachers College in Conway prepared many performers for educational careers. ASTC graduate Roy Cost worked as a band director at Augusta High School and for nearly twenty years as an elementary school principal. Cost's "day job" in Arkansas schools was matched by numerous recordings on Vega Records and other labels, regional concerts, and media broadcasts, as well as induction into the Rockabilly Hall of Fame. Cost gained prominence in central Arkansas as the singer and band leader of the Shadows, a group that frequently played the Silver Moon in the early 1960s with Nance on piano.

"The Silver Moon was the favorite place in Arkansas to play," Cost wrote in his band history.[52] "Sonny Burgess, Joe Lewis and other celebrities would wander in off the street and we would let them sing and perform. By having Jack Nance in the band, we just had more people, as he was from Newport and was a bigger name since he played for Twitty and had once played for Sonny and the Pacers."

Another lesser-known Arkansas talent, Chuck Comer, chose a more stable career as a radio announcer. In 1953, a teenaged Comer was singing on his own early morning radio show, *The General Store*, at KNBY in Newport. He made his first recordings in 1959 for Vaden Records, a small enterprise established at Trumann, Arkansas.[53] The session produced the superb country rocker "Little More Lovin'." Country music was Comer's passion, but he took advantage of the popular new sound in the 1950s.

130

"If you didn't do something akin to what Elvis Presley and some of the others were doing you just didn't work the clubs," Comer said. "That's what people really wanted to hear. So I wrote a few rockabilly songs."

Comer also worked for Arkansas music entrepreneur Gene Williams of Tyronza, who established the Cotton Town Jubilee record label and music publishing company at West Memphis in 1962. That same year, Williams created a new country music stage show, also called *Cotton Town Jubilee*. The live show was held at the Rosewood Theater in Memphis and broadcast over KWAM every Saturday night. Williams also created a successful television program, the *Gene Williams Country Junction Show*, broadcast for nearly fifty years on KAIT-TV in Jonesboro.

Not many Arkansas rockabilly performers had the talent and good fortune to earn a living. Most would agree with the advice of Billy Lee Riley, who, approached by Larry Donn following a talent show at the 1957 Craighead County Fair, told the starry-eyed teenager, "The best advice I can give you is if you're not already in the music business, stay out of it."

Few young performers would be so easily dissuaded. And even fewer would have the business sense to protect their assets, as a clever Teddy Riedel did with his song "Judy." The Quitman piano player first recorded the tune in 1960 for Vaden Records. The following year, Elvis Presley's version of the song on RCA Records spent several weeks on the Billboard Hot 100 list. Riedel said he was able to obtain royalties only because he had secured a copyright for "Judy" from the Library of Congress.

"RCA called me after Elvis had recorded it and told me they had made a serious mistake," Riedel said. "They should have checked it out. They wanted to give me $5,000 to hush my mouth, but I wouldn't take it. I got it all back."

King Biscuit Time

With the clanging sound of a dinner bell and the announcer's famil-iar refrain, "Pass the Biscuits. It's King Biscuit Time," America's longest-running daily radio show takes to the air each weekday as it has since 1941. These days, the announcer is "Sunshine" Sonny Payne, who has hosted the program since 1951. Live broadcasts from Helena's KFFA radio station originally featured blues artists Sonny Boy Williamson II (Aleck "Rice" Miller), Robert Lockwood Jr., Pinetop Perkins, and others. The show's noontime slot was chosen to coincide with the lunch break of Delta field workers.

By the early 1950s, young black blues musicians and their white rockabilly counterparts in Arkansas and Mississippi were listening attentively, hoping to gain the musical chops that would free them from a future of chopping cotton. To a young Levon Helm, tuning in on his family's battery-powered radio from nearby Turkey Scratch, the elec-trified country music was "like a metallic jolt of energy, a twang, a whip, a raw, sharp, grating sound."[54] The radio station itself had a drawing power much like the Sun Records studio in Memphis. It was a place where young musicians met the men whose music they emulated, where they hoped for an invitation to play on the air.

Similar to Memphis, Helena's blues heritage originated in the remarkable number of talented black musicians who performed on its radio station and appeared in its numerous clubs, coming to the city to add their voices in the last celebration of the all-encompassing cotton economy. But Helena declined, as did other Delta towns whose fortunes were based on agricultural labor. The city's stores and clubs shut down and people moved away. Its musical vitality was lost. Decades of poverty, racism, and a pervasive social lethargy followed.

Signs of progress did not appear until the 1980s. By this time, Memphis had cultivated Beale Street as a vibrant tourist destination and Mississippi had begun promoting the cultural heritage of its exten-sive blues history. In Helena, the abandoned train depot was renovated as a state museum and cultural center focusing on the people and music of the Delta. That heritage has been celebrated each year since 1986 with the King Biscuit Blues Festival. One of the nation's top blues events, the Helena festival is an outdoor, multi-day event that attracts more than 100,000 fans to its open stages and grassy slopes of the Arkansas River levee. As the festival is held in October, a large moon often rises beyond the levee on festival nights, creating an evocative setting for the once-flourishing river town.

In 2011, Helena conducted the first annual Arkansas Delta Rockabilly Festival, showcasing pioneer artists—Sonny Burgess and the Legendary Pacers, J. M. Van Eaton, D. J. Fontana, and Ace Cannon—as well as younger contemporary bands playing in the energetic style of their early rock and roll heroes. Veteran musicians Will "Pop" Jones and Phillips County drummer Jerry Nolan attended the second Arkansas Rockabilly Festival in 2012. The two musicians had long since retired from performing, and both showed the wearing effects of hard-lived lives. But Nolan's eyes lit up as he put his hand on the arm of his old friend and said, "Will's rides were blazing. He made a lead instrument out of the piano."

"I was inspired by Little Richard," Jones said. "He was a natural talent, the architect and creator of rock and roll." Referring to the 1950s-era headliners in Helena that day, Jones added, "All these musicians did their part. All contributed to rockabilly."

C. W. Gatlin, a Helena native and Rockabilly Hall of Fame guitar player, was on stage at both the 2011 and 2012 festivals. Gatlin began playing at KFFA and in Helena clubs in 1959 when he was fourteen years old. He had learned his blues licks from older local black musicians such as Robert Nighthawk, Houston Stackhouse, Frank Frost, and Sam Carr. Gatlin joined a cadre of young white musicians who blended country music with blues and played rockabilly. The wealth of musical talent with roots in Phillips County also includes the Hughey family of Elaine, among whose eight children were Gene, a prominent bass player with local bands, and John, widely recognized as the finest steel guitar player of his generation.[55]

"There was good money in the clubs then," Gatlin said, "and people wanted to see live shows. The radio sound was so poor; they came to the clubs to hear the good music."

Ronnie Hawkins and the Boys of Phillips County

Ronnie Hawkins could make anyone smile and love music.
—Sonny Burgess

The rockabilly flair for excess in performance as well as off stage was brought to new heights by the irrepressible Ronnie Hawkins, a man who never winced in the glare of the limelight and whose showmanship and talent were accompanied by a flamboyant disregard for anyone or anything that took itself too seriously or interfered with his outrageous behavior.

Born in 1935 in Huntsville, Arkansas, Hawkins had an early start defying authority by running bootleg whiskey from Missouri to Oklahoma. He also learned to defy gravity as a gymnast and stunt diver, a skill he transferred to his stage act by doing flips and landing in a split.

"Ronnie Hawkins was one of the best showmen I've ever seen," Sonny said. "He'd do anything to keep you laughing. If there was a wall at the side of the stage, he'd run up and turn a back flip off it, still holding the mike. He did the camel walk, which is the moonwalk that Michael Jackson did years later. He got it off some old black guy, he told me."

The black mentor was a musician named Half Pint who shined shoes in Hawkins' father's barber shop in Fayetteville, where the family had relocated in 1945. By the mid-1950s, Hawkins had formed his first bands, and he played Fayetteville venues such as the Tee Table and the Bubble Club. He was also part owner of the Rockwood Club, one of the area's larger venues. Along with musicians such as the Cate Brothers, Tommy McClelland, and John Tolleson, Hawkins became a leading promoter of the country-style rock and roll that flourished in the northwest Arkansas region.

Helena native Ed Burks played Dixieland music at the fraternity house parties on the University of Arkansas (UA) campus and at local clubs with his college band, the Tee Cups. Burks first met Hawkins in the early 1950s at the Tee Table club when Hawkins would sing folk songs such as "John Henry," a tune made popular at the time by Harry Belafonte. Burks remembered Hawkins as a boxer in college and friend of UA football stars Donny Stone and Billy Ray Smith Sr., the latter giving Hawkins' face a varicose skin pattern from a punch to the jaw during a sparring match.

The Pacers first met Hawkins when they played at the Sigma Chi house. "They had a big party and hired us," Sonny said. "The kids there said this guy was a really good singer. We got him up, but all he knew was Roy Orbison and Carl Perkins songs. That's all he sang, but he put on a little show." Orbison spoke of a similar encounter, Sonny added, when the Texas singer played in Fayetteville. Invited on stage, Hawkins sang all of Orbison's songs immediately before Orbison performed.

Hawkins turned the original work of others to his advantage with hit songs that included "Thirty Days" by Chuck Berry (re-titled "Forty Days" by Hawkins) and "Mary Lou" by Young Jessie (Obediah Donnell Jessie, an African American singer and songwriter from Texas). When Chuck Berry challenged Roulette Records concerning the origins of "Forty Days," Hawkins cleverly thwarted the claim by showing the similarities of both songs to "When the Saints Go Marching In." "This is the song that took us from the hills and the stills and put us on the pills," Hawkins later said.

During his college years in the early 1950s, Hawkins made summer trips to Memphis and Helena to learn the blues. On one of these trips, he was introduced to Helena businessman Charlie Halbert, a former University of California at Los Angeles football player whom Hawkins said loved music, played a little guitar, and sponsored athletes to attend UA.[56]

Halbert had several key roles in local businesses. He was an owner of the popular Delta Supper Club, and he built and operated the Rainbow Inn, a motel and restaurant where he allowed many Phillips County musicians to stay at no charge. He also renovated Helena's Cleburne Hotel and established another club, the Pot of Gold, inside it. A handsome man who had been a stand-in for movie star Buster Crabbe, Halbert made his early fortune in a California trucking business. He returned to his home state of Arkansas and married the beauty queen Carolyn Simon, Miss Mississippi of 1940. Halbert bought the ferry service at Helena and met Floyd and Thelma Jenkins. Jenkins piloted the ferry *The Belle of Chester* and occasionally worked on riverboats on the Mississippi. Halbert became godfather to their son Harold, later known as Conway Twitty.

In 1957, Hawkins went to Memphis to join a new band created by Jimmy Ray "Luke" Paulman, a Helena guitarist who later played with the Pacers. Paulman had just returned to Arkansas after a Canadian gig with Conway Twitty's band. Now, his newest group had broken up just as Hawkins arrived. Invited to Helena, Hawkins ran into Ed Burks who, having completed college and military service, was back home working in his father's insurance business. Despite sage advice from Halbert on the stability and rewards of insurance sales, Burks was more interested in music.

The Burks family was well established in Helena. Ed's grandfather, James Pinckney Burks, had been editor of the newspaper the *Helena Daily World*. Ed Burks suggested Hawkins move into his widowed grandmother's rooming house, a large structure called the Dogwood House, whose sitting room contained hundreds of books from his grandfather's personal library. Burks was also living there, and he recalled nights when the young men would sit up late in each other's rooms, talking of their future as rock and roll stars.

A new band, Ronnie Hawkins and the Hawks, was soon formed with Paulman on guitar and his cousin Will "Pop" Jones on piano. Hawkins wanted Burks to play drums, but Burks instead suggested local teenager Levon Helm. With Helm on drums, the band began rehearsals in the basement of the Floyd Truck Lines building, the Helena site that housed the KFFA radio station and broadcast the live *King Biscuit Time* show. The Hawks originally borrowed the show's old bass drum with the words "King Biscuit" on its side, until Halbert decided to lend them money to purchase a new drum set and other equipment.

Helm said he learned to twirl his drumsticks from watching the Pacers' drummer Jack Nance. The Newport musician was also helpful when the scheming Hawkins found a way to reduce his debt. "Jack Nance bought our new drums and we used his old set with its snares worn out and loose skins," Hawkins said. "That way, we didn't have any payments."

The group's first job was at the Rebel Club in Osceola. The Hawks' popular sound and early success led to shows at the Silver Moon in Newport and other Arkansas Delta clubs. As front man for the group, the irrepressible Hawkins dubbed Jones "Will Pop 'Hoochie Coochie Mau Mau Jerry Lee' Jones" in tribute to his pounding piano style.

"You can see a video of us as the Hawks when we played the Dick Clark television show in 1959," Paulman said. "Will is at the upright piano. His hands are so large and he's hitting the keys so hard, the hammers are flying out of the piano top."

Through his friendship with Halbert, Hawkins met Harold Kudlets, the booking agent from Hamilton, Ontario, who placed southern bands in Canadian and northern U.S. cities. According to Burks, Halbert persuaded Kudlets to give the Arkansas musicians a chance, offering to cover Kudlets' costs if the band was not successful in Canada. The Hawks went to Ontario, worked at the Golden Rail Club, and made their first recording in a Toronto garage in 1958. The band traveled extensively between Canada and the United States, garnering success with hits on Roulette Records and appearances on national television shows. Back in Helena, the Hawks stayed at Halbert's Rainbow Inn. They played frequently in Jackson County. "Newport was one of the best club scenes I ever played," Hawkins said. "It was always full. It was always rockin'. Sonny Burgess was the king of that area."[57]

Through the early 1960s, the Hawks went through numerous changes, a predictable scenario for young men whose initial enthusiasm was rewarded with low-budget travel and transient lodgings along a seemingly endless series of beer joints and high school sock hops. But as original band members grew weary of the road life and Hawkins' stern management, other talented musicians—Roy Buchanan and Fred Carter Jr. among them—joined and left the group. Hawkins rallied on, his popularity in Canada increasing all the while.

By 1964, the revised Hawks decided to strike out on their own. Helm, the last remaining American in the group, brought the band to Arkansas. Accompanying him were four Canadians: Rick Danko, Garth Hudson, Richard Emmanuel, and Robbie Robertson. Starting in Helena and rooming at the Rainbow Inn, the young musicians called themselves "Levon and the Hawks." Like other start-up bands, they began the itinerant lifestyle of late-night shows at low-end clubs. At one point, the group was staying in a small trailer near the Rockwood Club in Fayetteville. When the Pacers played in town, Bobby Crafford went to see them, and he booked the band at the 11/70 Club in Hazen and at Jarvis' in Newport. The talented group eventually became back-up musicians for Bob Dylan. Within a few years, they would gain immense popularity and critical acclaim as the Band.

Hawkins' musical career continued to thrive in Canada, and he made Ontario his permanent home. Though he has won numerous awards, performed worldwide, and recorded more than twenty-five albums, his lifestyle never changed. Most 1950s-era performers have not survived the decades of riotous indulgence. Yet Hawkins, a 2002 pancreatic cancer survivor who had been given only a few months to live, has embodied pop music's hedonistic battle cry, "Sex, Drugs and Rock and Roll!" In biographies of both Hawkins and Helm, detailed examples are offered of a lifelong celebration of drinking, crude humor, back-stage and hotel room carnage, and long nights of high-energy music.

Those who knew him in the early days now smile and shake their heads, allowing the years to obscure the wild memories. "Ronnie played at the Silver Moon one Friday," Doc Hawk said. "Then I went on a spree with him, riding in his Rolls Royce for days to Little Rock and Nashville."

Sonny recalled catching up with Hawkins when the veteran Memphis musicians known as the Sun Rhythm Section played in Toronto in the 1990s. "We were playing, wearing these bright red shirts," Sonny said. "He came in and of course everybody knew him. So I brought him on stage and introduced him as my old buddy from Arkansas. The first thing he said was, 'These boys have been gone from home two weeks, and they're horny as hell.' I looked over at Smoochie Smith at the piano. His face got as red as his shirt."

Hawkins today still sees himself as a mature version of rockabilly's wild boy, driven since the beginning of his career by a self-deprecating humor and a born performer's innate ambition. "I was trying to play with any band in the world," Hawkins said. "I've been a show-off since 1952."

Conway Twitty

When Twitty got in the growling part, them little ole gals would hang on the edge of the stage, tears just a falling. And Twitty would say to me, "You think I'm on to something with this?"

—Sonny Burgess

Harold Lloyd Jenkins was born east of the river, on the blues side, where generations of black Mississippi field hands sang of their troubled lives and loves. But country music had greater appeal to white families like the Jenkinses. In 1937, four-year-old Harold was given his first guitar, the same Sears acoustic model that a young Sonny Burgess learned to play. He was ten when his family moved from Friars Point, Mississippi, to Helena. Within a few years, Jenkins had formed his first country group, the Phillips County Ramblers, and secured a weekly radio show on KFFA.

Conway Twitty at the Newport baseball park; 1962. Similar to Sonny Burgess, Twitty was a talented ball player invited to a major league training camp.

Similar to Sonny, Jenkins developed two skills in his high school years: music and baseball. Jenkins, as well, was offered a chance to play professional ball, but he was drafted into military service before his first pro season. In the army, he organized the Cimarrons, a band that took second place in an all-army talent show.

Back home in Helena after his military service, Jenkins put country music aside after hearing Elvis' 1955 version of "Mystery Train." The new band Harold Jenkins and the Rockhousers gained confidence playing the local clubs, and Jenkins took his act to Memphis to audition for Sam Phillips.[58] Like most of the eager young men who showed up at the Sun studio, he was given a chance and then sent away. "We worked with him a lot," recalled studio engineer Jack Clement, "but we didn't get what we wanted."

Eight songs were recorded, and a shrewd Phillips obtained the publishing rights. Though none of the songs were released until well after his success on other labels, Jenkins' potential was recognized by Phillips. He gave Jenkins' song "Rockhouse" to Roy Orbison, who rewrote some of the lyrics and recorded it.

Jenkins had talent, good looks, and rockabilly showmanship. He also had a hometown environment with established performance venues and appreciative audiences. Levon Helm described a show at the Delta Supper Club. "Conway's doing 'Jenny, Jenny,' and the place is just going nuts. He had all the rock moves—the stutter, the twitches, the strut—and the band...provided a raw rockabilly jolt. Girls loved Conway's big, heavy-lidded good looks and long hair...reminded 'em a little of Elvis."[59]

As Twitty gained success, he bought a motel and club at nearby Moon Lake, Mississippi. His mother Thelma was manager of "Conway's Place," and the lodgings there, like Halbert's Rainbow Inn in Helena, became a haven for musicians. The Moon Lake business provided a livelihood for Twitty's parents following the 1960 construction of a highway bridge at Helena. The new span, another sign of Delta modernization, replaced the ferry service where Twitty's father Floyd Jenkins had worked, where passengers once played the onboard slot machines, and where the adolescent Twitty first gained

Halbert's admiration as he played guitar on the open deck on the thirty-minute crossing.

Twitty's band played the clubs in Jackson County, and he became close friends with Bob King. A newspaper account of the friendship tells of the evening Twitty lost his band's payment in King's gambling room. King returned the money and had Twitty promise never again to gamble, a promise he upheld.[60] "When Harold got down and out, Bob took care of him and hired him when nobody else would," Sonny said. "So over the years, Harold would come back and play Bob's once or twice a year for nothing. He never forgot them."

Jenkins' career took off in 1957. Through Charlie Halbert, Jenkins met Harold Kudlets and began working in Canada. Several accounts tell of Jenkins seeking a better show business name and the involvement of his manager Don Seat in the selection of names from towns in Arkansas and Texas. The choice of "Conway Twitty" left some of his music friends wondering. "What's wrong with the name Harold Jenkins?" Jack Clement asked. "I thought his new name would never go over," Jimmy Ray "Luke" Paulman recalled.

In 1957, Memphis drummer J. M. Van Eaton and saxophone player Martin Willis played with Twitty for a stint at the Flamingo Lounge in Hamilton, Ontario. A year earlier, the two young musicians played together in Memphis high school talent shows. When the gig with Twitty ended, both men were hired by Billy Lee Riley, who was performing at a nearby Ontario club. Van Eaton and Willis became part of Riley's group the Little Green Men, recording with him and others at Sun Records. Willis also traveled and performed with the Pacers in the spring of 1958.

Twitty, now without a band, came back to Arkansas. He learned that the Pacers had also broken up, and he hired Joe Lewis and Jack Nance to return with him to Canada. Helena bass player Blackie Preston (Preston Wilkerson) was also hired at this time.

Twitty had two valuable resources supporting his success. The first was the multi-talented Nance, who was co-writer of Twitty's first major hit, "It's Only Make Believe." The other was the wealthy and well-connected Halbert, who had unfailing confidence in his godson's talent.

"Charlie Halbert sent Conway Twitty to MGM Records with 'It's Only Make Believe,'" C. W. Gatlin said. "He called a guy he knew up there and said, 'If this song doesn't hit, I'll pay for it myself.'" Sonny said he first heard the song in 1959 when the Pacers were on tour. "We were traveling out west with Cash and that thing was playing on the radio everywhere," Sonny recalled. "I said Ole Harold's got him a hit there."

Twitty's star status attracted top musicians to his group, including the Canadian guitar player Al Bruno, who joined Twitty's band in 1959. Bruno played with Twitty until 1963, going on to an accomplished career as a performer and studio musician. Five decades later, Bruno, who continues to perform, was a fourteen-time winner of the Best Guitar Player Award from the Academy of Country Music and a recipient of the California Country Music Association Living Legend Award.

Bruno moved from Canada to Newport in 1959, living in the Dorsey Arms, the apartment complex that was temporary home to several Pacers band members. In 1960, a new tenant moved in across the hall. This was Louise Beebe, a single mother who worked as a waitress at a nearby Front Street café. Bruno gave guitar lessons to her fourteen-year-old son, Mike. The teenager's early music training may have prepared him for a successful political career in Arkansas. Governor Mike Beebe, serving from 2007 through 2014, was preceded by two other popular governors with roots in rock and roll: saxophone player Bill Clinton and bass player Mike Huckabee.

Twitty peaked as a rock and roll star between 1957 and 1960. In 1959, he appeared in three teen exploitation films for MGM, writing the title songs and soundtrack for *Sex Kittens Go to College* with Mamie Van Doren and, with co-writer Nance, the title song for "Platinum High." In 1960, the Broadway musical *Bye Bye Birdie* was inspired by the media circus surrounding Elvis' military service. The show's lead character was named Conway Twitty, but it was changed to Conrad Birdie when Twitty threatened to sue.

By 1960, Sonny was performing nightly in Hamilton, Ontario, as a member of Twitty's band. Jack Nance had left the group by this time, replaced by drummer Tommy "Pork Chop" Markham, another Arkansas musician who attended ASTC in Conway. The band's name changed from the Rockhousers to the Lonely Blue Boys to its final name the Twitty Birds.

"Twitty was hot as a firecracker and drawing the crowds," Sonny said. "He had a big white Cadillac and a station wagon."

While Twitty was active in movies, Sonny and the band often performed in Canada without him. On tour, their paychecks were $150 per week, with Twitty drawing twice that amount as group leader. The formula was standard to the musicians' union at the time, although Sonny said Twitty gave him an extra $25 from his share. After each show, Twitty collected the money and wired it to New York.

With their steady income and Twitty frequently away on other activities, the band was unaware of growing problems between the star and his manager Don Seat. The conflict peaked when Twitty learned that Seat and MGM Records had control over his songs and money. The band was in Hamilton when Twitty called them to return to the States for a three-week tour. The final stop was at the Silver Moon, an April 1, 1961, show that drew a huge crowd. Arkansas State Police officers told manager Charles Watson that parked cars blocked the highway as people rushed to get inside. "At that last show at the Silver Moon, Twitty divided all the money among the band," Sonny said. "He didn't send it to New York and he didn't report it to his manager."

That night, Twitty told the band that he was making a change. He encouraged Sonny to return with the band to Canada and continue playing music there. But Sonny chose to stay in Newport, and the band dispersed. Sonny found work at a service station, and Joe Lewis worked at a hardware store. A year later, Lewis, Markham, and Preston rejoined Twitty, and the Twitty Birds resumed their rock and roll careers. Sonny again chose to stay in Arkansas.

Twitty's return to rock and roll lasted only a few years. In 1965, he signed with Decca Records as a country artist and moved to Oklahoma City where he and other country musicians performed at the Spring Lake Amusement Park. Twitty had already written "Walk Me to the Door," which was a Top 10 country hit for Ray Price in 1963. In 1968, Twitty wrote and recorded his first country No. 1 hit, "Next In Line."

In 1968, Twitty established a fast-food restaurant corporation named Twitty Burger with a flagship restaurant in Oklahoma City that could seat 120 people. The restaurant sign, the menus, and glassware all featured the singer's logo: a bird playing a guitar. The restaurant's feature sandwich—which included bacon, American cheese, and a slice of pineapple fried in graham cracker crumbs—came in three sizes: Papa Twitty, Mama Twitty, and the child's size Itty Bitty Twitty.

When the business went bankrupt in 1971, Twitty repaid investors and identified those funds as a tax deduction. Challenged by the IRS, the case resulted in a rare display of humor when the appeals court judge and the government auditor, both amateur musicians, wrote songs about the case and attached them to the court records.[61]

By the time of his death in 1993, Twitty had sold more than fifty million records and had recorded 110 albums. He held the record with forty No. 1 Billboard Country hits until George Strait surpassed him in 2006. From 1971 to 1976, Twitty received a string of Country Music Association awards for duets with Loretta Lynn and was inducted into the Country Music Hall of Fame.

Twitty's financial success generated conflicting opinions that persist two decades after his death. Some early band members and their surviving family contend that Twitty withheld money or co-authorship rights and thwarted their careers by limiting record distribution. And lawsuits were filed and counterfiled by Twitty and his manager Don Seat concerning payments due.

Sonny, however, has no negative memories of the Phillips County musician he often calls "Ole Harold." "He was one of the nice guys in the business," Sonny said. "Super talented, a good songwriter, and he had a good head on him. He was the king of rock and roll in 1960 when Elvis was in the army."

Charlie Rich

Charlie Rich was the best piano player that ever played at Sun.
— Sonny Burgess

The biggest star with rockabilly roots from central Arkansas was too much of an individualist and solo performer to be a member of anyone else's band. Charlie Rich was born in 1932 and raised in Colt, a Delta town in St. Francis County. His upbringing matched most of the essential rockabilly profile. Though his family was not poor, Rich was raised in a rural environment. He had strong influences of church music (white gospel) through his parents, and he learned to play blues through a family friendship with a black sharecropper, C. J. Allen. The talented Rich also developed proficiency in jazz, rock and roll, country, and vocal styling.

In the mid-1950s, Rich tried to grow cotton. In true rockabilly pattern, the failure of his farming efforts accelerated his musical career. Rich signed with Sun Records as a songwriter and studio musician in 1957. He played on the Pacers' single "Itchy" / "Thunderbird" that year, later gaining prominence as a solo performer with his 1960 hit "Lonely Weekends."

Much has been written about the highs and lows of Rich's career, the range of his extraordinary talent, his numerous hits and awards, his struggles with alcohol, and his disdain for the artistic compromises imposed by the mainstream entertainment industry.

His wife, Margaret Ann, called him a "natural born loner," a man whose temperament was unsuited for the public exposure of stardom.[62] Sonny Burgess recalled a frustrating experience when he booked Rich in Newport in the 1960s. "Charlie called me when he got to town that afternoon," Sonny said. "I told him we had Jarvis' sold out, and that was about four hundred people. Just before the show, he called back and said he couldn't stay, that he had to go back to Benton because his wife was sick. I knew he and Mouse Hockersmith had been drinking pretty heavy. He left, and I had to get up there and tell the crowd that we would give their money back."

Like others struggling with inner conflict, Rich lost many professional opportunities. He had two blockbuster hits in 1973, "Behind Closed Doors" (No. 1 on the country charts) and "The Most Beautiful Girl" (No. 1 on both pop and country charts), that earned him a Grammy and the Country Music Association's Male Vocalist of the Year award in 1974. A year later, Rich was blacklisted by the CMA after he showed contempt for the selection of John Denver as the 1975 honoree, setting fire to the paper announcement on stage at the televised awards ceremony.

Family and friends who remained close understood his challenges and his core emotions. His son Alan, a piano player who has shared the stage with the Pacers and performs today using his father's name, spoke of Rich's admiration for his Newport friends. "When I was seven or eight years old," Rich recalled, "Dad and his bass player Mouse Hockersmith managed to sneak me into a night club near Little Rock called the Red Gate. I remember hearing a song that was a hit in Arkansas at that time, 'Short Squashed Texan,' a state anthem lauding the praises of our Arkansas Razorbacks over those big bad Texas Longhorns. The band playing turned out to be the Pacers. That's the first time I heard Sonny Burgess and the Legendary Pacers live. Even as a kid I could tell these guys were great. Charlie always loved the Pacers. He considered them one of the Sun Studio legends that formed the original Memphis and Delta rockabilly sound."

Billy Lee Riley

Billy Lee Riley is a prophet without honor in his own hometown.
—Marvin Thaxton, Newport civic leader

Rock and roll history, similar to that of any topic, includes a number of random events that inexplicably fall into sequence. It also includes unpredictable chance meetings that bring together people whose destinies seem to have prepared them for that exact strategic moment.

Sonny Burgess with Billy Lee Riley in Newport; 2005.

Consider the turbulent life of Billy Lee Riley, a man of explosive talent, widely recognized as one of the most natural rockabilly artists that ever strutted the stage. Riley's life changed when he spontaneously gave rides to two hitchhikers on Christmas morning 1955 near Jonesboro, Arkansas. The men were Slim Wallace and Jack Clement, Memphis musicians hitchhiking home after spending the night in jail in Paragould.

Riley's life was about to blossom. His random act of kindness that frozen morning was rewarded by strangers who revealed a new world awaiting. Some sixty miles away, the cold body of Fats Callis was lying on the morgue slab at a Newport hospital, as Fats had been shot dead hours earlier by Sheriff Jake Winningham in the parking lot of the Silver Moon. But the distant omen of Callis' death, unknown to Riley at the time, did not diminish the white light of his rising star.

How Wallace and Clement came to be hitchhiking home was the fault of a drunken woman who got them arrested. The musicians had performed in Paragould the night before, Christmas Eve, at the Plantation Club, which Wallace owned. Wallace's wife was with them, and the wife brought a girlfriend, who got drunk and began roaming the streets. When Clement tried to control her, he and the woman were arrested by Paragould's overzealous police officers. The woman was released, and Wallace's wife drove her back to Memphis that night. Clement spent the night in the drunk tank, and Wallace stayed over to hitchhike home with him the next day.

At this time, Riley was twenty-two years old, married, and living in Memphis. He had been raised in Arkansas, picking cotton with other impoverished families, black and white. Riley's musical ambitions had been strengthened by winning a talent contest while in the army. In 1953, he moved back to Arkansas and formed the KBTM Ranch Boys, a country band that played on the radio at Jonesboro and at dances. Two years later, he moved to Memphis and opened a restaurant, which lasted three months. Now he was working as a meat cutter while trying to break into the Memphis music scene.

The events of that Christmas morning are well documented in rock and roll lore. Riley took his passengers to Memphis, where he was shown the basic recording studio being built in Wallace's garage on Fernwood Street. He began playing in their band, the Dixie Ramblers, at the Paragould club. In March 1956, Riley cut his first tapes at "Fernwood Studios" and Clement secured him an audition at Sun. Riley got a Sun contract, and Clements was hired as a Sun engineer. "Flying Saucers Rock and Roll" and "Red Hot" were released the following year, and Riley was launched into rock and roll's dizzying stratosphere.

Riley's band was the Little Green Men. Science fiction and UFOs were popular, and rock and roll was thought strange enough to have come from aliens. Also, their stage outfits were cut from billiard table felt, a material that caused profuse sweating and stained the wearer's skin bright green. The core band included Jerry Lee Lewis on piano, Roland Janes on guitar, and J. M. Van Eaton on drums. Riley also toured with Sun Records stars, backing up Cash, Orbison, Perkins, and others.

Riley came storming onto the vibrant music scene in Memphis, a handsome, talented, and ambitious young man entering a market that was at its peak. Things happened fast. Others drank as much and lived the road life as fully as Riley. Others rose as high and fell as low. Many where cheated along the way by their managers and record labels. And there was Riley, his raw music and his raw life, his short temper. He got local attention but not the national exposure he believed he deserved.

Riley rampaged through Sun offices in late 1957 in a drunken rage, knocking over furniture and pouring whiskey on the files. He contends that earlier that day he had seen orders requesting shipment of tens of thousands of copies of his single "Red Hot." He said he actually heard Phillips cancel the order and tell the distributor he would be promoting a bigger hit. To add further irony, Riley played bass on Lewis' "Great Balls of Fire," the record Philips waved like a flag of triumph, and Lewis had played piano on "Red Hot."

That night, an intoxicated Riley was found amidst the wreckage of Phillips' trashed business. In the moments before he entered the studio, Phillips may have considered having Riley arrested and banned from the label. Instead, he brought a bottle of liquor that he and Riley would empty that night. At dawn, Riley would leave the studio convinced by Phillips that he would be the next great rock and roll star. He clung to that belief for a career of over sixty years.

Riley's hard feelings toward Phillips can be seen in the 2001 documentary *Good Rockin' Tonight*.[63] In the video, Riley and Phillips are seated at a table in the former Taylor's café, the coffee shop next door to Sun Studios where Phillips had a makeshift office and where Riley once lived in the apartments upstairs. The video shows Riley staring at Phillips as he insists that wrongs were done, his career derailed, and his true earnings unaccounted for. But Riley states that he has resolved his internal conflicts. Though he continues to hold Phillips responsible, Riley says he no longer bears animosity; he no longer hates.

"Riley had a bad case of feeling like he was overlooked," Sonny said. "I believe everything happens for a reason. If we were meant to be stars, we would have been stars. We weren't supposed to be like Elvis."

The closing scene in the documentary shows a solitary Riley standing in a sheltered doorway of a hauntingly empty Beale Street. A blues harp is cupped in his hands, and his solitary music is carried off in the blowing mist, the last of his frustration and bitterness dissipating in the gray light of the late afternoon.

Within the brash assertions of rockabilly lay the quiet humility of the blues. Riley returned to country blues in the last years of his life. Performing at a 2007 Jackson County Historical Society meeting, Riley played a gleaming, all-steel acoustic Gibson guitar and sang a few of the quiet songs he learned from his mentor, Jericho "Lightning" Leon Carter. He spoke of the blues music he heard as a child in the black sections of Osceola. He seemed at peace.

Riley died in 2009 after a lengthy illness. He was the first honoree at Newport's Depot Days Rock and Roll Highway 67 Festival that year. A benefit concert, planned before his death by Bobby Crafford and Sonny Burgess, was held at the rebuilt Silver Moon club and announced on a Rockabilly Hall of Fame website. The concert drew a standing-room-only crowd for a five-hour show. The Batesville newspaper reported that numerous Arkansas and regional stars performed and paid tribute to a man loved and respected by his peers. Among them was Dale Hawkins, making his last public performance before succumbing to cancer five months later.

One surprise guest was veteran musician Sleepy LaBeef, who said, "I heard about it and pulled into the parking lot and saw Sonny and said, 'Can I do a couple of songs?'"[64]

Chapter 6.
Portraits of the Pacers

Legendary Pacers

Bobby Crafford

If Bobby Crafford could predict the future, a moment in 1957 might have offered a glimpse into the next fifty years of his rock and roll career.

The twenty-one-year-old Crafford from Cotton Plant, Arkansas, had recently bought his first set of drums. Home for the summer from college, he was working with a local band, the Night Owls, at clubs in small Delta towns. At a talent show one night, the Night Owls won top prize. Their winning performance was a lively version of the Pacers' hit "Red Headed Woman."

The Pacers were well known in Arkansas by this time and had become role models for young rock and roll bands across the state. When the club owner of the Spot, a popular roadhouse in Des Arc, Arkansas, mentioned that the Newport band was looking for a drummer, Bobby was immediately interested.

"He told me I wasn't good enough to play with the Pacers," Bobby said. "But I called their manager and auditioned. I never dreamed I'd be playing with those guys."

A week later, when the Pacers' green Cadillac pulled up at the Spot for a show, Bobby presented himself to the owner as the newest member of the group.

"By the end of summer, the music took over my life. Instead of going back to college, I moved to Newport and went on salary with the band for seventy-five dollars a week. That was big money for me."

*Bobby Crafford (drums) with his original band, the Night
Owls, from Cotton Plant, Arkansas. (From left: R. J.
Greenwood, Buddy Clark, and Larry Bunch); 1956.*

Music Every Night

It was exciting times for Bobby, living in his own apartment, playing
music almost every night, and recording at Sun Studios with Roy
Orbison, Charlie Rich, Billy Lee Riley, and others. Bobby's home club
was the Silver Moon, where his drums, perched on the upper back row
of the two-tiered stage, gave him unique views of the crowds and the
wild dancing incited by the band's antics.

The Pacers traveled in their green Cadillac limousine, their equipment packed inside or strapped to the roof racks. After shows in other
Delta towns and the ride home to Newport, Bobby and Johnny Ray
Hubbard, the band's two bachelors, would go to the Silver Moon to
listen to the jukebox and talk with the late-night gamblers. Bobby's life
was a far cry from Cotton Plant, where guys his age were stacking blocks
at the ice plant for minimum wage. "We dressed real sharp and put on
a show," Bobby recalled. "We wore red tuxedos and bought all our
clothes at Lansky's in Memphis."

When the band was not performing, the guys traveled to radio stations to personally promote their new record, an up-tempo version of
Hank Williams' "My Bucket's Got a Hole in It." Kennedy and Hubbard
went north to Illinois and Missouri. Bobby and Sonny went to Tennessee
and Alabama. "Sonny knew it would help if we got out and hit those stations," Bobby said. "A lot of DJs liked it if you laid a record in their hands."

In Nashville, they dropped in on Ralph Emery's late-night show at WSM-AM. Emery was a successful country music disc jockey whose show could be heard over most of the eastern and central United States. The all-night show was a mecca for country music stars, many of whom were personal friends of Emery and would often drop in unannounced. Bobby and Sonny had not met the famous announcer, but they knew Emery could give them national exposure. So they just showed up with no appointment. Bobby recalled knocking on the radio station door and a janitor letting them in. Emery brought them into the sound booth, where another guest was already seated. That was Jimmy Davis, former governor of Louisiana and a country music star with the national No. 1 record "You Are My Sunshine."

Keeping the Band Together

As the Pacers continued to change, Bobby kept the band together, finding new members and booking new shows. Following Sonny's departure in 1960 to join Twitty in Canada, Bobby began looking for a singer. A friend from Swifton, Tommy Wagner, joined them for a few weeks, but he, too, moved on.

"When we played at Ronnie Hawkins' club at Fayetteville, I told him we needed a singer," Bobby said. "He said 'Luke' Paulman would be a good fit." Despite early success as a guitar player with Harold Jenkins and the Rockhousers and with Ronnie Hawkins and the Hawks, Paulman was out of work and living in his parents' house in Marianna, Arkansas, when Bobby contacted him. "We moved him and his family to Newport in the green Cadillac," Bobby said. "Luke was a fantastic singer, and the girls really liked him. We were working six nights a week and thought we were setting the world on fire."

The Pacers were active, but they rarely played outside the southern region. The challenges were formidable for maintaining full-time employment for the group. Paulman left the band within a year. Hubbard also departed at this time. But new members came on board: Jim Aldridge on saxophone and Fred Douglas on bass. Joe Cyr was originally hired as a singer, but he played trumpet when backing up Aldridge's Tom Jones-style act. The Pacers' popularity continued through the changes.

When Kennedy began a new career with the Union Pacific Railroad, Bobby began looking for a replacement piano player. At a 1964 show in Cairo, Illinois, the Pacers ran into Jerry Kattawar, a friend of the band from Helena, Arkansas. Kattawar needed a job, and he joined the band that night, returning with them to Arkansas where he moved into the Newport apartment recently vacated by Paulman.

For the next three years, with Kattawar and Aldridge inciting each other to an energetic stage performance, the Pacers regained their status as the top show band at the Silver Moon. Kattawar would jump up and down on the piano, one time breaking the top casing and falling into the strings.

"In the early '60s, we probably had about as good a band as we ever had," Bobby said.

Despite their talent and local popularity, the Pacers had no record label contract. In 1967, the band had a regional hit with "New Wildwood Flower" / "The Pace." The songs were produced by United Southern Artists, a recording studio and artist agency established that year in Hot Springs, Arkansas. As band manager, Bobby became more aware of the shady activities of some record companies.

"'The Pace' was probably one of the best records we did, but United Southern Artists was the worst company we ever dealt with," Bobby said. "About the only company we worked for that wasn't crooks was our own."

Razorback Records

Bobby created the new label Razorback Records, which produced records for the Pacers and others. Master recordings were made at studios in several Arkansas towns and in Memphis. The first release was "Dessa" / "Baby Done Left This Town."

From 1962 to 1967, Razorback produced nearly forty singles and three albums for Pacer musicians under their own names or as studio groups for others. Bobby was sometimes listed as "Rapid Robert." A lot of Delta talent was available. Friends and former band members who recorded on Razorback include Sonny, Paulman, and Teddy Riedel, a piano player from Quitman, Arkansas.

Bobby Crafford; 2010.

Bobby had learned from Sam Phillips that a small recording studio could be a profitable local business. Having a tight band to back up an aspiring singer was another draw. Among the diverse Arkansans and bands that came to Razorback Records was Gennifer Flowers, the model and actress who would later claim to have a sexual relationship with Bill Clinton. Flowers was fourteen years old when she had a 1964 release titled "Do the Itch" / "When the Saints Go Marching In." Flowers used the name "Little Scooter Bill," a nickname her father gave her, Bobby recalled. The Pacers were her back-up band.

Bobby also worked as a booking agent, and he arranged two weeks of Arkansas shows for Ronnie Hawkins in 1965. The irrepressible Hawkins was in his peak years of wild rock and roll behavior, and Bobby recalled often searching for him in the apartments of young women in Little Rock. One spree concluded with Bobby, Doc Hawk, Hawkins, and a young woman driving to Nashville for a recording session. The men later learned the woman was a minor, and they had risked criminal charges for transporting her across state lines.

At the Nashville session, Hawkins recorded the Gordon Lightfoot song "Early Morning Rain." Impressed by the rendition, Bobby arranged for a Pacers' version and convinced Jim Aldridge and J. C. Caughron, who had left the band by this time, to sit in on the session. With Bobby on vocals, the song was recorded at Little Rock's E & M Studios, released on Razorback Records, and later leased to Dot Records in Los Angeles.

"Short Squashed Texan"

When the Pacers moved from Newport to Little Rock in the early 1960s, Bobby found a new niche audience that matched his Razorback Records logo. These were football fans devoted to the University of Arkansas team.

In the 1965 season, the Arkansas Razorbacks had a spirited rivalry with the Longhorns from the University of Texas. On October 16, the two teams played a showdown game to determine the Southwest Conference Championship. Texas was ranked first in the nation. Arkansas was number three.

In the days before the game, Bobby was visiting Pat Walsh at the KAAY radio station in Little Rock. A popular song at the time was "Long Tall Texan," a simple repetitive tune with a boastful refrain ("I'm a long tall Texan / I ride a big white horse"). The song was first recorded in 1959 and then covered by several artists, including the Beach Boys in 1964. It got a lot of air play in Arkansas and Texas as the game day approached. Bobby decided to create a satire of the song. He had local songwriter Jim Scott create new lyrics:

> I'm a short squashed Texan
> I had the No. 1 crown
> Now people look at me and say,
> That big red pig he put you down.

"The Pacers recorded it on the morning of game day, and I gave a few copies to local DJs," Bobby said. "I told them to play it only if Arkansas won."

Arkansas beat Texas 27–24, and the Pacers' song played all over town. The record continued to get air play through the year, a popularity boosted by the Razorbacks being undefeated for the football season. "Short Squashed Texan" became extremely popular among dedicated Razorback fans. With its simple lyrics and "yackety yack" saxophone melody, the comic song had people dancing, strutting, and acting out. More than forty-five years later, the song and three additional Pacers' tunes were featured in a 2013 documentary, *The Big Shootout*, which focused on a 1969 national championship game between the rival teams. Researching for the film, Dallas-based producer Mike Looney said he discovered that "Short Squashed Texan" had been played nearly nonstop on Arkansas radio stations at the time.

"Those guys captured the feel of that game at the time," Looney said. "Their music fits so well the hills of Arkansas and the feeling of the rural Fayetteville setting. The Pacers were a huge contributor to the film."

A series of Razorback fan songs followed, but the record label and its featured band were facing a dwindling market. Razorback Records ended in 1967.

"By 1967, we had families and were ready to settle down," Kattawar said. "In Little Rock, everybody went their own way. We still played, but the guys started getting day jobs. Music became a sideline for them." Increasingly dissatisfied, Kattawar left the band after a three-night set at the Club 70 in North Little Rock. The rest of the band also found other involvements, and by the mid-1970s, the Pacers disbanded, ending a fifteen-year span of shows and recordings after Sonny Burgess' 1960 departure.

The band's last recording was made at Roland Janes' Sonic Studio in Memphis and released in 1975. Bobby began working for United Van Lines. He later took a sales position with a photography and magazine distributor. "I thought it was all over in the 1970s," Bobby said. "I put my stuff in a corner and gave it up."

Kern Kennedy

It's a Saturday night, and the Pacers are on stage ready to begin. Kern Kennedy is sitting behind his broad electronic keyboard. He is wearing a bright red blazer and matching tie, set against a black shirt. The diamond and gold rings on each finger of his hands glitter in the stage lights. Kern is smiling even before the music begins. He kicks off the set, pounding out a boogie-woogie beat that immediately draws dancers to the floor. He is still smiling when the song ends and the dancers step away.

"If you like what you're doing, people will feel it," he said. "People will like you, and you'll be successful."

A lifetime of musical performances is sketched into the lines around his eyes. The smooth features and blond hair of the handsome young man are long gone. The smile lines remain.

"With many guys, their egos outgrow them," Kern said. "I try to remain as humble as I can. People compliment me on my playing, so your ego needs to be deflated once in a while." To prove his point, Kern recalled a moment at the end of a recent show where an elderly lady sat glumly in the corner through the evening and never smiled. "She called me over at the end and said, 'I don't like noise, and you made a lot of it.'"

Noise in the Church Basement

Kern has made a lot of noise over the years. It started in the 1940s when he and his twin brother Keith would walk from their family's farm home to the small Arkansas town of Tuckerman. The brothers taught themselves to play piano in the basement of the Methodist church, each twin banging away on the opposite ends of the keyboard. Their musical inspiration came from the radio. Like other homes in their rural community, the Kennedy household had no electricity. A rooftop wire served as an antenna for the family's battery-powered radio.

"We listened to KNBY Newport and WREC Memphis," he said. "A group from Memphis I enjoyed was Buck Turner and the Buckaroos. They had a blind piano player named Paul Whiteside that really inspired me. As a kid, I liked Sister Rosetta Tharpe and the blues feeling she put into her hit 'Strange Things Happening Every Day.' We would listen to the black musicians on the radio and go to the clubs where they played in Newport. We loved the black artists but we couldn't mix with them, so we stood outside and listened through the open windows."

Kern Kennedy; 1950.

It was a time when a large number of black and white families made a meager living picking cotton. The drudgery of that work held little appeal for Kern. "I always wanted to play music," he said. "Picking cotton is a great incentive to do better in life, and I wasn't that good at picking cotton."

His first break came in 1947 as a result of those church basement sessions. The music was overheard by Jimmy Davidson, owner of Tuckerman's radio repair shop, located next door to the church.

Davidson was also a musician, serving as a band leader and drummer in a local group that played regular shows at the Silver Moon club. Sixteen-year-old Kern got his first paying job in Davidson's band, earning $17 for a night's work. Davidson, who became a custom jeweler among his many successful endeavors, crafted the flashy rings that Kern wore in his later performances.

In Newport in the late 1940s, Kern met other aspiring musicians, local teenagers like himself drawn to the boogie-woogie sounds of the time. Sonny Burgess was among them, and the boys soon formed their first group, the Rocky Road Ramblers. They played at country schoolhouses and churches in shows sponsored by the local electric company Farmers Electric Co-op, which was installing the first electric lines in the rural areas of Jackson County. They played at community dances, and when they got a little older, they played at clubs and juke joints along Jackson County's famed Highway 67.

The Pacers Go Wild

Kern's keyboard skills continued to improve, and the band gained popularity. They became the Moonlighters, and then the Pacers, famous for their wild on-stage antics.

"The Pacers were a great show group, with lots of energy on stage, but I couldn't get in on that," Kern said.

The band's front men—Sonny, Johnny Ray Hubbard, and Joe Lewis—climbed on the bass for their human pyramid act, but Kern and drummer Russ Smith could not leave their instruments to join the acrobatics. Even sitting at the piano, however, Kern had no assurance he would remain uninvolved.

"One time at the Strand Theater in Newport, Sonny jumped off the stage and the microphone cord wrapped around my neck, nearly choked me to death," Kern said.

Kern recalled the Pacers' first touring vehicle, a used Cadillac limousine bought from a funeral home. He remembered shreds of the recapped tires flying off the vehicle on trips to western states and Canada. And there was the memorable winter trip when the driver's window failed to close. While the band members leaned close to the car's heaters, Hubbard, who was driving, wrapped a hotel towel around his head in a hilarious effort to keep warm.

"There were lots of miles and shows in those years," Kern said. "We were young and full of piss and vinegar, thinking we would live forever."

Kern Kennedy; 2006.

Kern laughed as he recalled the juke joints and clubs where he and the Pacers entertained raucous crowds. He mentioned OT's in Des Arc, a notorious club where local rice farmers came in from the fields in sweaty overalls and rubber boots. OT's used bucket lids for ashtrays and beer kegs for seats. The club had an old piano, its broken keys tied with rubber bands. One night as women crowded the stage, a fight started near the piano. "I ran into the bathroom, but the fight followed me in there," he said. "I climbed through the bathroom window and landed in the mud outside."

At a club in Newport one night, a couple of guys got into a brawl, Kern said, and the band's singer at the time, Bob Howard, announced to the group that we would throw them out of the club if they did not quit.

"The next day, Bob showed up with two black eyes," Kern said. "I told him, Partner, you were a little reckless with that word 'we.' I'm not here for hand-to-hand combat."

In his eighties, Kern has a lifetime of stories from the road and the roadhouses where the Pacers played. A favorite story tells about the time he turned down an offer from Elvis. Local saxophone player Punky Caldwell joined them for the B&I show that night, when Elvis, impressed with the Pacers' sound, invited Kern and Caldwell to join his group and begin touring.

"Presley always appeared to me to be a three-chord musician and that was about it," Kern said. "He was just this phenomenon to come along and maybe the first guy in that particular field to step out there and do all the shaking and wiggling."

"My interest was already with the Pacers, and I've never regretted that," Kern added. "Elvis was the guy who ended up making the money, and Scotty and Bill were out on the sideline. That's where I would have been, just another sideman for the group. Those guys never shared in the fortune."

Kern's understanding was accurate. In 1960, another Arkansas musician, Jimmy Newell, hired Bill Black, by then no longer with Elvis. Newell recalled picking up Black in the parking lot of a Memphis radio station where the bass player, after touring with Elvis for four years, was driving an old Studebaker with "Bill Black Appliance Repair" painted on the door. In Scotty Moore's book, *Scotty and Elvis: Aboard the Mystery Train*, the guitar player lists his income at an annual average of $12,000 during the fourteen years he performed with Elvis.[65]

Kern's decision to stay with the Pacers brought him to Memphis for the band's first recording session at Sun Records, where he first encountered Phillips' demanding expectations for enthusiasm and originality.

"I remember being terrified and exhilarated to be there," Kern said. "I was the son of a sharecropper and had never recorded before. But Sam wanted us to play like it was a concert for thousands of people. We worked with a single track recorder and had to get it right."

In 1956, the Pacers had the sound Phillips wanted, a rough-edged authenticity that placed higher value on a performer's sincere efforts rather than polished and precise music.

"When you're recording, if you think you'll make a mistake, you will," Kern said. "But Sam Phillips put you at ease. He had an uncanny way of getting you to do what you never thought possible. I admired him for trying different things to help you do better."

Kern also admires the band-leadership skills of his lifelong friend Sonny Burgess. "Sonny makes the calls to give each of us a chance on stage, and he's wise to do that. He watches the crowd and knows what they want to dance to. If it's country or a wild rock and roll show, Sonny knows what works."

Music in the Heart

Despite the Pacers' best efforts and the popularity of their recordings and road shows, Kern made the difficult decision in 1962 to permanently leave the band for a more stable career. He took a job with the Missouri Pacific Railroad, and for the next twenty years he worked as a detective and in corporate security areas. But his love of music, especially the western swing style of Bob Wills, remained in his heart.

By 1984, the railroad had merged with Union Pacific, and a company band was established to promote the new identity. Though more than eighty people showed up at the Little Rock auditions, Kern was chosen to lead the Union Pacific Country Band. The band was a phenomenal success. For the next ten years, he once again performed the music he loved, but this time all transportation, equipment, and wardrobe were provided by the railroad.

After Kern retired in 1993, a call came from Sonny, who was seeking to reunite the Pacers. A rockabilly revival movement was underway, and the Pacers were again in demand. World-wide recognition of the Pacers' role in the origins of rock and roll has increased in the past twenty years. As a member of the "Legendary Pacers," Kern has traveled the world, and untold thousands of fans have danced to his music.

Recalling the day in 1957 when he threw away what he thought were his worthless Sun singles, Kern laughs at his youthful error, his face once again lighting up in a smile.

"My thrill has always been in the playing itself," he said. "A few times in my lifetime I have asked how much a job pays. But if you really love what you do and put your heart in it, you'll make money. I've been one of a very few people that have done what they've always wanted to do. That love has got to be at the heart of it."

Jim Aldridge

In the early 1960s, the Pacers added a new routine to their wild on-stage antics. As the band began a lively rendition of the Ray Stevens tune "Ahab the Arab," Jim Aldridge appeared in a blonde wig and with veils across his face. A muscular man with his open shirt showing a hairy chest, Jim went skipping into the audience dressed as Fatima, the song's "Queen of the desert sands." Jim worked his floor show as screams of laughter filled the room.

When the Pacers switched the tune to "New Wildwood Flower," Jim found a bald man in the audience, sat in his lap, and stroked his blushing head, the Fatima wig thrown to the middle of the dance floor. Before the song was over, Jim was back on stage, his saxophone wailing, swaying in choreographed rhythm with the other members of the band.

Though he made it look easy, Jim's performances were created from his two most essential professional attributes: an inherent love of music and a natural on-stage poise. With a show business career encompassing more than 12,000 performances over fifty years, the saxophone player has earned his nickname of "Mr. Entertainer."

"Music has been so good to me," Jim said in a 1999 interview in *Rock & Blues News*. "I'm enjoying my days and my nights and working harder than ever. It's amazing to me that I'm getting to play this old music so many years later. I have been blessed."

Raised in North Little Rock, Jim had a musical heritage that began with several aunts and uncles who were piano players. One of his earliest memories is sitting in a rocking chair with his grandmother, Dora

Patterson of Stuttgart, Arkansas, and learning the old folk songs she played on the harmonica.

"By the age of eleven, I had already played trombone, piano, and saxophone," Jim said. "In 1952, when I was fifteen, I put together a nine-piece group that played the big band jazz of Glenn Miller, the Dorsey brothers, and Artie Shaw."

Jim Aldridge, high school band leader; 1955.

Jim prepared the musical arrangements for his first band, which at its peak had seventeen members, and they played sock hops through his high school and college years. By the late 1950s, when the nightclub music scene in Little Rock was mostly country or big band, Jim began listening to emerging new genres. These were the early rock and roll sounds known as "doo wop" and the records of Elvis Presley and others that brought the music of black artists to a new white audience.

"There were no more swing bands in night clubs," he said. "When I first heard rock and roll, I realized I could sing Elvis songs. I loved the singing part and shaking my booty, seeing the audiences smile at my showmanship."

A trip to Los Angeles and Hollywood in 1960 made Jim realize he could "hold my own with any horn player anywhere." But he did not find many saxophone players on the West Coast who played what he called "my Southern boy, rocking blues style," a combination of rock and roll with a jazzy be-bop sound.

Back in North Little Rock and playing at the popular Club 70, notorious for its rough crowds and fights, Jim made the connection that would change his life. Next door was another local bar, the Top Hat Club. As word got out that Jim was back from Los Angeles, the Top Hat crowd flocked to see their hometown favorite. At break time, Jim noticed that band members from the Top Hat had also come over to see where their crowd had gone.

That band was the Pacers, now without Sonny Burgess, but still maintaining an active work and traveling schedule. Recognizing the value of adding Jim's sax to their sound, the Pacers offered him a position in the band.

"I was impressed when they told me the band's history and that they worked somewhere every night," Jim said.

Jim joined the Pacers and moved to Newport. For the next six years, he enjoyed a consistent work schedule, traveling with the band from Canada to Alabama.

"We played all the hit records of the day that fit our sound and our style," Jim said. "I was always a showman, a Tom Jones-Elvis type of guy. The Pacers now had a real marketable product—showmanship. We packed the clubs everywhere we went."

In 1962, Jim put his creative talents into a new tune, "Do the Frog," modeled on the Rufus Thomas song, "Do the Dog," which had been banned on the radio. In the days of early rock and roll, Jim's song was among a cluster of popular records, hits such as "The Pony," "The Mashed Potato," and "The Watusi," that introduced wild new dance steps to high-energy teenaged audiences.

Living in Newport through the mid-1960s, Jim enjoyed the charms of small-town life. He drove a white Cadillac and had a matching white speed boat. He recalls summer days on the White River fishing and skiing, and fall mornings deer hunting in the Arkansas woods. He was playing in the clubs six nights a week, but he was interested in leading a band again.

In 1966, Jim returned to Little Rock and became front man for his own group. Three former Pacers joined him: Fred Douglas, bass; Bob Dalton, guitar; and Jerry Little (Kattawar), piano.

Though the crowds at the Top Hat, Club 70, and other clubs enjoyed the music, the rough atmosphere was always a challenge. Chicken wire occasionally surrounded the stage at Club 70, offering some protection to musicians when tables were knocked over and bodies stumbled across the room. Jim recalled "fighting our way out" many times. "I've seen beer bottles busted on heads and fights with women in high heels," Jim said. "I've seen folks chased off parking lots with hammers and car jacks. I wasn't scared to fight, but there's a time to fight and a time to run."

In 1970, Jim's night life settled down considerably when he accepted an invitation to perform in Houston. He moved to Texas and formed a new band "Water Brother," recording under the stage name of Jamie Rich. He composed and performed "Read Your Mind" and "Flute Sweet," records that reached No. 1 in Texas and California. His label was Westpark Records, published by Soundsville music and released by Mercury Records.

"My largest show was in 1972 when we played for the returning Apollo 17 astronauts," Jim said. "President Nixon and 110,000 people were at the Houston Air Terminal that day."

But Jim's success attracted some unscrupulous characters. Offered an opportunity to record directly for Mercury, Jim discovered his con-

tract with Soundsville had been changed by a man he called "an uneth-
ical booking agent." Jim, his manager, and the studio were the targets
of a $1.5 million lawsuit. "I settled and finished the contract, but I lost
the chance for a hit record," he said. "I came back to Arkansas and put
together another band. I just wanted to go back to playing my music,
being the Jim Aldridge show band again without all the problems."

Jim Aldridge; 2006.

Back on home turf, Jim resumed the business management style
and work ethic he learned from his parents, performing six nights a
week at local clubs and paying his bills on time. In 1981, he released
an album *Jim Aldridge* on his own label, Square Records. He also developed a popular lounge act, and through the 1980s his group, "Jim
Aldridge and the Al Di La Band," was a headliner show at top Little
Rock hotels. National stars such as Robert Goulet, Huey Lewis, and
Wayne Newton, performing in Little Rock, often joined him on stage
at the Hilton Hotel for late night singing and fun, Jim said.

The 1970s and 1980s were peak years. Jim was honored with the
"Entertainer of the Year" and "Entertainer of the Decade" awards by

the Arkansas Association of Country Music. A fan club was created, and for several years, he participated in the music industry event Fan Fare at Nashville. In 1984, he appeared on four segments of *You Can Be a Star*, the TNN Nashville television show hosted by country superstar Jim Ed Brown, finishing among the top four performers.

Brown and his sisters Maxine and Bonnie had started their show business careers as a trio, and the Pacers had more than once shared the bill with the Browns at the family's Trio Club in Pine Bluff, Arkansas. Aldridge and Brown had been friends for years, but old friendships carried little weight with the new television show. Brown advised Jim not tell anyone of their background to avoid rumors of favoritism.

By the 1990s, after three decades of working some 300 shows a year, Jim began to cut back. At the same time, he was asked to perform again with the Pacers. The first was a 1993 tribute show at Bob King's club in Swifton. Jim rejoined his old bandmates, and the bookings continued for the band now called the Legendary Pacers.

In the past ten years, the band has found new audiences in Europe and Asia, having been recognized as authentic pioneers of American music. Jim said the international bookings began soon after distinctive fans were noticed at Pacers shows in the United States. Many of the young people who came up for autographs were rockabilly fans from England, Sweden, Spain, and other European countries.

"It was like they discovered Elvis again," Jim said. "They study American music, and they pride themselves in their knowledge of artists and dates. They know as much rockabilly as we do."

In addition to the Pacers, Jim continued to perform locally, at times as a duo with Kern Kennedy or with his own rock and roll band. Having been "discovered" again and connecting with a new generation of fans is a surprise and a thrill, he said.

"They are recognizing rockabilly as their music," Jim said, smiling. "It's amazing, and I'm delighted."

Fred Douglas

Fred Douglas is the Pacers' "straight man," not given to exaggeration or comedy. When he speaks of the band he has been playing with for more than fifty years, his voice is measured and understated. "The Pacers are older than the Rolling Stones," he said in a matter-of-fact tone. "We may be the oldest rock and roll band in the world."

Fred was born in 1939 in the rural Arkansas community of Smithville, about forty-five miles north of Newport.

"I grew up with a guitar in the family, and I've been fooling with one since I was six," Fred said with a hint of pride. "I was going to church some back then, but church music had nothing to do with me playing."

As for others of his generation, the music of his youth came over the radio. Grand Ole Opry performers Hank Williams and the Wilburn Brothers were his favorites, until a new sound dominated the airwaves in 1955. "When Elvis and others came along, I had to get into that stuff," Fred said. "I started playing at the clubs when I was fifteen."

A Profusion of Talent

Fred's teenaged musical abilities caught the attention of Slim Rhodes. The popular country and rockabilly singer was among the judges at a youth talent show in Pocahontas, Arkansas. Rhodes was born in that Delta town in 1913 as Ethmer Cletus Rhodes. Since 1939, he had been heard daily on WMC-AM in Memphis. "Slim Rhodes & the Mother's Best Mountaineers" were sponsored by Mother's Best Flour, which also sponsored Hank Williams' radio shows. The Rhodes band was popular in Memphis, and Sun Records had signed them to a recording contract in the 1950s. The band also had a thirty-minute live show on KATV-TV in Pine Bluff, Arkansas, every Tuesday.

As a teenager, Fred was unaware of the profusion of musical talent emerging in northeast Arkansas. Winner of the talent contest that day and the prize of appearing on the *Grand Ole Opry* show in Nashville was another musical son of the Arkansas Delta, Bill Rice. Born in the hamlet of Datto (Clay County), Rice went on to a career that has included seventy-three awards from ASCAP (the most received by any songwriter), several Grammy nominations, and original recordings on the country charts. Fred played guitar on several of Rice's recordings in the early 1960s.

"Slim said I should have won the talent show," Fred recalled. "But that started it; Slim became a friend of our family."

Fred Douglas, twenty-one years old, playing guitar with Teddy Riedel's band; 1960.

By the 1950s, the Douglas family had moved to Walnut Ridge, Arkansas. When Rhodes traveled to the area, he would visit the Douglases and stay for a home-cooked meal. While still a teenager, Fred performed with the legendary star and appeared on his television program. He gained exposure to some of the top musicians of the time, as Rhodes' band featured two outstanding musicians who later achieved great individual success. The electric guitar player was Brad "Pee Wee" Suggs, who became one of Sun's most recorded musicians. Pedal steel guitar was played by "Buttermilk" John Huey, who grew up near Helena,

Arkansas, and was a childhood friend and later a band member with Conway Twitty, Vince Gill, and others. Huey became one of the most renowned pedal steel guitar players in the music industry.

By 1957, Rhodes believed Fred was ready to audition at Sun Records. Once again, the Arkansas youth was in good hands. "Slim took me to Sun to audition," Fred said. "When Sam Phillips ran the tape afterward, he told Slim, 'The boy's got a good voice but he needs something different.' I was just trying to sound like Elvis."

The Sun rejection did not trouble him. Fred was a teenager, playing the music he liked and getting paid. He had a regular gig with Teddy Riedel, playing VFWs and clubs across Arkansas. Riedel was two years older than Fred, but he, too, had similar experiences with an older successful Arkansas musician. Riedel had been befriended by Wayne Raney, a harmonica virtuoso who came from the tiny community of Wolf Bayou (Cleburne County), and Riedel performed on Raney's television program in Jefferson City, Missouri. Riedel's most successful song was "Judy," recorded in 1960 with Fred on guitar and later covered by Elvis Presley. In 1962, Riedel recorded an album with the Pacers on Razorback Records.

Raney's story is another example of the wealth of musical talent emerging from Arkansas at this time. Raney had achieved immense success in partnership with Lonnie Glosson, a harmonica player who was born in Judsonia (White County). The two men established a mail-order business that sold millions of harmonicas and played a major role in turning the harmonica into a widely popular instrument. By 1938, Raney and Glosson had a program on KARK radio in Little Rock, later hosting a national show on WCKY in Cincinnati, Ohio. In 1949, their "Why Don't You Haul Off and Love Me," with Raney on vocals and Hot Springs (Garland County) native Henry Glover producing, reached No. 1 on the charts. Raney and Glosson recorded several songs with the Delmore Brothers, including the hit, "Blues Stay Away from Me," co-written and produced by Glover, the same year.

Learning from the Best

Fred was playing with and learning from some of the best musicians in the area. It prepared him for his later years when the Pacers played with rockers such as Jerry Lee Lewis and Carl Perkins. He was also helping new talent get started. One of those was J. C. Caughron, a lead guitar player hired by Sonny when the Pacers went to California in 1958 to join Johnny Cash.

"Caughron was a friend of mine in Walnut Ridge," Fred said. "I knew him when he couldn't play at all. He used to come to my house and fool around with me on the guitar. He picked it up fast. It wasn't long before he could play pretty good."

Like other Arkansas rock and roll musicians, Fred was familiar with the Pacers well before he joined the band. He saw Sonny perform at the 1958 benefit concert in Memphis for the family of Jay Perkins. Ernest Tubb, Hank Snow, and other Nashville stars performed at the Ellis Auditorium that night, but Sonny's act was the only one brought back for an encore, Fred remembered.

Fred joined the Pacers in 1959, about the time Sonny began working with Conway Twitty in Canada. The band still performed its wild floor show, and Johnny Ray Hubbard was still the showman and the clown. He would lie down on the floor and "waller," Fred said, and the guys would build a human pyramid on the bass. People loved the show, and Fred enjoyed being part of a successful and popular act.

But the steady work lasted only a short time. In the 1960s, Fred had to shift bands to keep the bills paid. He left the Pacers and rejoined Teddy Riedel in 1961, then a few years later came back to the Pacers and stayed with them until the band broke up.

"We played till about 1966 or 1967," he said. "Then we all took day jobs and did a little music on the side. I started working for state government. I was married with a couple of kids, trying to make a living."

As the occasional jobs grew fewer, Fred gradually put his music aside. By the mid-1990s, he was living in the central Arkansas town of Heber Springs when an announcement for a community event caught his attention. The nearby Ozark Mountain town of Shirley, Arkansas, was hosting a concert, and Fred knew he had to attend. The headline performers were a group now known as Sonny Burgess and the Legendary Pacers.

A Second Chance at Life

Fred caught up with his old friends that night in 1995. The band has been together again ever since. "It felt good to be back with these guys, all real good musicians," Fred said. "Back in my younger days when I was doing it fulltime, it got a little old with the traveling and everything. Now it's like being given a second chance at life."

Fred Douglas; 2006.

Today, the Legendary Pacer speaks of a 2009 concert in Sweden as one of the best shows the group has ever done. His most memorable musical experience of recent years was playing at the 1997 Elvis Presley Festival in Tupelo, Mississippi, when he joined Elvis' original sidemen, D. J. Fontana and Scotty Moore, musicians Fred said he idolized.

What Fred rarely talks about is how a rock and roll band can stay together for more than fifty years. The mystery and magic of the Pacers is an insight that Fred, in his quiet, matter-of-fact manner, still keeps to himself. "I don't know how we all got along," he said. "We had arguments, but we always got over them. We worked out the problems. We just slid it off."

Additional Pacers

The Pacers were a real good, original band. They always had a crowd. They played the best music ever made, and they played it right.

—Willard "Pop" Jones

Front cover of promotional flier for the Pacers; 1965.

J. C. Caughron

J. C. Caughron joined the Pacers in 1958 as a lead guitar player, free-ing up Sonny Burgess to focus more on singing. Prior to joining the band, Caughron, a native of Swifton, Arkansas, was working in Tuckerman at his uncle's gas station and grist mill, playing music on the side.

"When I first met him in 1956, he was pumping gas at Busters gas station," Sonny said. "Someone told us he could play a little guitar. He was pretty good, and after a time, he got even better."

From left: Johnny Ray Hubbard, Bobby Crafford, Jimmy Ray Paulman, J. C. Caughron, and Kern Kennedy); 1960.

Kern Kennedy, a distant cousin, remembered Caughron as a musi-cal perfectionist, a stickler for accurate chords, whose smooth sound was highly appreciated by Roy Orbison. Caughron made several western tours with the Pacers, and he recorded eight singles with them at Sun Studios in 1958 and 1959. Caughron's guitar work is featured on the Pacers' "The Pace" and "Wildwood Flower. " He also played on Chuck

Comer's 1959 Vaden recording "Little More Lovin'" made at the KLCN studio at Blytheville and on Jimmy Ray Paulman's "Be Mine," recorded in 1960 at Phillips International in Memphis.

Caughron battled an alcohol addiction for many years, causing some erratic behavior and interfering with his work as a musician. Nevertheless, he performed with the Pacers intermittently for nearly twenty years, and he joined them for band reunions in the 1990s. Caughron and his wife died in a vehicle accident in 2009. Kennedy and Aldridge played at his graveside service in Swifton.

In May 1995, Larry Donn wrote in his "Rockabilly Days" column for *Now Dig This* magazine: "J. C. Caughron was something like a 'legend' to me in the late '50s....At the time, he was one of the best guitar players I had ever heard. He had a driving feeling in his playing that reeked with the very essence of rock 'n' roll. He wasn't fancy, nor particularly fast, but his playing made me want to boogie all over town."

Johnny Ray Hubbard

In the days before rock and roll guitar players began to strut their stuff and flail with their shiny electronic toys, the showman of the band played the bass fiddle, an instrument also called the double bass or the doghouse bass. For the Pacers, the guy who spun and slapped this large acoustic instrument, who swung it up into the air and carried it with him as he jumped out among the dancers, was Newport native Johnny Ray Hubbard. "I clowned and put on a show and never stopped playing," Johnny Ray said. "I was the jolly man and kept them laughing."

As a young man, Johnny Ray was agile enough to lie on his back on the stage floor and balance his oversized device on his extended feet like a circus acrobat, inviting his willing bandmates Joe Lewis and Jack Nance to climb on board, all the while maintaining the thumping heartbeat of a rocking tune.

Though Johnny Ray's blue eyes dimmed with age, they still shone with merriment as he recalled the antics that made the Pacers one of the best show bands of the 1950s. "We never practiced the moves. We were young and we did whatever we felt like," he said. "Once in Mobile a woman threw her bloomers on stage, and the boys dared me to put them on. We got the biggest laugh. No other band was putting on a show like that."

Johnny Ray started exploring Newport's notorious night life as a sixteen-year-old boy in 1947. The most alluring club along Highway 67 was the Silver Moon, its marquee motto "Home of Famous Bands" suggesting a world far more exciting than chopping and picking cotton on his father's farm. "When I was a boy, the cover charge at the Silver Moon as $1," he said. "I got me a phony ID and worked there as bartender. On band nights, I'd take the door. I was a rounder, and I cut my teeth on that bar."

The Rocky Road Ramblers

Johnny Ray began playing bass as a teenager with the Rocky Road Ramblers. With Sonny and other Jackson County adolescents, he performed at makeshift theaters where local entrepreneurs set up a portable movie projector, hung a bed sheet on the wall, and showed western movies. "We'd play a little show, make maybe twenty-five cents a night," Johnny Ray recalled.

Another early venue was the Alamo Theater, a movie house built in the residential area of the Newport Air Base. The small community in east Newport had its own stores, social clubs, and baseball team, the Airbase Indians. The Rocky Road Ramblers soon became a popular dance band at the site, and Johnny Ray's stage antics got an early start there. A March 30, 1950, article in the Newport Daily Independent stated that he was voted "ugliest boy" at an airbase theater benefit program for the baseball team.

Military service interrupted the fun, but by 1953, Johnny Ray was back home from Korea and ready once again to rock. There was more work now than ever, and the group rapidly became known at clubs in Swifton and Newport.

Johnny Ray Hubbard at the annual Farmers Day show in Newport; 1957.

Johnny Ray was no stranger at Jackson County's most notorious music venue. As a former bartender and doorman at the Silver Moon, he knew all the regulars. He developed a special friendship with local tough man and brawler Francis "Fats" Callis, the Batesville native who made the Silver Moon his shore leave home when not on active duty in the navy. Johnny Ray had seen Fats lift men from their barstools and throw them through the screen door of the club. And Johnny Ray was on hand the fateful night when Fats had his deadly confrontation with the Jackson County sheriff.

Out of the Cotton Patch, On the Road

By 1956, the Pacers were an established band that opened shows in Jackson County for Elvis Presley and other top stars from Sun Records. They recorded their first single at Sun that year and began nationwide travel. "Sun took me out of the cotton patch and put me on the road," Johnny Ray said.

When traveling, the band members shared a hotel room, sleeping two to a bed, their usual practice to save money. Each man brought along five or six band outfits, which also served as extra blankets in poorly heated hotel rooms.

Often the driver of the Pacers' Cadillac limousine, Johnny Ray remembered some challenging moments behind the wheel, such as the time in a heavy rain when a large object passed them on the road. "It was my bass," he said. "It just broke loose from the roof rack and slid around the side of us on the road. Jack Nance pulled his clothes off and went after it."

One winter trip to Canada, the driver's window would not shut, and blowing snow and freezing air filled the car. "I put my coat in the open window, and the wind caught it like a balloon," Johnny Ray said. "The fenders were all caked with ice."

Lively Nights, Good Money

When the band came home from road trips, people followed them down the highway and honked their horns as the word spread through Newport that the Pacers were back in town. There was "good money" to be made back then, Johnny Ray said, about $18,000 in 1957, his best year.

That atmosphere changed as the work became more demanding. Playing music full time, Johnny Ray spent less of his free time at Newport clubs. He married in 1959 and joined a local church. Though his lifestyle changed, Johnny Ray's buoyant personality never diminished. "I never met a stranger," he said. "I liked to meet people, to shake hands and introduce myself."

Johnny Ray stayed with the Pacers through the early 1960s, recording on Razorback Records and performing in Arkansas clubs as new band members joined and left the group. In 1965, he retired from music, and for nearly thirty years, he worked at a local factory, living in a modest house not far from his childhood home and the fields his father once farmed. Health issues prevented him from rejoining the Pacers when the band regrouped in the 1990s, and he was unable to travel with them to Jackson, Tennessee, for induction into the Rockabilly Hall of Fame. The framed certificate from that honor hangs on his living room wall in his small home. A rear bedroom holds scrapbooks, posters, and other memorabilia from his younger days.

"I miss my friends. I miss my boys," he said, his blue eyes growing moist. "It gets me a lot to listen to the old rock and roll. It brings back a lot of memories."

Johnny Ray died in 2014 and is buried in Newport. His funeral service was conducted at the Air Base Church of Christ, a small building close to the former military site and the farmland his father once worked. Placed beside him in his open casket were a tri-folded American flag provided by the Veterans Administration and a Sun Records album cover of his Pacers songs.

Jerry Kattawar

Jerry Kattawar replaced Kern Kennedy as the Pacers' piano payer in 1964. The Greenville, Mississippi, native describes his musical genre as "Mud Bottom Boogie and Blues." His energetic style fit well with the Pacers' act. Among his favorite moves, Kattawar would jump up and down on the piano. If the piano top broke and he fell into the instrument, or if the piano fell off the stage, it was all part of his irrepressible showmanship.

As a teenager, Kattawar played in clubs across the Delta, falling in with the cluster of talented musicians from the Helena area. He was befriended by local businessman and music club owner Charley Halbert, and in 1961, Kattawar, then seventeen years old, lived in Halbert's motel, the legendary Rainbow Inn.

"Charley loved music and let us musicians stay at his motel while we practiced and got ready to go on the road," Kattawar said. "I started doing shows with all the Arkansas boys—Luke Paulman, Will Pop Jones, Conway Twitty, Ronnie Hawkins."

In 1963, Kattawar and his wife Millie moved to Peoria, Illinois, to work with the Shades, a band that had been started in Helena. Within a year, the young couple was facing some predictable challenges. He was unemployed and she was pregnant. When the Pacers played in Peoria in 1964, Kattawar went to see his Arkansas friends. He learned that Kern Kennedy had left the group. A piano player was needed. "I packed up that night and went with them," Kattawar said. "I left my pregnant wife with her mother to have the baby."

Jerry Kattawar (far right), an exuberant piano player from Greenville, MS, added a lively stage presence to the Pacers. (From left: Joe Cyr, Jim Aldridge, Fred Douglas, Bob Dalton, Bobby Crafford, and Kattawar); 1962.

Laughing at his youthful behavior, he told of a Pacers' trip to Canada, a three-month outing, when Millie called to tell him the grocery store had shut off her credit. Now married to Millie nearly fifty years, Kattawar said, "If a woman thinks a young man has character and will mature, she may make up her mind to stay with him."

In Newport, Kattawar lived in the Dorsey Arms apartment recently vacated by Paulman. Times were flush for the band in the mid-1960s, and the Pacers played five and six nights per week, sometimes up to three shows in one night, a seemingly endless stream of high school proms and graduation parties across the state. Their popularity was fueled by the high energy of their performances.

"Jim Aldridge was always there," Kattawar said, "and in those years we were like brothers competing on stage. We'd climb on furniture and swing from the ceiling."

When Bobby Crafford booked Ronnie Hawkins back in Arkansas and the Pacers opened for him, Kattawar, who occasionally used the stage name Jerry Little, said there were huge shows at the Silver Moon and reunions of Arkansas musicians.

"The Pacers were an Arkansas band. They loved the state and the people," he said. "That's where their heart was, and that's the reason they got so famous. We were all over the place."

By 1966, however, the Pacers had relocated to Little Rock. Most of the band members were married and worked at day jobs. "Everyone grew up and had families that demanded more of their time," Kattawar said. "Music became a sideline for them."

Kattawar left the Pacers after a three-night gig at Club 70 in North Little Rock. He returned to Greenville and developed a career in the trucking industry, a successful business he continues to operate today. He also started a new group with his brother Mike on drums. Forty-five years later, the Kattawar brothers continue to perform and are well known in Memphis and across the Delta. An irrepressible showman, Kattawar compares his longevity in music and freight with that of another Memphis musician and one-time truck driver.

"Elvis left trucking and got into music and is gone," Kattawar said. "I left music and got into trucking. And I'm still going."

Joe Lewis

He first showed up as a tall thirteen-year-old boy, already over six feet, who heard the music from a neighbor's house and came by to sit in with guys nearly ten years older than himself. His family lived in the residential area at the former Newport Air Base, and in 1953, the Rocky Road Ramblers often rehearsed there at band member A. L. Wilson's house.

Photos of Lewis from the time show him holding a mandolin, standing behind a microphone with several other teenaged boys, each of them wearing identical cowboy hats and western style shirts, outfits provided to them by the Newport Farmers Electric Co-op. Lewis and his bandmates were among the local performers at rural meetings conducted by the electric utility. In the photos, Lewis appears as an awkward, oversized kid staring glumly at the camera.

Fourteen-year-old Joe Lewis on mandolin auditioning at KNBY with his cowboy band; 1951.

Within three years, however, Lewis had matured into the Pacers' lead guitar player, his charismatic stage presence inciting a nearly hysterical adoration by local teenaged girls.

"The night the Pacers were playing at a dance not far from here, big Joe Lewis had the mike and was giving his usual enthusiastic song delivery, planting his adequate feet on the platform and writhing for emphasis, some ecstatic teenage girls stormed the platform. They got so carried away, they attempted to carry Joe away. Joe escaped, but not before they yanked off his flashy pink jacket."

—*Newport Daily Independent*, August 20, 1956

It was Lewis who came up with the band's new name. He had grown up at the air base and had seen the Piper PA-20 Pacer airplane there. Lewis joined the Pacers in 1955, his good looks and guitar antics adding to the band's athletic showmanship, and he was with the band when the first Sun recordings were made the following year.

"We should have made Joe our front man," Sonny said. "The women loved him."

When the Pacers changed in 1957, Lewis had the performance skills and the confidence to strike out on his own.

Another Rock and Roll Band Here:
Joe Lewis Gets up His Own Outfit

"Joe Lewis, broad shouldered rock and roller from Newport, who rates almost as many teen aged screams as Elvis Presley hereabouts, announced today that he is forming his own band. Lewis, who sings and strums a guitar, has joined with drummer Russ Smith, also of Newport, both former players with the Pacers, who have attracted much attention in this area....Opening tomorrow night at the Silver Moon, the 6-5 former high school football player doesn't know for sure what his future plans will be...but first he intends to finish high school."

—*Newport Daily Independent*, February 8, 1957

Newspaper articles from 1957 call Lewis "Newport's skyrocketing rock 'n' roll star" and identify his appearances on Memphis television programs and regional radio stations. In his two years with the Pacers, Lewis performed with Elvis Presley, Carl Perkins, Roy Orbison, Johnny Cash, and many other top stars. After that, Lewis recorded at Sun Studios with Jack Nance on vocals and piano. They called themselves "Joe and Jack," and they recorded seven original tunes that were never published.

Lewis' solo career never materialized. Instead, he joined Conway Twitty's Rockhousers and began performing in Canada. When members of that group returned to the United States, Twitty sent Lewis back to recruit new musicians. Lewis returned with his old friend Jack Nance. The band changed its name to the Lonely Blue Boys and eventually to the Twitty Birds. Lewis' showmanship at this time was noted in a Twitty biography: "The dominating presence in the group was Joe Lewis.... Blond and handsome, Big Joe stood a solid six foot six, had a unique electric bass style, and sang a marvelously blended harmony to Conway's gutsy baritone."[66]

When Twitty and Nance toured in England in 1960, Lewis created the four-man group Friday Nights, which included Sonny, Blackie Preston, and Tommy Markham. The quartet played in Canada during Twitty's absence. Lewis remained faithful, despite a challenging period in 1961 when Twitty's band dispersed and Lewis worked as a salesman with Banner Hardware of St. Louis. He rejoined Twitty the next year and moved with him to Oklahoma City in 1965. For nearly twenty years, Lewis was a member of Twitty's immensely successful rock and roll and country music bands.

Lewis was thirty-nine years old in 1976 when he died in a vehicle accident. Buried at Newport, he has a large gravestone that reads "Joe E. Lewis, Professional Musician" and is adorned with musical notes and an image of his guitar.

Jack Nance

In 1955, Jack Nance he got an offer he couldn't refuse. Newport's most popular band, the Moonlighters, had returned from an audition at Sun Studios, where Sam Phillips suggested the group develop a more unique sound. Now, Sonny Burgess was looking for new talent.

Nance had a college education and a steady job in his hometown as the assistant band director at Newport High School. He played a variety of instruments: drums, piano, trumpet, and bass. The Pacers already had Russ Smith on drums, so Nance was offered a job on trumpet. His performance style matched the Pacers' wild energy.

Jack Nance, on trumpet.

"In the clubs, Jack played that trumpet loud and was a good showman," Sonny said. "That was great for us because all the other bands had saxophones. Nobody else had a trumpet. But Jack would get hit a lot. People would reach up to touch us and hit his trumpet, which put things out of whack."

Nance's frenzied trumpet solos, a counterpoint to Sonny's growling vocals, gave the Pacers their distinctive sound, what music writer Colin Escott described as "total abandon: coarse, untutored singing, unintelligible lyrics, ragged drumming, distorted guitar, capped by a wildly bleating trumpet. Even Little Richard paled in comparison."

And when Sonny sang *"Red headed woman make you wish you'd never been born. All you want to do is hear Gabriel blowing his horn,"* Nance's trumpet pushed the song to new highs, punching out a crisp phrasing and rhythm like a boxer working a speed bag. Years later,

Nance told his son Richard that he patterned his music with the Pacers after the 1920s jazz trumpet player Bix Beiderbecke.

Nance was with the Pacers in 1956 and 1957 when the first Sun recordings were made. When he left the Pacers, Nance performed for a short time with Joe Lewis before both men joined Conway Twitty, who was performing in Canada and northern U.S. cities. In 1957, they had a nine-week gig at the Flamingo Lounge in Hamilton, Ontario. Nance found a piano in an upstairs room and worked up new tunes. He started one song while on break during a show. On the next break, Twitty finished composing the song with him. The new song took seven minutes to complete, Nance later wrote.

"It's Only Make Believe" was pitched to MGM Records, which set up a Nashville recording session. In May 1958, the three Arkansans—Nance, Twitty, and Lewis—found themselves with some studio heavyweights: Floyd Cramer on piano, the Jordanaires providing vocal backing, and Hank Garland playing guitar.

"It's Only Make Believe" became one of the most successful songs in popular music, but it was not an immediate hit. The song went unnoticed for a few months, long enough for the band to decide on a career change. Nance wrote about the events in his music memoir *The Jack Nance Songbook*, which contains sheet music, lyrics, and commentary on the twenty-seven songs he wrote or co-wrote with Twitty:

> We decided to give up the music business, go back home, and do something else. We had been at home about two weeks and I was really feeling down and defeated when Conway called. He was really excited and shouting, "We've got a hit record!" A DJ in Columbus Ohio named Dr. Bop had flipped the record over and played "It's Only Make Believe." The people had liked it and bought it, and it had become number one in Columbus.

The band regrouped and, joined by bass player Blackie Preston, headed for Ohio, where fans were waiting. Nance described the excitement of driving up to that first show where Dr. Bop, in a live remote radio broadcast, was telling the audience that Twitty was coming:

When we got to the drive-in, there were thousands of people there and cars parked two blocks away. We had a sign on top of the car that read, "Conway Twitty and his MGM Recording Band." When Dr. Bop saw that, he yelled, "There he is." The people treated us like stars. That was something new and exciting and a feeling I'll never forget.

By the end of 1958, "It's Only Make Believe" was No. 1 in the nation and sold over one million copies. The band performed on top television shows such as *Your Hit Parade* and *The Andy Williams Show*, and in concert with the Everly Brothers, Connie Francis, and others. Nance and Twitty toured in England and Australia, and the Newport newspaper reported that the performers signed a ten-year songwriting contract with a New York publishing firm.[67]

The contract, if it ever existed, did not have much weight. Musicians and songwriters were commonly taken advantage of in a time when outright theft of musical material was common. Shirlene Nance, Jack's first wife, stated that Nance received no payment for "It's Only Make Believe" and he was short-changed on royalties and song titles.

Nance's memoir also includes passages about financial promises unfulfilled by Twitty's manager Don Seat. Twitty also had financial disagreements with Seat. Lawsuits were filed, and Nance left Twitty's band with hard feelings. He returned to central Arkansas and began playing piano for a popular band called the Shadows.

By 1962, with more than six years experience as a traveling musician, Nance had developed an expertise in performance logistics. It was a business skill that would carry him to the highest levels of the music industry.

Nance joined Dick Clark Productions, working in tour management and promotion, as well as serving as a road manager for a variety of new artists. This was followed by similar work at Concerts West and Motown Records. In the mid-1960s, Nance was associate producer for the NBC *Swingin' Country* television show. He also worked as tour manager, agent, and promoter with artists such as Dionne Warwick, the Monkees (one tour had Jimi Hendrix as the opening act), the Moody Blues, the Fifth Dimension, Paul Revere and the Raiders, the Rolling Stones, Three Dog Night, the Temptations, Herman's Hermits, and the

Jackson Five. Nance managed four road shows for Elvis Presley, and he was a personal manager for Michael Jackson and the road manager for Jackson's 1984 Victory Tour. He also had a song on the soundtrack of the 1999 animated movie *The Iron Giant*.

Nance died from lung cancer in 2000. He was sixty-five years old. In a series of tribute articles in the *Batesville Guard Daily* in 2010, he is quoted on changes in the music industry since his early days as a drummer for Conway Twitty's rock and roll band.

> We put all of us and our instruments in a station wagon and drove from club date to club date. For [Michael Jackson's] last big tour in 1994, I hired two of the largest airplanes in the world, the Russian Antonov 27, just to carry the stage and all the special effects. I hired a 727 to carry singers, dancers and stage hands. Michael had his own plane for family and friends. Conway's old station wagon would have been lost in the packing cases we carried on the flight to Bangkok....
> I kind of miss the old days. We were kids with the juices flowing. A bunch of us created the music for a generation. We created an era of music that will never die. I was there from the beginning.

Nance is buried at Newport. His large gravestone, shaped like a piano, is engraved with *"It's Only Make Believe," #1, 1959—Conway Twitty, 1970—Glen Campbell, 1989—Ronnie McDowell.*

Jimmy Ray "Luke" Paulman

> *Me and Levon wouldn't be heard of if it hadn't been for Jimmy Ray Paulman. He was the best rockabilly guitar I ever heard.*
> —Ronnie Hawkins

Jimmy Ray Paulman was a member of the Pacers for a less than a year, filling in the lead guitar and vocals role vacated by Sonny Burgess in 1960. Paulman was already well known on the southern music scene as an original member of two successful bands: Harold Jenkins' Rockhousers band and Ronnie Hawkins' the Hawks. His nickname was "Luke," a moniker later made famous by Levon Helm, who sang "Hey Luke, my friend, what about young Anna Lee?" in his song "The Weight."

Jimmy Ray "Luke" Paulman (center) with the Pacers; 1960.

Paulman had already quit the Hawks when Bobby Crafford offered him a job. The relocation to Newport did not last, as Paulman, who admits to being "young and foolish" at the time, refused to cut his long hair and conform to the Pacers' stage presence. Following the Pacers, Paulman moved to New Mexico, where he started a new band.

Paulman's career includes recordings on several record labels and work as a studio session player. He currently lives near Jackson, Tennessee, and continues a music writing and publishing business in partnership with Billy Weir, a drummer with the former Rockhousers whom Paulman has known for more than fifty years.

Russ Smith

The Pacers' original drummer was a member of the band from 1954 to 1957. During that time, the Newport native Russ Smith shared the stage with Elvis, toured the United States and Canada, and performed on the Pacers' first two Sun records. Following his departure in early 1957, Smith had a brief duo act with Joe Lewis until the young guitar player joined with Conway Twitty. In March of that year, Smith was contacted by Bob Neal about becoming a drummer for Jerry Lee Lewis.

Smith began touring with Lewis, traveling to Australia, Canada, and across the United States. In New York, he appeared on television on *The Steve Allen Show* and on stage in Alan Freed's rock and roll revue show, where attendance records were set. Smith told the Newport newspaper that crowds of fans kept Broadway blocked for two hours and 100 extra policemen were called out to keep order.

In 1958, Lewis appeared briefly in the MGM film *High School Confidential*, and Smith was photographed in a publicity shot for the movie. The picture shows Smith playing a snare drum on a flat bed trailer as a standing Lewis pounds the keyboard beside him. It is one of the last public images of the drummer.

In mid-1958, the Pacers were playing in Lubbock, Texas, when Buddy Holly came backstage. Holly told Bobby Crafford that he had just seen Lewis in England and had met Smith there. In the aftermath of that disastrous tour, little was heard of Smith and other band members. Sonny recalled an evening in the early 1960s when Lewis and Smith played a show at Jarvis' in Newport, but Smith soon drifted into obscurity.

Crafford recalled rumors of Smith playing in the Gulf Coast area. A chance meeting occurred in the mid-1960s when the Pacers were playing at a club in Mobile, Alabama. Smith was in the audience and came up to speak with his former band members. Crafford remembered Smith drinking heavily that night. Crafford helped him start his stalled car. Then Smith abruptly said he had to leave. He drove off and was not heard from again. Crafford mentioned a reunion of Lewis' musicians in 2010 when people said Smith had died and was buried somewhere in Mississippi. The location of his grave is unknown.

Russ Smith; 1956.

Charles Watson II

Fiddle player Charles Watson II jokes that he was "born into the band." His father is a Newport native, a lifelong friend of Sonny Burgess, and former manager of the Silver Moon. Watson was two years old when his parents moved to Tupelo, Mississippi, in 1962, where his father currently owns another Silver Moon, a music club named in recognition of the legendary venue he left in Arkansas.

Raised in a world of music and clubs, Watson first played with the Pacers at a 1996 Tupelo music festival, earning an invitation to join the band at a reunion held at Bob King's club in Swifton later that year. For the next twelve years, he traveled with the Pacers, adding a unique new sound with his fiddle.

Charles Watson II with Sonny on the porch of Elvis Presley's Tupelo birth place.

"Most people never would have thought a fiddle could fit in a rockabilly band," Watson said. "But Sonny never cared what people thought. If the music fit and the person made it feel right, he would put it in. He was an innovator, a risk taker."

Watson spoke of several surprises from his years with the band. The first was the extraordinary vitality of Arkansas musicians who were his parents' age. The Pacers frequently performed more than 120 shows per year in those days, often playing for two hours at a time without a break.

The Pacers at the Boom Boom Room, Bossier City, Louisiana; 1962.

"It doesn't matter where we went or what the venue was," Watson said. "At a show in Australia or some little Arkansas town, we would get out there and leave it all on the stage. You could count on that."

Another surprise came at a 2006 concert in London when the Pacers opened the show for Ike Turner. "In Arkansas, I was used to older crowds at the festivals and casinos, but in London, it was everyone, kids and older folks," Watson said. "When the band signed autographs in the lobby for an hour and a half, I realized how big Sonny was in Europe."

Having recorded several albums with the Pacers, Watson recognized Sonny's professionalism in the studio. "We would usually complete an album in two days, with everything down live, not revised on multi-channel systems," Watson said. "If you couldn't get a song in one or two takes, it wouldn't get on the album."

He also credited Sonny with being one of the few group leaders who split performance payments evenly and shared honors among the band members. "You don't hear about the lead artists sharing at all," Watson said, adding, "He even wanted me on stage for the Pacers' induction into Rockabilly Hall of Fame. I didn't expect to be included in that."

By 2010, medical issues forced Watson to postpone his musical career. Following a two-year recovery period, he has returned to the activity he loves, and he currently plays fiddle with several Tupelo-area bands.

"I still consider myself a Pacers' band member in reserve," he said.

Chapter 7.
Keep on Rocking

Sonny Burgess and the Legendary Pacers: 1996-

When the Pacers hit the stage, you wouldn't know their age. You'll be dancing, clapping your hands, and tapping your feet. They play the real music, and they play it well.

—Travis Wammack

By chance, two old friends run into each other and spend a few minutes catching up on the years of separation. The random meeting includes a brief nostalgic conversation about the divergent paths their lives have taken. The moment passes, and the men depart with a handshake.

Sonny Burgess; 1998.

This meeting took place at a music store in a North Little Rock shopping mall in 1981. At the time, Bobby Crafford lived in Little Rock and worked for a book and magazine distributor. Sonny had never moved from Newport, where he was then working for a cloth and sewing supply business.

"We ought to get back together and play one day," Bobby suggested.

Sonny was amenable, but neither man had any sense of how their talents would once again combine. Professional gigs had first brought them to the stage and the recording studio twenty-five years earlier; they were not amateurs who would gather to simply play for fun. The Pacers had last played together in 1976, recording a reunion album, The Old Gang. The session was arranged by Lake Country Records of Switzerland, and the recording took place at Jim Porter's MusAd Studio in Little Rock. Sonny wanted the cuts on The Old Gang to have the characteristic rockabilly echo originally heard in Sun recordings. That was not possible because some equipment at the Little Rock studio had been damaged in a fire a week earlier. The album was recorded, and Sonny, dissatisfied with its sound, gave it little thought. Nearly ten years later, Sonny had his first glimpse of The Old Gang album when he performed in England and a fan gave him a gift copy.

By the mid-1980s, a rockabilly revival was underway in Europe. New international businesses such as Lake Country, the French-British Charly Records, and the German Bear Family Records were keenly interested in recording or reissuing American rock and roll classics. Rockabilly concerts and festivals were being held overseas. Warren Smith and Charlie Feathers were the first Sun artists to play the shows. Sonny said his first European performance was in England in 1986 after he had been contacted by old friend Ronnie Hawkins. "It seemed that everyone had gone over but me," Sonny said. "Hawkins called and said I needed to go over there, that it was like stepping into a time tunnel."

Within a short time after the chance meeting in North Little Rock, Bobby was contacted by a woman from Cotton Plant who was opening a new duck hunting club. When she asked for his help in booking a band from Nashville for her large private party, Bobby arranged for Sonny and Kern Kennedy, still active with the Union Pacific show band,

198

to play with him. Sporadic bookings continued through the 1980s and early 1990s, and as the jobs increased, former Pacers Jim Aldridge and Fred Douglas were called in.

Sonny remained active during this time, playing with the Sun Rhythm Section and recording with Rounder and High Tone Records. But the enthusiasm of European rockabilly audiences and a new slate of bookings in the United States convinced the Pacers to formally reunite. The results of that decision were noted in May 1995 when Larry Donn wrote about the man he performed with some thirty years earlier.

What Rock and Roll Can Do

"On the evening of December 22nd, I fired up the ride and motored to Bob King's club, near Swifton, Arkansas, for the fortieth anniversary of Sonny Burgess & The Pacers. I will just mention that Jim [Aldridge] and Sonny were constantly dancing about the stage, acting like a couple of sixteen year olds throughout the evening. It is truly amazing what rock 'n' roll can do in the matter of energizing the body to writhe about with flailing limbs that otherwise would be stiff and sore."

—Larry Donn, *Now Dig This*, January 1997

Sonny believes a Pacers' 1996 performance at a Smithsonian Institution festival was key to formally re-establishing the band. Bobby thinks it was a huge show at Horseshoe Casino in Tunica. By 1998, when the renamed "Sonny Burgess and the Legendary Pacers" band performed in the documentary *Good Rockin' Tonight*, there was no doubt the band was back in business.

European Rockabilly Revival

The Europeans try to dress like we did in the '50s, but they don't, they dress like city people. We didn't wear them rolled up blue jeans. We tried to wear dress pants if we had them, and we wore suits when we were playing. I like a band to look like a band.

—Sonny Burgess

The death of Elvis in 1977 prompted a global curiosity about the lives of early rockabilly performers. Music that might have been forgotten was suddenly rediscovered in Europe. New fans traveled to the United States and discovered records on music store "vintage" shelves or purchased through wholesale outlets. The 45s and LPs were highly desired by Europeans who had a romanticized vision of the 1950s in America. The demand led to the reissuing of thousands of early rockabilly songs by companies in England, France, the Netherlands, and Germany. Songs that had been mostly forgotten in the United States suddenly made the musical charts overseas.

"Everything revolves around Sun and Elvis," Sonny said. "They think everybody was on Sun. It's a hotbed of music for these fans."

Most early rock and roll performers received limited royalties from the record labels that produced their work. As the European revival began, that pattern was continued by companies that reissued the original music on new compilation albums without compensating the performers. But the exposure and growing fan base did lead to invitations to revival shows and festivals, the earliest of these held at Hemsby and Weymouth, England. Sonny and other Arkansas performers—Larry Donn, Billy Lee Riley, and Sleepy LaBeef—were initially invited as solo performers. Local rock musicians, decades younger than their American idols, were thrilled to be selected for the back-up bands. When the Pacers were recognized as one of the few acts that included original musicians, their status rose at the festivals. The Arkansans found they had a choice of shows if they were willing to go abroad. Fans in England, France, Sweden, and Germany were eager to see them. Similar to the Sun package tours fifty years earlier, the Pacers were frequently grouped with other artists from the mid-South. Tours were arranged in Japan, Australia, and other distant venues.

"We all got a little hotter fifteen years ago," Ace Cannon said in a 2011 interview. "I hadn't done any rockabilly until the festivals started giving us the jobs. Now I do a lot of shows with the Pacers."

The European enthusiasm is also reflected in the colorful names of their festivals. In recent years, the Pacers have been on stage at the Rockin' Race Jamboree and the Screamin' Summer Festival, both in Spain, as well as the Rhythm Riot, the Rockabilly Rave, and the Wildest Cats In Town Festival, all in England. In Sweden, the Pacers have been featured performers on the cruise ship weekend Rocking at Sea.

Following a 2007 performance at the Crossroads Festival in Oviedo, a city in the northwestern Asturias region of Spain, the Pacers recorded locally. At the festival, the Pacers' show was interrupted by a mid-set power failure, but they came back forty minutes later to thrill the crowd, which had been waiting in the dark. The next day, after only a few hours of sleep, the band recorded nine songs in a studio in the coastal town of Gijon, much to the delight of record producer Mike Mariconda, who wrote in the *Gijon Stomp* album liner notes:

> That afternoon I heard the kind of RnR that after years of working in the studio, many attempted to duplicate. Many failed. There behind the studio glass were the people responsible for inventing it. Jorge and I furiously rolled tape trying to keep the pace with the Pacers. The sound immediately transported me back to the U S of A. A rock solid backbeat and a Jimmy Reed shuffle that no drummer in the country could master. Roadhouse piano that was up to snuff with the Killer's wildest poundings. A hillbilly yodel cured for years in Arkansas corn likker, drenched in tape echo. And blues holler, well, that made Elvis sound a little more like Pat Boone and a little less than Arthur "Big Boy" Crudup. This was not the normal noise you hear on a Sunday in our barrio in Gijon. Or London, or New York or even Memphis anymore, for that matter. This was some archaic language that only the elders could speak and the youngsters could only hope to understand. Damas y Caballeros, se llama Rock and Roll.

Mariconda's enthusiasm for his own production was affirmed in a review in the American music website Allmusic.com:

The band is ferocious, with guitar and saxophone solos ripping out of the speakers and Burgess' voice as strong as ever....."Gijon Breakdown" is an instrumental showcase for the band, which lets them cut loose with sandpaper guitar riffing, and raucous, bar-walking saxophone at a tempo that's practically hardcore punk. This is the sound of a bunch of grandfathers ripping it up one side and down the other in a way that would put half the young bands out there to shame.[68]

Sonny, as always, downplays the international recordings and the shows, but he admits that the European venues have been "a life saver for all these Sun guys." Flights to the overseas festivals are easy to arrange, the payment is good, and large audiences, sometimes 5,000 people or more, attend, making it seem that flush times have returned, he said. He is even willing to play in the style his new fans desire. "Europeans have a certain beat they want to hear," he said. "The Europeans want it fast."

At a 2012 rockabilly festival in Vara, Sweden, the Pacers sold out their merchandise of CDs, T-shirts, and caps and took two encores, eventually leaving the stage only because the building had to be cleared. As they did in Spain a few years earlier, the Pacers followed the show with a recording session that created *Live in Sweden*, a selection of original tunes and rock and roll classics. The album had a CD release party in 2013 at the Center for Southern Folklore when the Pacers played at the Memphis Music and Heritage Festival.

"We knocked 'em out," Bobby said about the Sweden show. "The people there are amazing. They know the dances and they understand the songs. They dress in '50s style, with jeans rolled up, girls in poodle skirts, and fuzzy dice hanging in cars. The parties we play in Europe and the wild dancing remind me of the old days at the Silver Moon."

In recent years, the Pacers have also reached new fans in Canada, where more than fifty years ago, clubs in Ontario and Toronto provided the first international stage for southern rockers. The band was a featured performer among a host of eager young Canadian rockabilly groups at the seventh annual "Red Hot and Blue Rockabilly Weekend" at Montreal in 2011. The Pacers' distinctive original sound and seemingly ageless showmanship astonished local audiences and impressed *Montreal Gazette* music critic Sylvain Cormier, whose review was titled "No Pacemaker for the Pacers."[69]

> These rockabilly grandpas were astounding Saturday. Tackled, thrown to the ground, steamrolled, knocked down. Crushed, this is how we felt. All with great fun…it was an hour and forty minutes jam packed with boogie, R 'n' B, rockabilly and big beat. Living joy in a pure form, big laughing happiness….You had to see Sonny the Giant handling his Fender as a toy, and Kennedy! Again the most fabulous hands on the piano; good Kern came to the stage using his walker, but once he sat down, move over Jerry Lee!
>
> From there, thinking that rockabilly prolongs active life, it's just a small step and I take it. Just think that these grandpas were leaving the country the next morning at 6 a.m. and playing the same night in Memphis, Tennessee. Over there, just like here, they will have broken the house down: this is the only thing the Pacers can do.

Rock and Roll Pioneers

Sonny Burgess: Roots-Rock Rocket

> *Although less visible than the King and the Killer and Carl Perkins, Burgess was rockabilly's real wild child—hootin' and hollerin' and flat-out screaming, pouncing off the stage in mid performance with the Pacers to lead the audience in Indian war dances and human pyramid-building, then jumping back on the bandstand and tearing up the fretboard. Which makes him a hero if you're into any kind of wild-ass rock and roll.*
> —Carly Carioli, *The Boston Phoenix*, June 6, 1996

In recent years, recognition of Sonny and the Pacers by U.S. fans has increased rapidly. In 2010, the band had a special evening in Chicago when they were invited on stage by members of the "Million Dollar Quartet," the musical show that celebrates the 1956 impromptu jam session with Elvis Presley, Jerry Lee Lewis, Carl Perkins, and Johnny

Cash. Bobby said the show's publicist, learning that the Pacers were to perform in Chicago, asked if they would join the cast on the anniversary of the original event.

"We were in the audience that night," Bobby recalled, "and at the end of the show, the musicians introduced us to the packed house. We went on stage and played 'Bucket's Got a Hole in It,' 'Red Headed Woman,' and 'Shake Rattle and Roll.' The place went wild."

The Pacers made a new friend that night in Chicago, the piano player Lance Lipsky, who performs the role of Jerry Lee Lewis in the stage show with a powerful energy and talent that recreates Lewis' performance style. Lipsky has played several shows with the Pacers since then, including a guest appearance at the 2013 Arkansas Delta Rockabilly Festival in Helena-West Helena.

In balance with their more glamorous venues, the Pacers play at small-town dance halls in Arkansas several times a year, such as in Ward, some sixty miles south of Newport on Highway 67.

"Ward Country Dance, Live Band Every Friday Night"

Two young girls, both long haired and barefoot, ride their bicycles on tree-shaded streets. Cars and pickup trucks drive slowly, windows open to the warm evening air, drivers raising a hand or nodding to those they pass. The parking lot of the large metal building is full, but the only people outside are a trio of women smoking, their cigarettes not permitted inside. The small sign near the doors states "Pacers" in a scrawled print. Cicadas buzz in the trees. At eight o'clock on this July evening, 2011, the twilight sky is glowing with a soft dusky haze. Ward, Arkansas, population 4,085, settles in for another quiet Friday night.

The inside of Ward Country Dance Hall smells of popcorn, sold at $1 a bag, the same price as a cold can of Dr Pepper or a bottle of water. Strings of twinkling holiday lights shine overhead, attached to the bare metal beams and the matting insulation fitted between the ribs of the ceiling. The large linoleum dance floor is flanked by folding tables and metal chairs. Plastic Christmas trees with red lights adorn the stage, along with rows of small American flags and leather cowboy boots holding plastic roses and snapdragons. The band is on stage, and Sonny is crooning the high notes of "Judy," the Teddy Riedel hit. Many older couples are on dance floor. The men wear western hats and boots, jeans with large belt buckles. The women's white hair is styled into soft, airy orbs that do not move when they dance. One woman is dancing on her own. She wears an attractive Mexican peasant style dress with an open lacey collar and embroidered flowers at the hem.

Among the dancers, a ten-year-old girl is two-stepping alongside her grandfather. Her blonde hair is done up with white ribbons, with matching white shorts and boots. Later in the evening she will be on stage singing "Be My Good Luck Charm" and "Your Cheating Heart," invited to the microphone by Sonny after he is called aside by her grandmother. Several dancers show their enthusiasm for the young singer by forming a bridge of hands, and the line of dancers passes beneath it in single file. The line circles the floor and returns, the dancers bending at the knees to fit below their neighbor's arms.

Two older women come to a side table and drop heavily into the chairs. Though the air conditioning is ample, they fan themselves with their hands in exaggerated fatigue.

"Hell, if I rest now and then, I might make it," the first one says.

"I didn't bring my inhaler with me tonight," her partner replies.

In a few minutes, the women are back out on the floor, joining their friends, perhaps two hundred of them in all, in a gentle polka as the Pacers play crowd favorites "Roll Out the Barrel" and "Down Yonder."

"Best turnout we've had in a while," Bobby Crafford said, standing at the band merchandise table during a break. He said the band played the Ward dance hall frequently that summer. They also played senior centers and community theaters, county fairs and school reunions. The smaller bookings provided a modest payment, but their value, Sonny later explained, was in keeping the band active between high profile and higher-paying gigs.

Later that summer, the Pacers played at Lincoln Center in New York City, part of a rockabilly show for 7,000 enthusiastic fans. Other bookings have put them on stage at the Smithsonian Institution's American Folk Festival in Bangor, Maine, and the National Folk Festival in Virginia, where they celebrated their 50th anniversary in show business in 2005. The Pacers have played at the Library of Congress and the Kennedy Center in Washington DC, and at the huge Memphis in May festival. The Pacers have been repeated stars at rock and roll festivals in Tupelo, Mississippi; Las Vegas, Nevada; and Green Bay, Wisconsin. They have rocked the house at birthday celebrations for Elvis, Scotty Moore, and Sam Phillips in Tennessee and Mississippi. And they have been repeat guests at Clear Lake, Iowa, where the annual Fifties in February is held in the building where Buddy Holly made his last performance before the 1959 airplane crash. They were featured performers in 2000 at the opening of the Rock and Soul Museum in Memphis, which includes an exhibit on them, and at their own induction into the Rockabilly Hall of Fame in Jackson, Tennessee.

The list of shows goes on and on, and at many Arkansas venues, the same dedicated fans have come out to enjoy the performances. Among these fans have been highly energetic dancers whose elaborate footwork and hand exchanges are commonly seen at a Cajun/Zydeco Fais Do Do. Other dancers are older and more sedate, such as the line of five women who stepped and turned in measured cadence before the stage at a Helena festival, each of them wearing a pastel blue 1950s-style satin jacket with "Rockabilly Filly" embroidered in sparkling letters across the back.

Sonny with E Street band bass player Garry Tallent, Bruce Springsteen, and D. J. Fontana backstage at a 9/11 benefit show in New Jersey; 2001.

The Pacers were in top form at a 2006 performance at the Gem Theater in Heber Springs. All band members wore bright red blazers that glowed in the stage spotlights and white silk ties set off against their black shirts. Kern Kennedy seemed to be shooting off sparks from the oversized jeweled rings on both hands as he played his wide electronic keyboard with an enthusiasm that belied his seventy-five years. The stage lights bounced off Jim Aldridge's swaying saxophone, glinting like a mirror as the energized sixty-nine-year-old musician swung his horn in time with the lively music. And Sonny's white goatee glowed silver beneath his dark glasses and black hat as he stood at the microphone, a relaxed smile on his face, his gravelly voice resonant with a country inflection as he told the familiar jokes: the one about Ricky Nelson changing "beer" to "milk" when he copied the Pacers' 1957 version of "My Bucket's Got a Hole in It"; another when he introduced Kern's up-tempo piano solo ("Ladies and gentleman, notice that Kern's fingers never leave his hand"); and a story of when Bobby Crafford took his blindfolded drum break.

On stage, the seventy-seven-year-old rock and roller stood in a comfortable, slightly bowlegged stance, his graceful dips and rhythmic swaying keeping perfect time with a music tempo set for dancing. With the long-neck Fender guitar hung low on his lean frame, the wide leather strap across one shoulder, the easy loping play of his body moving in time with the music, Sonny seemed much like another classic American icon—the western horseman sitting astride his saddle, his broad-brimmed hat pulled low over his eyes, horse and rider moving as one in slow cadence, waltzing across Texas, as Ernest Tubb once sang, in the fluid rhythm of the bygone open range. Legendary cowboy and veteran rock and roller, two archetypal heroes of our national heritage.

Current Recordings and Recognition

Sonny is an innovator, then and now. He and the band play with a wild joyous abandon that is totally lost on today's mostly formulaic and uninspiring music scene.

—John Lappen, Cleopatra Records

In 2012, Rockabilly Records, a division of Cleopatra Records of Los Angeles, issued the album *Sonny Burgess, Live at Sun Studios*, a collection of recordings not released during the 1950s. The LP was manufactured on translucent red vinyl, and its cover featured a vintage photograph of a handsome young man against a bright yellow background. The smiling man, however, was not Sonny.

The original album sleeve put a photo of a young Hayden Thompson on the cover. Thompson, a Mississippi native and Rockabilly Hall of Fame inductee, looked similar to Sonny in the early years. His publicity photos from that era feature classic rockabilly big hair, tailored suits, and dramatic poses with guitar and microphone. Thompson's popularity with European audiences in rockabilly revival shows, a current market for which the album was targeted, may account for the error. A second printing of the cover correctly replaced Thompson with a photo of the young Sonny Burgess.

Also in 2012, Cleopatra Records showed a more accurate recognition of Sonny's talent by inviting him and the Pacers to participate in *Rockin' Legends Pay Tribute to Jack White*. The band was selected for the album by project coordinator John Lappen, who sent them a copy of White's song "Steady As She Goes."

"Sonny was chosen for the project because we were looking for different takes and outlooks on Jack's music," Lappen said. "Sonny and the band not only dived right in on this project but did a great, timeless version of Jack's 'Steady As She Goes.' I feel they really made the song their own by virtue of their performance. I've probably listened to it one hundred times by now and still get goose bumps every time."

Sonny is also in top form on *The River of Song* album where he sings Jimmie Rodgers' "Blue Yodel #1 (T For Texas)," calling out in his throaty, growling voice, "Get 'em, Jim boy" and "Get 'em, KK," prompting hot solos from Aldridge and Kennedy. The album and accompanying educational outreach package was produced for a 1999 Smithsonian Institution project that celebrated American music with cultural ties to the Mississippi River.

The Mississippi and Arkansas Delta region was a thematic identity for the Legendary Pacers in another Smithsonian Institution project, a 1998 video performance titled *Rockin' on the River*. Also in the late 1990s, the Pacers recorded two LPs, *They Came from the South* and *Still Rockin' and Rollin'*, the latter voted best new album in the country and roots field in Europe in June 2000.

Sonny performed at the Montreux Jazz Festival in Switzerland in July 2001, joining Bill Wyman, Billy Lee Riley, Little Milton, and others in a concert promoted as "Good Rockin' Tonight, A Tribute to Sun Records, Exploring the Roots of Rock 'n' Roll." The show also featured a special performance by retired Led Zeppelin stars Robert Plant and Jimmy Page. According to Dan Griffin, who was promoting Sonny at the time, the British duo agreed to play together again because of their appreciation for the Pacers' 1957 recording of "My Bucket's Got a Hole in It."

Once brought back into the limelight, Sonny's original talent was quickly rediscovered by reviewers, particularly by music writers from the *New York Times*. In 2001, following a performance at the Lincoln Center Out-of-Doors Festival in New York, a critic stated: "Sonny Burgess' jubilantly feral howls and punchy guitar solos reverberate with same raw energy and excitement as during rockabilly heyday in Memphis." In 2006, following another Lincoln Center show, the newspaper called him "a legend who began his career as an opening act for Elvis Presley in 1955." And in 2008, the newspaper stated that at the 7th Annual Ponderosa Stomp in New Orleans, his "startling guitar solos [leapt] between country twang and jazzy chords."

Sonny's flailing limbs have earned him and the band multiple honors. In 1999, he was inducted into the European Rockabilly Hall of Fame sponsored by *Now Dig This* magazine, and in 2002, he joined the U.S. Rockabilly Hall of Fame at Jackson, Tennessee. Arkansas has honored its native son with a 2007 induction into the Arkansas Entertainers Hall of Fame and a star for the Legendary Pacers at the Hot Springs Walk of Fame. In 2011, in recognition of his lifetime achievement, Sonny was awarded an honorary Doctorate of Music degree from Arkansas State University in Jonesboro. And in a light-hearted moment when the band performed at a campus benefit concert in 2013, the university issued an official pardon that lifted the 1958 ban imposed on the Pacers for playing too loudly at a campus dance.

Public appreciation of Sonny and the Pacers in recent years has influenced their contemporary performances, Rosie Flores said. Ten years after the two artists toured together in 1996, Flores said she was invited to join the Pacers at a show in Green Bay, Wisconsin. At that 2007 show, Flores saw a band that had been revitalized by its success and the love of its fans.

"When you feel celebrated, you look like a star," Flores said. "Sonny looked younger and more handsome. His vocals hadn't lost a thing, and there was a fire in his voice and his showmanship. The band had gotten so much appreciation and love shining down on them. That's infectious to the audience. You walk taller and smile bigger when you feel loved. Those guys at Green Bay were happy and joyous. There was a light around them like a polished diamond."

Current Bookings

As a result of Bobby Crafford's diligent booking, the Legendary Pacers continue to perform three to five shows a month throughout the year, an impressive schedule for a band whose members' average age in 2013 was seventy-nine. Recent bookings have put the band on stage at the Hemsby Rock & Roll Weekend in England, as well as at the American Folk Festival in Maine, the Arkansas State Fair, and numerous festivals and shows across the mid-South, including ten shows at the Ward Country Dance Club.

"We're tough and we can handle it," Jim Aldridge said. Bobby agrees, but he does concede to the compromises of aging: "Used to be we'd chase women and drink a lot," he said. "Now we take Advil and bring our wives with us."

Similar to his bandmates, Bobby's motivation is fueled by fans' increasing enthusiasm for the music. "It's grown bigger than I ever thought and coming on stronger every day," he said. "In 1998, we played a show at a Tunica club that held 1,000 people, and it was packed. When we walked off the stage, the Kentucky Headhunters shook our hands. It made us feel like we still had a little bit left."

"Nothing's changed," Sonny mused. "We still haven't gotten rich or famous, but we're still trying. If it hadn't been for Sun Records, I wouldn't still be around playing. Those old records have been pretty good to me."

Like many musicians of his generation, Sonny believes that many modern recordings rely too heavily on production technology, studio equipment that can correct notes and make a song sound perfect. He sees the Nashville Top 40 genre as more like pop music, with performers only singing a song but not truly feeling the music.

"If it hits you, if you feel it, that's what you want," Sonny said. "What Nashville has done is made everything perfect but took the soul out of the music. Once in a while there will be one that has got the feel to it."

Travis Wammack called it the "dying art of the player," a contemporary process that produces talented young musicians who have perfected their skills through videos, technology, and formal training, but sound much alike. Wammack said the best musicians were self taught, such as Sonny and several of his peers, such as J. M. Van Eaton, Martin Willis, and Ace Cannon, who began playing as Memphis teenagers. "You can take the best young guitar player, and you can't tell one from another," Wammack said. "That's what's lacking in these musicians. They didn't learn like we did, by feel."

For Sonny, some country artists that "have stayed true the music" include Travis Tritt, Marty Stuart, and George Strait. Surprisingly, he also admires the rap artist Kid Rock and a 2003 duet, "Picture," recorded with Sheryl Crow. "Kid Rock really sings good, but he does most of that rap stuff that I can't understand," he said. "It's got a lot of cussing. I grew up with a lot of cussing. Today they get paid for it."

Sonny Burgess; 2010.

Chapter 8.
Arkansas Rock 'n' Roll
Highway 67

It's easier to pick a tourist than it is to pick cotton.
—Arkansas governor Orval Faubus,
visiting Newport's lakeside tourist park in the 1950s

Larry Donn called it a "fertile middle of nowhere," describing the strip of musical clubs surrounded by miles of cotton farms and a generation of talented musicians that emerged from the rural lifestyle of the Arkansas Delta. Unlike the meandering rivers that left their imprint in the curves of oxbow lakes and the sloughs of bottomland hardwood forests, the highway is man's signature on the land, an unwavering line of concrete and asphalt that once had a selection of roadhouses and clubs along its length.

Entering Jackson County from the south, motorists on Highway 67 are afforded a distinct perspective. Near the exit to the remnant communities of Possum Grape, Olyphant, and Old Grand Glaise, the rolling green slopes of the Ozark foothills can be seen on the driver's left, west of the highway. To the driver's east, the earth lies flat and featureless, the horizon marked by rows of trees across the precision-leveled farmland. With a bit of height, one might see all the way to the Mississippi River and the skyline of Memphis far off in the haze.

It was along this demarcated stretch between the hills and the Delta that the clubs flourished. The profusion of roadhouses and clubs began with the Wagon Wheel at Bald Knob in the south and continued north to the Current River Beach Dance Pavilion at Pocahontas near the Missouri border.

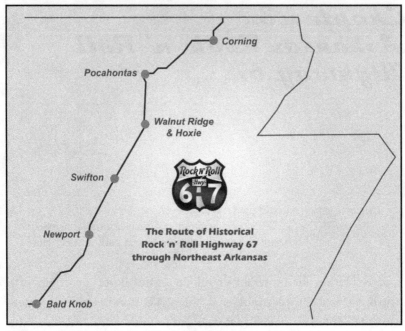

Highway 67 map. (Courtesy Charles Snapp)

"Highway 67 was the dividing line for rock and roll," Teddy Riedel said. "People went to Memphis to record, but all the musicians came to old 67 to play."

Robert Thompson, a professor of popular culture at Syracuse University, agrees that the distinctive musical heritage of the hundred-mile stretch of Arkansas highway has been overshadowed by the urban density of Memphis. "It's kind of like Beale Street in the middle of the sticks," Thompson said. "You have this stretch of road and it isn't Hollywood Boulevard. It isn't Broadway. It isn't Beale Street. We all know those places where a concentration of culture boiled over. What is so interesting about this, is here you have all of that."

The Highway Bill

Arkansas Act 497 was passed in March 2009, the highway bill formally naming a three-county portion of the historic road as the "Rock 'n' Roll Highway 67."[70] Governor Mike Beebe signed the official document in a public ceremony, then he strapped on a guitar and, playing some of the chords he learned from Conway Twitty's guitar player Al Bruno nearly fifty years earlier, joined Sonny Burgess and Billy Lee Riley in a rendition of "Red Hot."

The State Capitol's white marble walls echoed the rockabilly song, once considered a distasteful display of adolescent bragging. But as with Riley himself, who died five months afterward, public response has softened with age, and the song is now celebrated for its youthful energy and popularity. A cluster of smiling state legislators looked on, among them the leading sponsor of the bill, Representative J. R. Rogers of Walnut Ridge, a guitar player who sometimes joined the Pacers in northeast Arkansas shows.

Rogers and his colleagues had reason to smile. The bill's passage would allow state agencies to erect highway signs and create promotional materials to tout the cultural heritage of the area, efforts intended to bolster the depleted economy of their Delta districts with tourist dollars. The language of the bill also included a tribute to one of their own, the former state representative Bobby Lee Trammell of Jonesboro, listed among the "early rock 'n' roll legends" who regularly traveled Highway 67 and cited for "a hit known as 'Arkansas Twist.'"[71]

The similarities of stage performance and political posturing were well demonstrated at a celebration of the bill's passage that evening at a Little Rock club. Prior to the Pacers' performance, several state legislators took the stage to sing their favorite rock tunes, the enthusiasm of the amateur musicians far greater than their talent. Not to be outdone, Rogers performed with professional-level skill, though his setting a lighter-fluid blaze inside the stage piano, a pyrotechnical stunt to accompany his rendition of "Great Balls of Fire," nearly engulfed the room in smoke.

In recent years, Arkansas Rock 'n' Roll Highway towns have conducted music festivals to celebrate their heritage. Highway signs have been erected and towns along the route have installed plaques. Pocahontas leads the effort with five plaques recognizing its former rock and roll venues, including a boyhood home of Riley and the family home of Bill Rice, one of country music's most celebrated songwriters.[72]

Along Highway 67 in the far southwest corner of the state, Rock 'n' Roll Highway signs have been dedicated at Texarkana, recognizing that southwest Arkansas city for performances at the Arkansas Municipal Auditorium by Elvis and other early rock and rollers.

"This is more fun than any bill I've ever signed." —Governor Mike Beebe

Arkansas governor and rockabilly music fan Mike Beebe joins Billy Lee Riley (left), State Representative J. R. Rogers (second from left), and Sonny Burgess (right) for a little picking at the bill-signing ceremony designating Rock 'n' Roll Highway 67 in Little Rock; 2009. (Photo courtesy of Charles Snapp.)

But even as development of musical heritage tourism across the state made slow progress, another significant loss occurred. A 2010 fire at Swifton's King of Clubs destroyed the region's last original music site. The fire was a somber reminder of a remark by Sonny Burgess more than a decade earlier. "The sad thing is that if anybody had the sense back then, they could have taken the Silver Moon and turned it into a rock and roll museum," Sonny told the *Arkansas Democrat-Gazette* in 1997. "People from Europe and all over the world that now go to

Memphis would have trooped right over here to Newport, the site where all these people played."

The New Highway

In Newport, the original Highway 67 that brought musicians and travelers to town is still called Malcolm Avenue. The active street with its numerous stores runs through the town's main commercial districts. The businesses thin out as the old road heads north into the open countryside toward Tuckerman and Swifton. Running parallel to the Union Pacific rail line, the highway offers bleak remnants of a vanished economy: boarded-up buildings with rusty signage, the charred walls of structures lost to fire, and empty lots with littered concrete foundations.

Not far to the east, a new state highway has been constructed that bypasses Newport. The modern thoroughfare provides easy access to neighboring Lawrence and Randolph Counties. Like historic Route 66 in Oklahoma, now accessible only to travelers who exit Interstate 40, the small towns along Arkansas Rock 'n' Roll Highway 67 will once again find themselves bypassed by progress.

Sonny and Scotty Moore at Depot Days in Newport, Arkansas; 2010.

Creative development strategies by some civic leaders are trying to reverse that trend. In Newport, music fan Henry Boyce, currently prosecuting attorney for the 3rd Judicial District, a position his father Sam

Boyce held in the 1960s, has been a leading promoter of the town's Depot Days Festival. The free public event began in 1997 and is held each September at the old train station. The Pacers have performed at every festival, joined by local musicians, contemporary rock and roll bands, and veteran Sun Records artists. Boyce has also created the Rock 'n' Roll Highway 67 Museum, a display of photos and music memorabilia, much of it contributed by Sonny Burgess, housed in the Newport Economic Development Commission building.

Walnut Ridge Guitar Walk

A distinctive tribute to regional rock and roll history is the Guitar Walk at Walnut Ridge. Though none of the highway's clubs were located there, the town takes its music heritage seriously. Colorful banners are hung on downtown streets identifying the route of the historic highway through the town. A music park is located adjacent to the town's Amtrak Station along Highway 67. The park features a large concrete walkway in the shape of an Epiphone Casino electric guitar. A series of audio displays and tribute plaques identifies rock and roll musicians who played along Highway 67 in the heyday of the 1950s.

Entry to the Guitar Plaza, a park at Walnut Ridge, Arkansas, that pays tribute to the musical heritage of Highway 67.

Visitors to the Guitar Walk can stroll among the eleven stations surrounding the body of the walkway-embedded guitar and listen to music clips from Elvis, Jerry Lee Lewis, Johnny Cash, Sonny Burgess, and others. They can study period photographs and read biographical information about the artists. And they can hear Sonny's colorful narrative of the old days interspersed among the music, though the entertaining audio tracks are at times briefly overwhelmed by locomotive air horns and the rumbling of freight cars on the adjacent railroad track.

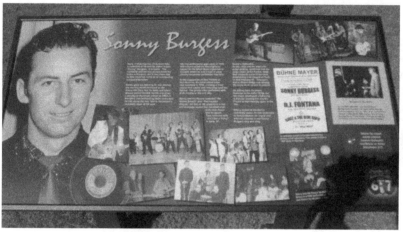

Sonny Burgess panel at the Walnut Ridge Guitar Plaza.

Walnut Ridge also celebrates another facet of rock and roll history, a brief encounter with greatness that the Delta community continues to cherish. In September 1964, the small municipal airport was a transition stop for the Beatles, who switched planes as they traveled to a ranch in southern Missouri, a weekend respite during a national tour that had brought them to Dallas. Only a few residents were aware of the group's first landing, but on their Sunday return, crowds of excited local fans, including many teens who skipped church services that morning, were on hand to catch a glimpse of the British sensation, their popularity in the United States as extreme as anything achieved by Elvis a decade earlier.

The moment passed, but Walnut Ridge has not forgotten. In 2011, the town started a Beatles-themed music festival called Beatles at the

Ridge, with local entertainment such as clogging, cheerleading teams, duck calling, dog costume contests, and a motorcycle show. The town has renamed a downtown street "Abbey Road" and created Beatles Park, with a sculpted tribute to the British musicians. The street corner park features a sculpture titled "The British Invasion of the Rock 'n' Roll Highway." Life-sized metal silhouettes of the four musicians stand before a 10' x 20' aluminum wall etched with details from the famous *Abbey Road* album cover. Close inspection of the etchings also reveals numerous hidden references to Beatles song titles and Arkansas images worked into the art.

"Walnut Ridge Arkansas is the only place in North America where Abbey Road meets the Rock-n-Roll Highway," local tourism promoter Charles Snapp said.

An Arkansas Tradition

Putting historical stories to music is an Arkansas tradition, a folk artistry advanced by Jimmy Driftwood, a prolific songwriter and preservationist who lived in the north-central Arkansas town of Mountain View.[73] Charley Sandage, also of Mountain View, has a large collection of songs based on Arkansas history.[74] His rockabilly-infused tune "Up on Highway 67," written years before the official state designation, remains a lively tribute to the musicians and venues that defined the distinctive sound.

"Up on Highway 67"
by Charley Sandage

Up on Highway 67, Saturday night, getting right
Wagon Wheel up to Porky's Rooftop
Gonna' be rockin', could be a fight
There's a Silver Moon winking in a cotton field heaven
Up on Highway 67

Got boys from the hills, got girls from town
Got Jerry Lee and Elvis and the Sun sound crowd
Carl he's a lookin' for a new way of cookin'
Slide them strings and play the back beat loud

220

BB's searching for R&B heaven
Up on Highway 67

They listened on the porches, they listened in the churches
They listened in the tonks for the licks they could use
Sounds a little like Hank, a little like preachin'
A little like Momma Thornton shoutin' the blues
It's a turn up collar, greasy sideburn heaven
Up on Highway 67

Up on Highway 67, Saturday night, getting right
Wagon Wheel up to Porky's Rooftop
Gonna' be rockin', could be a fight
There's a Silver Moon winking in a cotton field heaven
Up on Highway 67

The Town

Chapter 9.
Newport Origins

In little more than 100 years, Newport evolved from a frontier outpost with isolated pioneer settlements into a thriving model of post-war progress. From its origins through the 1950s, Newport's path of growth was paved with natural resources that provided one windfall after another. In an era of national confidence and growth, the scrappy river town and the outlying communities where the Burgesses and other farm families lived came of age, with its population motivated by the elusive rewards of wealth and social prestige.

The Military Road

While Route 66 is often called the Mother Road of America, U.S. Highway 67 might as easily be called the Mother Road of Arkansas. It is very likely the most historic route in the state.

—Ray Hanley, A Journey through
Arkansas Historic U.S. Highway 67 (Images of America)[75]

The immense triangle that is the Mississippi Delta has its northern tip at St. Louis; its southern base traverses the Gulf Coast from Texas to Florida. The western diagonal of the triangle bisects Arkansas from its northeast to its southwest corners, dividing the state into two geographical regions. The Ozark Mountains and foothills are located to the west. The Arkansas Delta lies in the east. Along this line, the U.S. Army created the Southwest Trail, originally a military road widely used by settlers to the new American wilderness after the Louisiana Purchase in 1803.

President Andrew Jackson signed an appropriations bill for the improvement of the Southwest Trail in 1831, identifying it as a national road, a designation equivalent to today's designation of interstate high-way, and securing the roadway as the future path of U.S. Highway 67, the main thoroughfare of Jackson County.

Early travelers on the Southwest Trail crossed the White River at Newport where enterprising pioneer Roland Tidwell began his ferry service in 1831. Originally called Tidwell's Landing, the site was iden-tified as "The Town of New Port" when Tidwell renewed his ferryman's license in 1835.

An American Diorama

Newport in the nineteenth century offered an American diorama Mark Twain and Walt Whitman would find familiar. Following Arkansas statehood in 1836, the pioneer White River crossing site became a robust riverfront town. Skiffs and keel boats carrying pelts down from the hills transferred their goods to large paddle wheelers coming upstream from the Arkansas and Mississippi Rivers. Bales of cotton were loaded and shipped to mills downriver. And Newport became known for its trading houses and betting rooms, as well as its brothels and saloons lined up on Front Street facing the sloping mud banks of the river dockage.

In the Delta, teams of laborers harvested the natural resources, work crews cut the timber and cleared the land for cotton, and railroad crews laid the first rail lines. These laborers were primarily unmarried men, a worker class that generated a host of local saloons and purveyors of spirits to engage the men in their non-working hours. The origins of the north Jackson County town of Swifton, for example, can be traced to the original Swift family farm and an enterprising son who opened the first saloon to sell whiskey to the Irish laborers building the Iron Mountain Railroad.[76] Years later, Swifton would be known for its pop-ular roadhouses and dance halls, such as the King of Clubs and Mike's Place, sites that rivaled Newport clubs for their crowds and exuberance.

Jackson County's location on the western edge of the Delta also gave it the business advantage of easy access from its dry neighbors. In adjacent Independence County, Batesville is one of Arkansas' oldest communities, a town with strong church affiliations. Only twenty-three miles by road from Newport, Batesville was a short drive for a man who wanted a drink. Newport mayor David Stewart recalled his years on the Newport Police Department when phone calls from anxious Batesville housewives frequently inquired if their errant husbands were in police custody.

Though Newport and Jackson County prospered, some residents knew only failure and dislocation. During the Depression and the rural exodus of the 1930s, when the land gave out—overused and under-nourished much like its people—thousands of Okies and Arkies traveled to California in search of work, following their dreams on Route 66. And again in the 1950s, southern farmers and rural people moved north as part of the Great Migration, an agrarian population seeking factory jobs in the steel mills and auto plants of Detroit, Flint, and other cities in the upper Midwest. This was the exodus of a generation of field workers replaced (and displaced) by mechanical cotton pickers.

Yet in the 1940s, when men and draft animals still labored on the land, Mann Shoffner established an empire of mules. He was the son of pioneer Anias Ephraim Shoffner, whose farming success created the Jackson County town with his family name. Mann Shoffner was known as a sharp dresser. He wore a vest, necktie, and high boots. He became one of the most successful mule dealers in the South and had a legendary ability to understand the mind and work potential of the stubborn creatures. Shoffner's sale barn in Newport was the site of sprawling auctions and trading, with hundreds of mules on the grounds. As money changed hands at the Thursday sales, games of dice and cards accompanied the transactions. So did drink and prostitutes. Local wags called it "hogs and whores day."

And farm workers came, some directly from the fields, straddling the fender of a tractor for the ride, still wearing their muddy gum boots, their week's pay stuffed inside their overalls, ready for a night of drinking and fighting. Years earlier, boatmen and river crews had come roaring up Newport's muddy gangways with similar intentions. In the mid-1950s, a new attraction brought customers to Jackson County's drinking establishments. A lively music was heard, up-tempo hillbilly tunes mixed with driving rhythm and blues that had people singing and dancing.

In *John Barleycorn Must Die: The War against Drink in Arkansas*, Southern Arkansas University history professor Ben Johnson documented the emergence of Arkansas' saloons from the pioneer era through the mid-1900s. He could have been describing Newport's roadhouses and clubs when he wrote:

> Changes in drinking patterns, increasing favor of beer over whiskey, and lack of home refrigeration, caused drinkers to seek out draft lager at the corner tavern. Competition among the beer manufacturers led brewers to set up their own saloons, keep businesses open past legal hours, entice drinkers with gambling and vaudeville style acts, and never ever tell a customer that he has had enough. [77]

Betting against the Railroad

The selection of Newport as the Jackson County seat is another windfall in the town's history. Three miles upriver, Jacksonport was the prior county seat and the original economic center of the county in the pre–Civil War steamboat era. But Jacksonport leaders made a catastrophic choice. Betting against the railroad, they brought the community to ruin.

Jacksonport's disastrous decision stemmed from an 1853 survey by the Cairo and Fulton Railroad for a rail line from St. Louis to Texas. The survey followed the western diagonal of the Mississippi Delta. Seeking the most direct path unencumbered by hills, it crossed the White River at Newport. Progress on the railroad was delayed by the Civil War. But in 1872, planners of the renamed St. Louis, Iron Mountain and Southern Railway approached Jacksonport with an offer. If the town provided a no-cost easement, the railroad would deviate from its survey and bring the rail line through Jacksonport. When the town's merchants and political leaders refused, the railroad defied the upstream river barons and chose Newport for its river-crossing site.

The consequences of Jacksonport's bad decision were immediate. The town rapidly declined, losing businesses and residents to its downstream neighbor. A period of desolation set in, evidenced by what Newport historian James Morgan described as "empty homes, boarded up businesses, burned blocks of businesses not replaced, the absence of a newspaper, the closing of churches. It was simple: the newspaper, the churches, and the people had moved to Newport."[78] Growing increasingly embittered and envious of Newport's boisterous prosperity, the *Jacksonport Herald* wrote in 1879 that "latest statistics show that one pint of Newport whiskey contains four fights, three knockdowns, one stealing of the ballot box, one contested election and one rape."

These shifting fortunes culminated in an 1891 election that established Newport as the Jackson County seat. The town celebrated its good fortune with profits from timber harvests, wood products, and cotton. Churches, schools, and hotels were built. The Singer Sewing Machine Company built a mill to supply wood for its cases. The Newport Club, a private venue for men offering rooms for poker, billiards, reading, and smoking, was open all week and until all hours. The Newport Opera House opened in December 1890, and William Jennings Bryan spoke there in 1911.

The river town was in its golden age at the turn of the century, but the river was no longer the vehicle of progress. In 1902, the Iron Mountain Railroad built a $10,000 depot across from the Front Street business area. By 1906, the depot was receiving twenty-three trains a day carrying freight, passengers, and livestock. People set their watches by the whistles.

One of Newport's most accomplished citizens from the time was U.S. Navy Rear Admiral Neill Phillips Jr. In a series of articles for the Jackson County Historical Society, Phillips tells of screeching train whistles and falling cinders, river-front swimming and log rafts, circuses and carnivals, wooden sidewalks, and women in wide skirts and plumed hats going to parties. Downtown commerce and crowds of shoppers were congested along Front Street on boisterous Saturdays when swarms of rural families came to Newport with money to spend, Phillips wrote. The activity often ended with drunken brawls at the many saloons:

> All the streets around were jammed with wagons carrying in folks from all over the county who were doing their shopping and enjoying a little of town life. By the late afternoon in those less than moral times, all the saloons would have done a rousing business and there would have been several lively fights. Town Constable George

Robinson would have the caboose full and the long lines of loaded up wagons, their loads of corn and cotton converted into store-bought goods would begin streaming out of town, drivers soused with Bourbon whiskey, bawling and swearing at their teams and each other, while their womenfolk, jolting as usual on splint bottomed chairs set in the wagon beds, patiently accepted in a matter of fact way this normal ending to Saturday in town.[79]

Tall Timber and King Cotton

Momma's a beauty operator.
Sister can weave and spin.
Daddy got an interest in an old cotton gin,
Just watching that money roll in.
        —Charley Monroe, "Roll in My Sweet Baby's Arms"

Timber and cotton flourished in a region with some of the richest topsoil in the world. The boom times allowed communities in Jackson County and northeast Arkansas to build conspicuous wealth. Vast stands of virgin hardwood supported the economic growth. As railroad lines were constructed and lumber crews cleared thousands of forest acres, the cut timber was floated down the Black River to sawmills and processing facilities at Newport. Wealthy families celebrated their good fortune, building large, expansive homes with elaborate parquet flooring, railings, and wall panels.

Following the timber boom, the land was reshaped. Newly cleared acres were leveled, wetlands drained, and irrigation ditches and levees built. Prosperity awaited the few families able to accumulate land and leverage equity. Those who did not own land became sharecroppers and tenant farmers, people who rarely accumulated wealth. Uneducated and unable to overcome the production systems that exploited them—systems whose structure capitalized on their work ethic and their penury—sharecropper families survived in a culture of subsistence farming. They worked the land according to the seasons and the sun. "You work till you can't" is an expression still used among Delta farmers, meaning that the day ended only when no more work was possible.

Through the late 1920s and into the Depression years that followed, government policies were introduced to stabilize the economics of cotton production. The new programs offered incentives to larger farm owners, an economic strategy advantageous to Jackson County's wealthier farm families but one that did little to offset the increasing challenges for black and white sharecroppers working the land.

Though sharecroppers faced a lifetime of struggle, the communities that supported them flourished. Newport's economy was structured in an agricultural pyramid with three tiers. Wealthy landowners were at the peak. These were farm families with title to thousands of acres, the owners of cotton gins, compresses, and plantation-style stores that gave rise to family-named towns such as Shoffner and Swifton.

In the center was the banker and merchant class, made up of the townsfolk who operated the retail stores, small businesses, insurance offices, cafés, and bars. This group was the middle class, the town's civic boosters and strivers for upward mobility, who responded to the community's material needs and extended annual credit to farm families.

Land workers, sharecroppers, and tenant farmers were at the base, a group whose only equity was the daily application of their labor, whose year-round purchases were made on credit. This was a low-educated group with a strong work ethic trapped in an annual survival mode.

Merchants and the Middle Class

Scarecrow and a yellow moon,
Pretty soon, a carnival on the edge of town.
    —Robbie Robertson, "King Harvest Has Surely Come"

Newport in 1900, Neill Phillips wrote, had it sidewalks "thronged not only with townspeople, but also with a sizeable transient population: gamblers, drummers, cotton buyers, and people brought in by trade and pearl fishing on the river, by traveling shows, and by the fact that the town was a railroad center." In the Front Street business district, the curbs were "blocked solidly with teams and wagons, the wagons packed with cotton bales if it were the fall, buyers moving among them…all the stores and sidewalks jammed with country people, white and black, doing their marketing and enjoying a dash of town life."[80] Newport also had visits from Ringling Brothers and other circuses and traveling minstrel shows. The circus visits often coincided with harvest time when farmers had money to spend.

By the late 1930s, Highway 67 was a paved road that brought travelers to town in increasing numbers. On Front Street, the Hazel Hotel, with its coffee shop and banquet facilities, was a popular stopping place. The hotel was remembered by Phillips for its long porch with rocking chairs and awnings and for its clientele of permanent lady guests who sat on the porch to keep watch on town affairs.

In contrast to the Hazel Hotel, Phillips wrote that the Planters Hotel attracted a less desirable trade. Its rooms were for "street carnival people, patent medicine men, second-rate drummers, and persons of occupations less definite and decidedly less savory." Saloons and bawdy houses provided additional entertainment. Drinking was a major activity, and prostitution was accepted. In Newport, "'The Houses' located along the river across the railroad tracks from the business district… provided 'entertainment' to the accompaniment of the 'tinkle of the mechanical pianos.'"[81]

Prostitutes and brothels were part of Newport's licentious history. Today, some older men will remember hearing of a Newport sheriff in the 1930s who loaded up the more conspicuous prostitutes in a railroad boxcar and deposited them in the countryside outside of town, suggesting that they use their long walk back to consider finding another place to work.

By the early 1950s in rural Arkansas, a young woman's most marketable asset was her attractiveness—still restricted to local beauty pageants or mirrored in suggestive movie posters featuring Jane Russell's cleavage in a low-cut blouse. "Cheesecake" photos were commonly printed in the Newport newspaper. The beach shots were as suggestive as the period allowed, showing attractive young women sitting in the surf or leaning toward the camera in low-cut bathing suits. The photos, which came to Newport through a media wire service, were the 1950s equivalent of the World War II pinups. Catering to the prurient interests of male readers, they appeared frequently through the first half of the decade. By the later years of the decade, a greater editorial discretion was applied, urged on perhaps by Newport churches, and the photos were rarely used.

Like other Delta communities at the time, Newport contained distinct male and female cultures. The masculine culture was one of "self-indulgence, bravado, and physical competitiveness, manifested...in drinking, fighting, gambling, and other forms of male recreation." The other was dominated by women and centered in the home and church. This was an evangelical culture that emphasized "piety, harmony, and self-control."[82]

Plucky Newport

The early years of the modern era were marked by numerous fires and floods. In 1882, a Newport fire was described in a *New York Times* headline: "Disastrous Fire in Arkansas. Sixty Buildings in Newport Burned to the Ground." Listing the damaged businesses, the newspaper identified numerous dry goods and grocery stores, but also noted that two jewelry stores and five saloons were among the structures lost to the blaze.[83]

The most destructive fire came in 1926, when more than 280 buildings in a thirty-block area of the downtown residential and business districts were destroyed, including many of Newport's glorious homes with their detailed woodwork and displays of wealth. The fire burned for more than a week, and auxiliary firefighting crews and equipment came by rail from Little Rock.

When the White River flooded Newport in 1915, covering tracks of the Iron Mountain and White River Railroads with twelve feet of water, an Associated Press story declared, "Newport, Ark. Is Still Completely Isolated. 4,000 Refugees From that Place are Crowded into Hotels at Little Rock."[84]

Another flood came in 1916, prompting local citizens to build a tax-funded, half-million-dollar levee. The levee was unable to contain a catastrophic flood that inundated the entire Mississippi River Valley in 1927, one of the worst natural disasters in the nation's history. Arkansas was the most severely affected, with nearly half the state, about 6,600 square miles, under water. Newport, however, was spared the severe damage and loss that took place in lower portions of the White River to the south and east. When the flood water receded, Newport showed a distinct resilience, an outlook fueled by the repeated discoveries of new sources of wealth. Never at a loss for civic optimism, the town's signage on Highway 67 in the late 1920s proclaimed to travelers that they were "Entering Plucky Newport."

Boom Times: Pearls, Buttons, and Rice

In the first half of the twentieth century, "Plucky Newport" received one infusion of wealth after another, each adding to the heady times of its early success in timber and cotton. The first of these windfalls occurred from 1900 to 1920 when Jackson County became the center of the freshwater pearl market in United States.

Prior to the development of cultured pearls, freshwater mollusks or saltwater oysters were the only source of the jewel. Findings were rare and sporadic until the discovery of a valuable freshwater pearl in New Jersey set off a national frenzy of prospecting. The rivers of northeast Arkansas were rich with mussel beds, and the region became a lucrative spot for pearling camps. River barges hauled tons of mussel shells, and pearl buyers came from across the country.

In 1902, the Newport Independent reported that a White River pearl sold for $1,625. By 1905, the Arkansas pearl market was valued at $1.2 million. Pink pearls, a rarer variety found in the Black and White Rivers, were sold for as high as $20,000. The Newport pearling rush ended when the pearls, like local timber, were over-harvested with little thought toward sustainability. But as the river jewels grew rarer, another windfall industry developed.

By the 1930s, Newport was a production center for pearl buttons. Vast quantities of mussel shells were harvested from the White and Black Rivers, and small disks called "button blanks" were drilled from the shells. One Newport factory reportedly could handle 76,000 pounds of shells per day, requiring 1,000 shell fishers to keep it active. Many button cutters worked for the Muscatine Pearl Works. Others owned their own cutting machines and had home businesses. At the button industry's peak, some 200 cutters were working in Newport.[85] Shell residue was so plentiful, it was used by the city for street paving. Mayor Stewart recalled the alley behind his father's Front Street shoestore paved with crushed shells, many with visible holes from the button drills.

The button industry declined during the 1930s, influenced by the Depression and the advent of plastics. But Newport continued to thrive. A new state highway bridge spanned the White River in 1930, replacing the ferry service that had been in place since the 1870s. Newport greeted the bridge opening with a two-day festival that featured baseball games, a parade, fireworks, and the crowning of a young woman as the White River Queen. Tolls for the bridge were fifty cents for a car, one dollar for a truck, and five cents for a cow. Pedestrians could cross for free. The removal of tolls in 1938 was occasion for another party, and people again celebrated at the bridge's base.

The *Arkansas Gazette*, in a 1936 article titled "Rice Gives Newport Best Year in Many," proclaimed the city was on the "threshold of a bright future." Rice became a lucrative replacement for labor-intensive cotton, a crop increasingly subject to federal regulation. Most remarkably, in a time of the Midwest dustbowls, farm foreclosures, and western migration of families desperate for work, W. A. Billingsley, president of the Bank of Newport, reported a rise in deposits, stating "people in the county owe less now than they have in years."

An endearing portrait of Newport during the Depression era can be found in lyrics written by Jack Clement, a Tennessee native with an extensive career in the music industry, including a stint as recording engineer for Sun Records when he coordinated sessions for the Pacers. Clement's grandparents, Jefferson Davis and Ella Henderson Clement, lived in Newport, where Clement would make extended summer and holiday visits as a child in the 1930s. His memories of small-town life include sleeping in a room with open windows and hearing the nighttime sounds of birds, crickets, and trains. In particular, Clement recalled the voices from a nearby house where young girls would sing "You Are My Sunshine."

Jack Clement, in the Sun studio, with Sonny and Sam Phillips; 2001.

Years later, Clement wrote the "Air Conditioner Song," describing a time before closed windows cut off outside noise and the cooling breezes of the White River on a summer night. Clement performs the song in a video posted on YouTube. He is shown on a shady Newport street with the White River levee at the end of the block. He points out the houses where the girls sang, and, sitting on the decayed porch of his grandfather's abandoned house, Clement tells the camera, "I ain't sat on this porch in about sixty years," before offering a melancholy rendition of his childhood memory.[86]

> *But the sound of their singing thrilled me*
> *As distantly but clearly it rang*
> *Though I never saw their faces*
> *And never knew their names*
>
> *And the gentle breezes brought sweet dreams*
> *Of sweethearts that I never saw*

Who sang, "You are my sunshine"
In Newport, Arkansas.
                  —Jack Clement, "The Air Conditioner Song"

The Newport Gypsy

Jack Clement's song, as well as Sonny Burgess' reference to Front Street in "We Wanna Boogie," were not the first musical tributes to the town. W. C. Handy wrote two songs that mention a Newport resident widely known in the early 1900s. In Handy's "The St. Louis Blues," published in 1914, the singer says, "been to de Gypsy to get mah fortune tole." In "Sundown Blues," published in 1923, Handy identifies the Gypsy as Aunt Caroline Dye, a black woman with supposed psychic abilities that brought her wealth and recognition.

I'm going to Newport, Arkansas
I'm going there to see Aunt Car'line Dye
Why she's a reader and I need her…
She reads your fortune and the cards don't lie
                  —W. C. Handy, "Sundown Blues"

Dye's fortune-telling skills advised hundreds of people, black and white. Newport merchants and planters sought her approval on business decisions, and large numbers of people seeking her consultation arrived at the Rock Island train depot, where local children brought them to Dye's home. Contrary to Handy's song, Dye reportedly turned away the lovelorn, advising them to work out their own problems.

At the time of her death in 1918, Dye was a celebrated woman whose estate included numerous farms and cash accounts exceeding $100,000.[87] Dye's success and the decorum of her downtown residence earned the respect of Newport's white community and contributed to a racial status quo that went unchallenged until school desegregation began in the 1960s.

Newport's black community, its farmers and townsfolk, comprised a world different from the white man's world only in scale. The same social networks existed—leading families, legitimate business, illegal gambling, and drinking clubs—but the black population was one-third the size of the white. Jackson County also had an immensely successful black farmer, Pickens Black, who owned some 9,000 acres of land and operated a cotton gin, sawmill, and grain elevator. Black established the independent community of Blackville ten miles east of Newport, selling land to black farm families.

Racial animosity toward Black's success, however, resulted in the burning of Blackville's general store on several occasions. Characteristic of the times, the black community voiced no overt public dissent. Newport white businesses provided jobs for blacks at the gins, the laundries, the cafés, and as janitors. Photos of Newport's thriving mercantile environment show black shoppers amid the Front Street crowds. Black audiences mixed with whites at the electric cooperative's annual Farmers Day fair. And the town newspaper included a weekly column, "With The Colored," that reported on school, business, and community news.

On May 9, 1955, the *Newport Daily Independent* reported on two significant events for the community. The first was the death of Pickens Black at ninety years old, signaling an end to an era of agricultural independence for small family farmers and the approaching loss of farming towns, black and white, across the rural landscape. The second news article told of the opening of a motel near Tuckerman. The Freeman Tourist Court was advertised as "For Colored. New. Completely Modern. Reasonable Rates." The availability of commercial lodgings reflected the increasing mobility of black families in the new age of paved highways and more affordable cars. The motels gradually replaced the practice of black travelers renting rooms at family homes, such as Louis Armstrong and his band members did when the nationally known entertainer performed at the Silver Moon in 1954.

Black-owned businesses had existed on Front Street for some time, but black clubs, pool halls, and barbershops were limited to the southern end of the street. In black communities across the South, such streets were often referred to as "the Stroll." The north end of Front Street, the white section, where Saturday night clubs also flourished, was not frequented by blacks.

"The lower part toward the bridge was the black section," Governor Mike Beebe said. "There were bars, dives, and a mixed culture of black and white. It was pretty rough. The other end of Front Street was a commercial area with retail stores and drugstores with soda fountains. The upper part of Front Street was not open at night. The lower part was not open in the daytime."

The ethnic divisions of the street—with white clubs on the north, black clubs on the south, and commerce in the middle—reflects Newport's model of social compromise, most evident in the curious manner of business at Fred's Café, one of the few Newport restaurants that accepted both black and white customers. The café had two front doors. Blacks entered on the left, whites on the right. Inside the restaurant, blacks sat on one side of a U-shaped serving counter, whites on the other. The segregated customers could look across the middle of the room as they ate.

Social norms for Newport's black population, such as restricted seating at movie theaters, tent shows, and cafés, were mild compared to the violence against blacks in other southern towns. Joe Black, a grandson of Pickens Black and a contemporary economic developer in the Delta region, grew up in a time when lynchings and murders were stark reminders to all African Americans that challenges to the racial status quo would not be tolerated. "The message of the black murders of that time, of Emmett Till and others, was one of terrorism," Joe Black said. "If you revoked that, you could not win. You could endanger your family. I recall some blacks were burned out."

Air Base and War Prosperity

I remember Newport during 1940s. There was Grover Phillips' sandwich joint at 2nd and Hazel, a café in the train depot, and two little greasy spoons at Front and Beech Streets. Homer Dunn had a pool hall near the Columbia Hotel. I remember the Star Café in "honky tonk," the skid row area along the railroad tracks toward Jacksonport, where whites and blacks were allowed. I was a boy hauling wood to town for $1.50 per rick. I could hear people cussing and raising hell, glass breaking. I was afraid they would spook my team.

—Nathan Elton Davenport

For others, Newport in the 1940s offered a traditional but active small town life.

> I went to Newport High School and got my team letter in football. I had a job dipping ice cream at Sam Walton's store on Front Street. I sold Grit on a corner, and I worked as an usher at the Strand Theater. I still have a photo of me with the marquee showing Tarzan's New York Adventure. I remember the crowds on Front Street. You'd want to get a good parking place just to watch the people. Some hot summer nights, we walked to the Pentecostal Church to watch the holy rollers. Men were out on the street, shouting and falling down.
>
> —Steve Stephens

Stephens' nostalgic, hometown memories also include a milestone moment in American history. "In December 1941, I walked out of the Strand Theater and heard a kid say the Japanese just attacked Pearl Harbor," Stephens said. "The Army Air Corps base went in, and Newport was changed."

In 1942, a U.S. Army airfield was constructed east of town. The site selection was influenced by Congressman Wilbur Mills, the White County native whose sway as a member and chairman of the House Ways and Means Committee brought numerous federal projects to Arkansas.

The Newport Air Base was one of seven flight training sites in the state during the war years. The base provided housing for some 4,800 people, more than doubling Newport's population at the time. The huge influx of people also found lodging in old houses in town, rented rooms, and garages. Overall, the airbase was a $10.7 million project with its own stores, a movie theater, and four 5,000-foot runways.

Like many others in Newport, Stephens' family fortunes changed with the new development. His grandfather Rufus Stephens had been a sharecropper, never able to overcome a world of credit and debt. His parents Owen and Allie Stephens worked in town at the Bridge Service Station, a small garage near the entry to the White River Bridge. During the Depression, the garage owner left Newport for work in northern auto plants and sold the business to the Stephenses for $100.

The family lived in a trailer behind the garage, and Stephens remembers his father responding to early morning phone calls, heading off in the pre-dawn darkness with his truck and air compressor to repair flat tires.

The Newport Air Base, one of seven training facilities in Arkansas during World War II, had extensive runways, hangars, housing, and other structures, nearly doubling the town's population; 1941. (Photo courtesy of Frank Plegge.)

"When soldiers came in, Dad bought the Strand Café next to the-ater," Stephens said. "We sold twenty-cent burgers and one-cent ciga-rettes. The soldiers played the jukebox, ate steak, and drank beer. My folks finally did well. They bought $25 war bonds and were able to pay $3,000 to build their first house in town."

In 1944, operation of the airbase was transferred to the U.S. Navy and the site was operated as the Marine Corps Auxiliary Air Field. The Marine fliers occupied the Newport airbase until it closed in 1946. Marine pilots were trained in the Douglas A26 and B26 Invaders.[88] These attack fighters were some of the fastest and most versatile U.S. aircraft of World War II, serving as a daylight bomber, a night fighter, and a ground-attack platform. The flight crews would certainly be among the "Top Gun" military personnel of the time, men whose advanced flying skills were often matched by macho attitudes.

Jug Wallace had numerous encounters with the soldiers when he played trumpet with the Townsmen, a local dance band in the 1940s.

"The Marines and sailors would always get into fighting," Wallace recalled. "One time at Paragould, a woman insisted we play 'Stardust' again even though we had already played it twice. She was drunk and spilled her beer on one of the musicians and fell on him. It wiped out our group. The Marines thought we had insulted her. They took off their belts and wrapped them around their hands to get at us. We had to play 'The Star-Spangled Banner' four times to stop them from fighting."

Baseball players for the Newport Air Base team: Billy Van Welch (left), Sonny Burgess (center), and Johnny Ray Hubbard (right); 1948.

During the war, the airbase had given the city a new export product: service to the defense industry. That opportunity, building on Newport's historical role as a profligate river town, led to new levels of a traditional activity. "The airbase attracted a lot of women," Sam Boyce, a Newport prosecuting attorney and 1966 Arkansas gubernatorial candidate, said. "Jackson County was wide open, and Newport was red hot."

Some Newport civic leaders provided a wholesome social venue for the soldiers, opening a United Services Organization (USO) operation at the downtown Newport Armory. But other local businessmen realized a different style of entertainment was better suited to the Marine flyers. "When Bob Fortune built the Silver Moon in 1944, the club brought in wild-ass Marines and sailors from Memphis always looking for a fight," Wallace said. "There was gambling in the back of the Silver Moon, and the soldiers from the airbase had money to spend."

Bob Fortune was well known in Newport as the owner of Fortune's Billiard Parlor and Liquor Store at 414 Front Street, a business he started in 1932. He was also part owner of a wholesale beer distributorship. Many people in town knew Fortune as an active gambler. His son Bill Fortune, a Newport motel owner today, recalled seeing Minnesota Fats and other pool hustlers coming into his father's business. The gamblers stopped in at Newport while traveling to more lucrative engagements at Hot Springs, Fortune said. He also remembered a betting room upstairs and a button behind the bar to unlock the betting room door.

With new profits to be made in alcohol sales and gambling, Bob Fortune partnered with Don Washam and George Langston, brothers-in-law who had started a small club at the airbase. The men located the Silver Moon on Highway 67 north of town outside the city limits. Nearby was Rube's Place, a beer joint with a small area for the jukebox and dancing, owned by Rube Stephens, uncle to Steve Stephens. Fortune hired Stephens to build the new club. The original Silver Moon was a simple tavern, but Washam bought out his partners and made several expansions and improvements over the years. Washam lived next door to the club in a small white house with a picket fence.

The original lack of decor was no impediment to the airbase crowds who made the Silver Moon an immediate success. Newport residents joined them, attracted by the live entertainment. Local bands and nationally recognized performers were regularly advertised in the *Newport Daily Independent.* Only beer was sold, but bottles of whiskey could be brought in. An indulgent atmosphere permeated the club, which rapidly gained notoriety among local teenagers as a place with lenient enforcement of age requirements. "If you were six-teen years old and had a quarter, you could get a beer at the Silver Moon," Doc Hawk said.

In the late 1940s, Jimmy Davidson's band the Rhythm Kings were popular at the Silver Moon (shown here with a Falstaff beer sign covering the "Moon") and on Davidson's radio program broadcast from Tuckerman. From left: Bob Armstrong, accordion; Paul Whaley, guitar; Davidson, drums; Charlie Martin, trumpet; Kern Kennedy, piano; and Dennis Ball, guitar. (Photo courtesy of Jimmy Davidson.)

Most teenagers came to the Silver Moon to dance, but some came as musicians. In 1947 and 1948, a young Ace Cannon played frequently at the club as a band member with Buck Turner and his Buckaroos and with Clyde Leopard and his Snearly Ranch Boys, two Memphis groups popular in Newport at the time.

"I played the Silver Moon with those hillbilly groups," Cannon, whose extensive career included stints with the Bill Black Combo and Billy Lee Riley's Little Green Men, said. "We were a six-piece group that worked the door. On Christmas Eve, we made $55 each, then we came back on New Year's Eve and made $80 each. I was thirteen years old, earning as much as the grown men."

By the mid-1950s, when Newport city limits expanded to include the site, the Silver Moon had a tiled floor entry, rock walls, and carpeting and mirrors inside. A music room was added with a low stage for bands and capacity for 800 or more people, making the club the largest in the region. The Silver Moon's customers came from all social strata, but Washam kept the music room at high standards.

"Don began a dress code soon. He would lend you a necktie if you didn't have one," Wallace said. "Boys would come in from the field. Folks with deodorant or perfume had to sit next to those guys."

The last expansion of the Silver Moon also added a large gambling room in the rear of the building. Other clubs in Jackson County had dice and card games in their back rooms, but none matched the level of play at the Silver Moon.

"In its time, gambling was very lively at the Silver Moon," Wallace said. "They were always looking for guys with a wad and willing to play. A lot of money changed hands."

Despite the high-dollar activity that transpired in the Silver Moon's back room and in Washam's house next door, the club's public persona was as a venue for live music. In the gravel parking lot along Highway 67, the roadside marquee proclaimed: "Silver Moon, Home to Famous Bands."

After the war, the decommissioned airbase was declared government surplus, and management was transferred to city government. The 1,100-acre site contained housing for several thousand people and large hangars suitable for factories, a ready-made industrial center and housing project combined. The Newport Chamber of Commerce created an industrial committee and began recruiting new manufacturing plants to provide jobs to returning vets.

Sam Walton

In the late 1940s, Newport's industrial recruiting efforts were assisted by a retail merchant who, like many others, sought commercial success on Newport's highly congested Front Street. Sam Walton opened his first retail store in Newport in 1945. Five years later, his departure was announced with a personal notice in the town newspaper:

> It is with regret that we are preparing to leave Newport and our many friends and customers. Being unable to renew our lease, we are moving to Bentonville, Ark, to make our future home....We sincerely appreciate your friendship and patronage during the past five and half years and assure you it has been a pleasure and a privilege to have been of service to you. Once again, friends, "Thanks for everything"—Sam and Helen Walton.
> —*Newport Daily Independent*, December 21, 1950

Walton's passion for retail was ideally located amid Front Street's shopkeepers and merchants. His initial opportunity was in an under-achieving Ben Franklin store, a small business once called a "five and ten cent store." Walton's energy and vision created a new business model of discounting: cutting prices to boost sales. To draw traffic to his store, he put a popcorn machine on his sidewalk. He put a soft-serve ice cream machine beside it. By his second year of operation, Walton's store had doubled previous sales. By his fifth year, sales had tripled.

The Waltons were a sociable, churchgoing family with four young children. They became deeply involved in community life and in country club bridge and tennis circles. As president of the Newport Chamber of Commerce, Walton recruited new industry to occupy the vacated airbase, among them Victor Metal Products Company, a New Jersey manufacturer that made metal tubes for Colgate toothpaste. Occupying a former hangar at the airbase, Victor became Newport's largest industrial employer with more than 600 jobs.

In 1950, Walton discovered a critical flaw in his business plan. In his enthusiasm to open his Ben Franklin store, he had overlooked a renewal option in the lease. Walton's contract was with the Butler Brothers Company, a Chicago and St. Louis firm that sold Ben Franklin franchises. When Walton took over the Newport store, the original lease came with it. The building itself was owned by Paul K. Holmes, whose family had been Newport merchants since 1882. Holmes watched his sons, P. K. Jr. and Douglas, grow up in the family business, a general merchandise store and a men's store. By 1950, the brothers were ready to operate their own businesses. "My father owned the original building, which burned in 1940," Douglas Holmes said. "He rebuilt it and leased it to the Butler Brothers. After that lease was up, Dad wanted the store for my brother and me."

Walton was notified that his lease would not be renewed. The decision came through the Butler Brothers, but it was Holmes who set conditions that were impossible to meet. Walton's attorney Fred Pickens tried to intercede, offering Holmes higher rent and other terms. But business competition and family loyalties were too strong.

"They're not going to let you keep the store," Pickens, quoted in a 1990 Walton biography, said. "The plain truth is they want Douglas Holmes to run the Ben Franklin in that building. You showed the whole town what a moneymaker it can be."[89]

By August of that year, the man who would revolutionize American retail marketing opened Walton's Variety Store in the Ozark Mountains town of Bentonville. Walton once again found himself in a small-town atmosphere among self-reliant people like those he had admired in the Delta. Newport friends regretted the family's relocation, but the town had no time to mourn the loss. Merchants and business owners were once again on the precipice of boom times. The Holmes brothers returned to the store at the corner of Front and Hazel Street, the site their father operated ten years earlier, now the busiest corner in town.

Walton's keen business sense recognized the need for a manufacturing presence to balance Newport's agricultural economy. Through his leadership, the town's industrial recruiting program had its first success. But Newport's economic growth through the late 1940s and 1950s was not sustained. By 1970, when Wal-Mart announced the initial public offering of its stock and Walton's wealth soared—leading to his repeated designation by *Forbes* magazine as the wealthiest man in America—Newport had been irrevocably drawn into the Delta's broad economic decline.

Chapter 10.
Newport in the 1950s

A Town's Peak, and Decline

W hen he was a young adult, Sonny Burgess' celebrity status in his hometown was part of Newport's larger celebration of the decade of the 1950s. As the decade came to an end, the community equilibrium was thrown off balance. When Newport's foundations began to erode, celebration changed to crisis and empowerment was replaced by debilitation.

A Merchant's Town

The postcard shows a lakeside park, lush with foliage. At a shaded table, a couple sits with their open picnic basket. Children play on the iron-frame swings. Boaters on the background lake wave to those fishing on the bank. Signs on the green grass read "Lake Newport Wayside Park" and "Welcome Tourists." Like hundreds of other lakes across the Delta, this ox bow slough was formed over the centuries by the flooding and receding White River. For the gregarious leaders of Newport, the lake was another means of civic promotion, attracting the increasingly mobile American traveler.

Newport was a merchant's town. It liked to count things, to know their measure. In 1958, the city reported a visitor count of 5,646 at the Lake Newport tourist park. The city reported on weekly earnings from the parking meters newly installed on Front Street. The county reported on rising poll tax earnings and population changes. The 1950 census revealed that Newport's population rose by forty-five percent since 1940, and the growing population created a housing boom. The expanded city limits took in sections of Highway 67 north of town where the Silver

Moon was located. To the east, large areas of the decommissioned Newport Air Base were used for new residential housing. The newspaper listed it all, with ample page space provided by strong advertising sales.

Newport Lake Tourist Park. A postcard promoting the park stated that it offered "free ice water and tourist facilities"; 1950s. (Photo courtesy of Ray Hanley.)

Attendance at Farmers Day celebrations was always noted. In 1951, the fifth gathering of the annual August event drew a record 10,000 people. Governor Sid McMath was the keynote speaker and Betty Castleberry, Miss Newport, sang. Additional performers included Buck Turner and the Buckaroos with lead singer Hayden Thompson[90] and a local black gospel group, the United Harmonizers.[91] Both acts were on the Farmers Day stage repeatedly through the 1950s. In crowd photos from 1956 and 1957, the years the Pacers headlined the shows, black and white audience members can be seen mingling freely on the high school football field.

In addition to the live music, Farmers Day included talent shows and radio broadcasts, drawings for prizes, kiddie rides, and fireworks.

The program ostensibly was a Farmers Electric Co-op meeting, but people came for the show. Newport's furniture and mercantile stores set up a large tent on the grounds two days in advance, and new refrigerators, washing machines, and televisions were displayed in an "appliance circus." Newspaper ads touted the all-electric kitchen, televisions, electric typewriters, and other modern devices to make life easier, challenging homemakers with a message that linked modernization with pride: "Are you proud of your kitchen? Does it have that dressed up, well groomed look that makes the time you spend in it a real pleasure?"[92] The women of Newport responded. In May 1951, 500 of them sat in the Strand Theater to watch an Arkansas Power and Light Company representative demonstrate the features of a new electric range.

The Pacers on stage at the annual Farmers Day show; 1956.

Access to stores in Newport and other local towns was improved when the last gravel section of Highway 14 was paved in June 1952. The new road was touted in a speech by Gov. McMath at a celebration at the east Jackson County town of Amagon. Crowds were treated to free barbeque and train rides on the Great Southern Railroad. Newport merchants likely viewed the new roadway as a mixed blessing, and newspaper editorials and cartoons were printed touting the economic benefits of shopping locally. Civic progress was welcome, but not when it facilitated Newport customers spending their dollars in Memphis.

Phyllis Holmes was newly married and living in the Dorsey Apartments by the White River bridge. Her husband, Doug, was operating the Ben Franklin store, recently acquired from Sam Walton. The business, according to Walton's autobiography, had become the largest and most successful of its kind in the state.

"On Saturdays, we opened at eight a.m. and closed whenever," Holmes said. "When the crops were in, we hired extra help, sometimes some three dozen people in the store. There was no self service then. We had different cash registers all around the store."

Across Front Street in another postcard tableau was a small park beside the railroad depot. A bandstand was shaded by large cottonwood trees. Breezes blowing off the nearby White River made the park an inviting resting spot for downtown shoppers.

"We thought of them as the golden days," Phyllis Holmes said of Newport in the 1950s, echoing Neil Phillips' descriptions of the town in the early 1900s. "Downtown Newport was the highlight of the week. You would park on Front Street and watch the people walk by."

A Prosperous Future

"*Newport an Industry-Studded Garden of Eden. The US Engineers say Yes!!*" declared a 1950 headline. Colonel Louis W. Prentiss, an engineer with the U.S. Army Corps of Engineers in Dallas, was a Chamber of Commerce keynote speaker. He told of potential projects, including construction of new reservoirs in the White River valley that would halt floods, provide water power to attract industry, and create a playground for the tourist trade.[93]

Newport had reason to believe in its prosperous future. In May 1951, the newspaper cited an industrial survey that showed Jackson County as one of the wealthiest counties in the nation, the bulk of its income from agriculture. Jackson County was listed as eighth in the nation in rice production, tenth in cotton, and eleventh in soybeans. Each of the crops was valued at several million dollars.

Newport also sent delegations to New York and Chicago, inviting corporate leaders to visit the city. In 1952, the city sent emissaries to Washington DC to pitch Newport as a site for an atomic energy plant. That effort was unsuccessful, as was a plan to reactivate the airbase as a commercial airport. But the city still had much to brag about. The Federal Reserve Bank of St. Louis heartily agreed.

In an extensive report released in July 1954, the Federal Reserve Bank cited Newport as an economic development model, praising the community for acting as an entrepreneur in a manner that was ingenious, imaginative, and enterprising.[94] The full report is a remarkable document, not just for its glowing assessment of Newport's future, but also for its recognition of the potential conflicts introduced by change.

The report suggests Newport's rapid growth offered a visual contrast of the old and new. "Tree shaded avenues and fine old houses of some sections give an impression of the timeless old river towns described in the pages of Mark Twain. But this impression is belied by sprouting television antennas and spreading subdivisions of ranch type houses on the city's outskirts."

The report also recognized the danger to growth and prosperity as technology reduced farm employment. This was the report's most direct and dire warning: changes in agricultural technology and productivity would reduce the number of farm families on the land, and Newport's tradesmen-centered economy, representing its rapidly growing middle class, would be left without support. As a reminder, the report recounted Jacksonport's refusal to accept the railroad offer, concluding that "Jacksonport faded away when the steamboat vanished, her people having failed to recognize a major change in technology which could have been used to their advantage."

But Newport leaders believed that the town's rapidly increasing industrial presence would create jobs and sustain the local economy. In 1955, Major Jud Hout showed off a planned city auto tag that featured local industry.[95] The new tag design showed a toothpaste tube and the caption "Where Victor Tube Supply [sic] the World," a tribute to the world's largest supplier of aluminum toothpaste tubes.

The good news kept coming. In 1959, the Brown Jordan Company, a national manufacturer of metal furniture, announced the expansion of its Jackson County plant to accommodate the recently purchased American Lantern Corp. That same year, voters approved a bond issue to recruit a shoe manufacturer. Newport's success in recruiting industry was a common topic at Chamber of Commerce meetings. Dave Grundfest, owner of Sterling Stores statewide, told the group that Newport realized "the cotton crop is on its way [out] in this part of the country and it is highly important that more industry be obtained." Grundfest further assured the local business leaders that "industrialists want to come to the South where we have a philosophy and haven't been indoctrinated that a union card is good for security for life."[96]

In 1956, Governor Orval Faubus extolled Newport for creating industrial jobs, stating, "If every town and county in this state had grown as yours has, then the problem of loss of population would not exist."[97]

In 1957, as the date neared for the transfer of airbase ownership to the city, Newport reminded its citizens of the opportunity that lay ahead with a newspaper headline: "County's at Threshold of an Industrial Boom."[98] City leaders also introduced a public relations campaign to spread the word that Newport had the right stuff to become a city of the future. The messaging included a "Dress Up For Industry Week" when residents were urged to clean up yards and streets in preparation for a visit by an industrial prospect.

In 1959, the *Arkansas Democrat* paid its tribute. "Newport Firms Position as Industrial Pacemaker," a headline declared, followed by an article on the rapid industrial growth.[99] Not to be outdone, the *Newport Daily Independent* followed with a full-front-page story of the city's latest boom times and growth. The headline shouted "Newport—the young, cosmopolitan city! NEWPORT IS OPPORTUNITY SPELLED WITH BIG LETTERS," using capital letters to drive home its point.[100]

Finally that year, the Newport Chamber announced a fundraising drive to erect two signs to share this message with Highway 67 travelers. The "Plucky Newport" message long discarded, the new signs would proclaim, "Welcome to Newport. City of Progress."[101]

Cultural Stereotypes

Newport, like most of post-war America, willingly accepted the nation's cultural stereotypes. Bigger cars, sleek and powerful, meant visual prestige. The Pacers' stretch Cadillac, Bobby Crafford recalled, once prompted a patron at the Batesville Country Club to remark, "They should be good. They're driving a Cadillac."

Beyond Newport's city limits, rural areas were confronted with the collapse of sharecropping and the reduced demand for field labor. Historian Pete Daniel described it as "an abrupt mid-century crash of a rural way of life, with millions of southerners emerging from the wreckage." New national stereotypes were formed at this time. The former southern sharecropper was seen as "volitionless and culturally bare, an individual who would lower values of property and propriety upon arrival in respectable neighborhoods."[102]

Jackson County's distinctive stereotype was the "suggin," a name assigned to uneducated and ill-mannered rural residents who held a low place on the social scale.

"Suggin is a Jackson County term of derision, never used anywhere else," Mike Beebe said. "It means uncouth, ignorant. There was a lot of pride for people in being from Newport. That was a step up from the county folk and their homes with no plumbing or running water."

Beebe was born in the tiny Jackson County community of Amagon. He was raised by his divorced mother, who worked as a waitress. In his earliest years in the 1940s, his family occupied a rural home with holes in the wooden flooring. His Saturday night rituals would have been viewed by Newport's society as suggin.

"I had baths in a washtub with my cousins, with heated water poured in," Beebe said. "I was the last of three cousins in the tub, and one ornery older cousin would say he peed in the water before me."

Years later, Newport artist Josephine Graham tried to gentrify the derogatory term. An accomplished watercolorist, educator, and author, Graham created "suggin" paintings depicting Jackson County Depression-era scenes. In 1974, she published *Suggin Cookbook*, a collection of old recipes from pioneer families. Graham also established the Suggin Folklife Society, which at its peak in 1981 had 200 members from eight states. She explained that "suggin" was used playfully and lovingly to mean a "somewhat uncouth and unsophisticated person living in a rural area or small town along the White River."[103]

Visitors in Town

Two visitors in the early 1950s illustrate Newport's social conformity and cultural stereotypes. On July 3, 1952, President Harry Truman made a brief pass-through visit, arriving by train after a dedication ceremony the previous day at the new dam on Bull Shoals Lake in north Arkansas. His departure from the Newport Air Base strengthened the belief of town leaders that the site had potential as a commercial airport.

Truman rode through Newport in an open car, waving to cheering crowds along streets decorated for the July 4th holiday. The people of Newport loved him despite his national popularity being at the lowest point of his political career, a result of U.S. involvement in Korea. The son of a farmer, Truman grew up with modest means. He was the last U.S. president without a college education. Prior to his political life, he operated a men's clothing shop in Kansas City, Missouri. He was a self-made, small-town man, unaffected by inner doubts or introspection, an ideal example of leadership for Newport's merchants and middle-class voters.

The other visitor was Aunt Jemima, a costumed black woman with a beaming smile who appeared at the Newport Kroger supermarket on January 24, 1953, to promote Aunt Jemima Pancake Mix. Named for the original "mammy" cook at Higbee's Landing plantation in Louisiana, the product first appeared at the 1893 Chicago Exposition, establishing the core American stereotype of the cheerful black servant whose life purpose was the comfort of white guests.

In the 1950s, Newport's segregation policies were well established. Articles about local black sports and church programs were included in the daily newspaper. Blacks attended the Negro elementary school and the black Branch High School. They sat in the balcony at the Strand Theater, their designated area, and they entered the theater through a side door. At the black drinking and gambling joints on the south end of Front Street, Kern Kennedy and other teenaged boys too

256

young and too fair skinned to enter, sat outside and listened to boogie woogie and rhythm and blues through the open windows.

National Fears

Despite its civic optimism and material abundance, Newport shared in the predominant national fears of the era. As newspaper articles showed polio-stricken children on crutches or encased in bulky respiratory devices known as "iron lungs," local women joined a national Mothers' March on Polio, later known as the March of Dimes. The door-to-door fundraising campaign, conducted annually by mothers from several Jackson County communities, urged all families to turn on their porch lights when the women collected donations in the early evening. In 1956, when a film was produced on local polio victims, Jackson County raised a record $5,404 in donations. The following year, the headline act at the Jackson County March of Dimes Ball was Sonny Burgess and the Pacers. By 1958, the Salk vaccine was in widespread use and crippling disease had virtually been eradicated.

Atomic warfare was another fear widely held during the decade. As U.S. bomb testing was conducted in the Nevada desert in 1951, a series of newspaper articles described the increased killing power of newly developed hydrogen and cobalt bombs. A speaker at the city Rotary Club gave the details of a hypothetical nuclear bomb explosion with Newport's post office as ground zero. The blast, explained Jerald Moleston, a former U.S. Navy officer who participated in the Enewetak tests in the Marshall Islands, would "completely vaporize the entire city of Newport…, its generated heat would burn down and flatten Tuckerman and Diaz," and deadly radioactive fallout could spread as far as Pine Bluff, 130 miles away.[104] Adding to the confusion and fear, the newspaper also printed a string of articles, "You Can Survive the Atom Bomb," which instructed Newport residents on personal safety measures to avoid nuclear annihilation.[105]

These apocalyptic scenarios were linked to the overriding threat of the atomic age: communism. Senator John McClellan, speaking to the 1954 Newport High School graduating class, identified a "hideous threat of conspiracy that is world wide in scope." Ruthless, barbaric

Soviet communism, McClellan said, "seeks to destroy every vestige of human freedom and to enslave all humanity."[106]

Though the Korean War was over at the time of McClellan's remarks, for the previous three years, the Newport newspaper had regularly published reports of communist atrocities during the Korean War and the killing of Allied prisoners. Anti-communism sentiment was rapidly gaining national public support.

Operation Skywatch

The fear of communist infiltration and military attack remained high throughout the decade. Jackson County citizens were encouraged to participate in "Operation Skywatch," a civil defense program sponsored by the U.S. Air Force's Ground Observers Corps. The volunteer program enlisted civilians equipped with binoculars to spend time in rural outposts and report sightings of Soviet bombers in flight to destroy American cities.

One program recruitment ad issued the following call: "You are wanted to watch the skies, to make sure that not even one enemy plane sneaks through without the warning being flashed. It's a lonely job, but a vital one. Become a volunteer Skywatcher."[107]

Another program announcement used comedian Groucho Marx to rally public participation, showing him with a false moustache and horn-rimmed eyeglasses in four captioned poses: WAKE UP, with an alarm clock; SIGN UP, with pen in hand; LOOK UP, pointing his cigar upward; and LIVE, with clasped hands over his head.[108]

The U.S. Air Force disbanded the Ground Observers Corps in 1958, conceding that the human eye was ineffective in the new age of jets, radar, and intercontinental missiles. But over a nine-year period, some 280,000 civilians had volunteered at 16,000 observation posts across the nation.[109] The number of participants from Jackson County is unknown, but volunteers surely responded, the service enthusiasm continuing from the legacy of security at Newport's airbase during World War II. Jimmy Davidson recalled his role at the base developing the Signal Corps, which managed all communications between the planes and pilots. Davidson said rumors circulated through town of local farmers who were

German sympathizers cutting their wheat fields into arrows visible from the air to point the way to the airbase for enemy bombers.

Public awareness of a potential communist attack and invasion continued through the 1950s, with fears escalating during the 1959 communist takeover of Cuba. Most Newport residents had heard little of the island since 1951 when nineteen-year-old Betty Castleberry, crowned Miss Newport that year, also won the Miss North Arkansas title at the Batesville Water Carnival and went on a publicity tour to Cuba, an American vacation site at the time. Photos sent to the Newport newspaper showed the auburn-haired local beauty in bathing suit and high heels posed poolside at a Havana beach hotel.

Betty Castleberry, Newport July 4th parade; 1951.

Beauty pageants and musical programs were very popular through the decade. In June 1952, Newport hosted the Miss Arkansas Pageant. A newspaper article promoting the event asked local homeowners to rent their spare rooms to the expected visitors. That same year, Newport introduced the Follies, a Broadway-style show with a large cast of local amateur talent. Sponsored by the Newport Service League as a charity fundraiser, the Follies often hired a professional choreographer from New York who resided in Newport for weeks in advance of the show. The Newport Follies program, a highpoint of the community social calendar, was conducted annually for more than thirty years before it ended in the 1980s.

Music programs were also conducted in the schools. Newport High School required music classes; students could choose band or choir. In its peak years in the 1950s, the high school band included some sixty uniformed musicians, as well as baton twirlers and drum majorettes. It marched in the Cotton Carnival at Memphis and in Mardi Gras parades in New Orleans.

Rural Wealth, Rural Poverty

"Headin' down Front Street baby, and all over town
Man you oughta see the lights when the sun goes down."
—Sonny Burgess, "We Wanna Boogie"

Newport's town life offered a lively venue for landowners who capitalized on the new agricultural economy, a process that included getting one's share of government subsidies.

"I loved those payments in July when we got those big checks," Jim Wood said. "My grandfather called it the 'plow up years.' He was paid not to plant. One year, he was paid a cash bonus to plow up a field that was already planted."

Larger landowners had the advantage. One of Jackson County's most successful agricultural families, the Wilmans, at one time farmed about 15,000 acres, mostly in cotton. When crop prices changed, the Wilmans switched to more profitable rice and soybeans. Rail cars bound for New Orleans were loaded at the Diaz grain silo. The Wilmans also introduced registered cattle sales and breeding services. As they were a prominent Newport family, most activity at the Wilmans' household was considered newsworthy. An article about a 1959 landscaping project stated that the family intended to buy 50,000 rose plants to become

260

a permanent living fence. Projected to grow to full size in three years, the living fence could extend for up to ten miles.

On the other side of the fence, the sharecropper's and tenant farmer's world was far removed from luxury or leisure. As was the case for many others of his generation, Billy Lee Riley's early years were shaped by the poverty and deprivation of the itinerant laborer. His childhood memories include a pair of shoes held together with glue and wire, his siblings searching the city dump for extra food, and a man knocking on the door seeking the dollar-per-week rent, often turned away empty handed.[110]

In the impoverished world of Riley's youth, school attendance was seasonal, limited to summer and winter months when the intensive field work was at a lull. Riley's schooling ended in the third grade, replaced by ten-to-twelve-hour work days, for which he rose at dawn to harness two mules to an array of plows, discs, harrows, and cultivators.

Braceros

Seasonal and migrant farm workers were additional rural residents whose lives were marked by hard labor and meager earnings. Their presence in Jackson County was thrust into public awareness in November 1958 when two migrant workers had an altercation at the Sale Barn Café on Front Street. Both had been drinking. One of them killed the other with a shotgun.

Newport was more crowded with laborers that season than it had been in previous years. Fewer farming areas in the Delta were still utilizing manual labor. Local farmers were expecting about 500 contracted Mexican laborers, hired through the cotton growers' association. But some 2,500 migrant workers arrived.

The Bracero Program (from Spanish, meaning "one who works with his arms") began in 1942 when the United States and Mexico entered agreements to address wartime labor shortages and allow Mexicans temporary, legal work. More than four million Mexican men entered the United States, initially in California and Texas, but eventually in the Mississippi River Delta as well. At its peak, the program provided a quarter of the cotton labor in the Delta region in Arkansas.[111]

The resource was a boon to large growers like the Burtons who could provide the required provisions: housing, cooking utensils, bedding, and transportation to and from the border. David Burton recalled his trips to Texas to hire up to 100 men at a time, sending trucks with bench seats built on the beds and overhead tarps, hauling the workers to and from Arkansas for the cotton harvest.

"They lived in empty sharecropper houses at first," Burton said. "We'd fix the beds out of cotton seed hulls poured in wood frames on the floor. Each man got two blankets; one for the cotton hulls below, the other to wrap in. Then we built barracks housing fifty men each. They had bunks with cot springs and a dining hall with tables. We hired a Mexican cook for them."

The braceros earned $25 to $35 per week based on their volume of picked cotton, a similar wage as local workers. Many of them sent money home, but as with other labor crews, some of the men spent their wages locally. On some farms, crew chiefs brought alcohol and prostitutes to the camps to keep the men from going to town.

"It was a loose situation the way these men were handled," Burton said. "The system rules changed every year, and there were always some workers disgruntled or disappointed that they weren't making enough. Some wanted to go home. Or they would run off, thinking they could walk to the Mexican consulate in Memphis."

The large number of braceros brought to Jackson County in the late 1950s harvested the cotton crop, but the program was troublesome. Nor did it address the larger problem causing the labor shortage.

"With the mechanical cotton pickers coming in and improving, we didn't need braceros anymore," Burton said. "We'd buy more machines."

Since 1950, the new mechanical cotton pickers had been rolling off the assembly line at the International Harvester plant in Memphis. The John Deere Company filed its own patent for the machines and marketed them extensively in cotton-growing areas. The first mechanical picker in Jackson County belonged to the Burton family and was used on the family's extensive land holdings near Tupelo. The one-row machine cost about $8,000, Burton recalled.

Witness to Change

The average farmer had neither the production volume nor capital to mechanize. Shelby Smith was one of thousands of southerners who went to the northern factories to find work. Smith, born in 1932, had childhood memories of a challenging life on his father's forty-acre farm with its horse-drawn plow, and his mother and older sister in the field chopping cotton. As a young farmer, Smith struggled to earn $30–$35 a week. In Flint, Michigan, Smith brought home $150 a week.

"At the Buick company where I worked, nearly seventy-five percent of us were southerners, black and white," Smith recalled. "They called us 'hungry southerners' because we were proud to work overtime and take those four extra hours on Saturday. Local people didn't want to work like that."

But Smith found life in the North too impersonal. It lacked the sense of community he and his wife had known in Arkansas.

"In Flint, people weren't friendly like in the South," he said. "You could live next to a person three years and not know them. We went up to get on our feet and come back home. I told my wife I don't know what we will do, but we'll make a living somehow."

Smith returned to Jackson County and farming in 1957. He retired in 1993 to a large, ranch-style home in Newport where pictures of his children and grandchildren cover the walls. Smith's life and values— his work ethic and his dedication to family—reflect the core character of those whose strength and focus are rooted in the land.

"Sue Ann and I were married forty-seven years," Smith said. "We were never wealthy, but we were rich in love and in our three children. We tried to provide for them."

End of the Decade

As the 1950s ended, Newport teenagers danced at the Silver Moon or the Farm Drive In, which had a jukebox and a large concrete dance floor. Those who had cars joined in the late-night parking at the "Pea Patch," an isolated area now used as the back nine holes of the Newport Country Club golf course. They would cruise past the

Dairy Queen or buy tamales from James Williams, a black man with a small store at the levee.

Other Newport teenagers were less conforming to community expectations. In 1959, school superintendent G. F. Castleberry issued a report that identified only 45 out of 140 graduating seniors planning for college. Half of the largest class in the history of Newport High School, the report stated, had no plans for higher education or employment.[112]

"This is a severe indictment of our educational system," Castleberry's report declared. At the time, Arkansas was ranked forty-eighth in the nation in expenditures in state schools. Its average teacher salary of $2,360 was the lowest in the nation.[113]

Following reports of vandalism at the city swimming pool and teens being disruptive at a local café, Castleberry warned the high school students that their behavior would not be tolerated.[114] Newport's restless teenagers and young adults had begun using the former runways of the airbase for late night fun, prompting Mayor Jud Hout to order their hot-rod drag racers off the site in 1956.

Newport's young adults were entertained by a new genre of movies that sensationalized unruly teen behavior. Replacing the animated family fare of top movies earlier in the decade—*Cinderella* in 1950, *Peter Pan* in 1953, and *Lady and the Tramp* in 1955—the Strand Theater in the late 1950s featured provocatively titled, B-grade films such as *High School Hellcats*, *Hot Rod Gang*, *Rock All Night*, and *Drag Strip Girl*. In *Running Wild*, Mamie Van Doren portrayed a buxom heroine described as "too young to be careful, too tough to be afraid." In *Jailhouse Rock*, Elvis Presley sang the title track in a style that demonstrated, as one critic noted, his "raw, sexual energy and sneering charisma."[115]

The combination of rock and roll, fast cars, and loose women was hard for the average young movie viewer to resist.

A State of Disrepair

Newport's jailhouse in the late 1950s was in poor condition. On June 12, 1957, three prisoners escaped from the aging county structure, sawing through an iron bar and pulling off a welded plate put there after a previous escape. And in 1959, seventeen-year-old Eric White surely set a local record when he escaped from the jail for the eighth time. White made his last getaway through a window whose bars had been bent years earlier by another escapee. Deputy jailer Bob Rush said the youth was not considered dangerous, but "he'll run from an officer and should be watched carefully if caught."[116]

In the final years of the 1950s, as the last remnants of the Arkansas frontier faded away, the newspaper reported the rare sightings of Jackson County's original wildlife—the timberwolves that preyed on rural poultry and the bears that wandered onto cotton fields, scaring pickers from their work. As a collapsing sharecropping system shifted agricultural wealth and sustenance to fewer and fewer families, and even as Newport's promising vision of industrial growth began to fade, teenaged escapee White, perhaps Newport's most clever and determined inmate, a suggin if there ever was one, finally gave up as well.

A month after his final escape, White phoned Deputy Rush to turn himself in. Through the early winter rains, he had been hiding in the duck blinds near his home. He was cold, wet, and tired. Now all he wanted was to serve his time and get it over with.

White's capitulation was a concession to the hard times that weakened his rural environment and dampened his spunk. A profound cultural shift was underway. Traditional lifestyles were now confronted by the new and changing world of mid-twentieth-century America.

Chapter 11.
Roadhouses and Rednecks

Club Life

Some of the Jackson County clubs where Sonny Burgess and the Pacers performed attempted a supper-club elegance with candles and tablecloths. Others found that concrete walls and metal chairs best suited their rough clientele. The musicians and the club owners created an atmosphere of indulgence during a decade of substantive social change. Rural patrons wildly expressed their appreciation by dancing, drinking, and gambling.

Dancers at the Silver Moon; 1950s.

Beer Joints and Brothels

At classy spots like the Silver Moon, well-dressed patrons danced to the music of Bob Wills and Louis Armstrong. Other clubs attracted farm workers with the dirt of the field and the stink of mules still on them, their faded cotton shirts showing dark lines where leather reins crossed their backs. Some of them walked miles into town to drink, dance, and fight on a Saturday night.

The north end of Newport was once called Honky Tonk. Among its clubs of distinction was the Sunset Inn, a beer joint where locals joked "when the sun went down, all hell set in." W. S. Holland, drummer with Carl Perkins' band, recalled the atmosphere of the small club. "It was so rough, they would sell bricks at the door," Holland joked.

Nearby was the Bloody Bucket, where a bear on a chair would guzzle your beer until it fell over drunk. Inside the club, brawlers sometimes fell against a large fan behind the bar. Charles Watson recalled a woman whose hair got caught in the fan.

"The worst kind of fight is women," Watson mused.

Marvin Thaxton remembered the Bloody Bucket in the 1940s when he drove an ambulance at the Newport Air Base. One summer, he mentioned the club to two new arrivals at the base who asked him where they could find a lively spot to drink. The men showed up the next morning at the base's infirmary.

"One of them came back with an imprint of a log chain on his head and both eyes blackened," Thaxton said. "He had been jumped in the parking lot and never even got inside."

Through the 1950s, numerous prostitutes frequented the Rainbow Bar and other establishments near the railroad depot at the southern end of Front Street. The women were continuing a tradition from the town's riverboat era when established bordellos were located across the tracks. Here was the Blue Room, a popular restaurant in the 1940s that later became notorious for gambling, prostitution, and drinking. Closer to the White River Bridge was the black neighborhood, the Vine Street area where whites and blacks alike bought Sunday booze from the town bootlegger, a black man called Shark, and where they shot dice late into the morning hours at Peg's gambling club. Stories still linger of a Newport mayor who supposedly bit off the nipple of a black woman.

"Down Front Street at the depot were beer joints, and the further you went, the worse it got," an older Newport man recalled. "There were so many whores back then, we used to say whores would starve to death in Newport."

A Front Street club with a brothel in the back was still operating in the late 1960s. Newport clubs never kept people out, never lost their riverboat mentality, Kaneaster Hodges suggested. Hodges was city attorney and Jackson County deputy prosecuting attorney from 1967 to 1974. He was later appointed by Governor David Pryor as interim U.S. senator following the death of incumbent John McClellan.

"I shut down Sylvia and Ray's, the last whorehouse in Newport," Hodges said of a 1967 conviction of Sylvia Prince and Ray Martin for operating a prostitution site at their tavern on lower Front Street.[117] The pair were fined but given suspended three-year jail sentences on the condition that they were absent from Newport during the term.

"When we got her shut down as a public nuisance," Hodges added, "Sylvia said, 'I'm glad to leave Newport, because it's hard to sell something everyone else is giving away.'"

In 1997, the *Arkansas Democrat-Gazette* wrote about the past profusion of Newport's music clubs and their lucrative business in alcohol sales.[118] Interviewed in the article, Johnny Ray Hubbard dismissed the simple explanation that wet Jackson County was located in a predominantly dry part of the state. Nearby towns such as Trumann and Marked Tree also allowed alcohol sales, he said, and people living in dry communities knew how to buy the items they desired.

"In a dry county you can buy just as much," Hubbard said. "It's just that it ain't legal. If you know the right people, it's still as wet as before."

Sonny Burgess believes the success of Newport's clubs was due to their ability to attract top performers. "In Little Rock or Memphis, they'd starve musicians to death. You were lucky if you got $75 for the whole band," Sonny said. "But you come here to Jackson County and you'd take home $200 to $300. That's why these bands played here and why the area was hot."

Ronnie Hawkins agreed. "Newport was one of the best club scenes I ever played," he said. "It was always full. It was always rockin'."

Gamblers and Lawyers

Newport club owners understood how things worked in their town. If they bought beer from an out-of-town provider, their pinball machines and jukeboxes, leased through a Newport distributor, would not be well serviced. And if portions of their gambling revenue were not shared with certain attorneys, club owners might get surprise inspections by the state Alcohol Beverage Control (ABC) Division.

Gambling in Jackson County was not limited to the clubs. At Mann Shoffner's sale barn in downtown Newport, all-night craps games were held on Thursdays after the mule auctions. When the city police raided the games one night, the wealthy Shoffner showed little concern for the $10 fine, telling an employee, "Pay that ticket. I got real money on the table."

Gamblers also met on Thursdays at a site on north Highway 67 across from the Silver Moon. This was the infamous "Green House" operated by gambler Joe Tarkington. The house attracted players from Newport and other towns for extended, high-stakes poker and dice games.

"The gambling might last two or three days until someone won all the money," Hubbard recalled. "They'd have fries and fish at the house, and then they'd go to hotels and motels. It was a booming thing back then."[119]

The Green House had metal plates on its windows and electric door locks. A buzzer in the vestibule added security for the interior rooms. Tarkington's installations, however, did not prevent the house from eventually going up in flames, a fire some locals considered non-accidental.

Among the half dozen gambling sites in Jackson County, the Silver Moon saw the most action. During Don Washam's ownership, a large windowless room for gambling was added. Entry was behind the bar and through a small storage area where an interior door with a peephole controlled access. The gambling room had an exterior door that could open to the street, but that door was kept locked and never used.

Washam originally lived next door to the Silver Moon in a small white house with a picket fence. The Silver Moon's dice games expanded into the house after Washam moved his family to downtown Newport. For a while, the three gambling sites—Tarkington's Green House, the Silver Moon's back room, and Washam's white house—operated in close proximity.

Gamblers often parked in the alley behind the club, their vehicles less visible to the street as the gaming continued into the morning hours long after music patrons were gone. When anti-gambling enforcement increased in the early 1960s, the Silver Moon responded with discretion. Washam installed a drop-down set of stairs in the ceiling above his office and moved the games to the club's attic where a dice table accommodated twelve to fifteen people.

"They didn't play every night, but when the big rollers came in from Missouri and elsewhere, the word would get out that a game would go that night," Jim Dupree said. "Several locals also played, but this wasn't for the common folks."

As long as Newport clubs maintained decorum, authorities were willing to disregard state laws prohibiting gambling. "Gambling was an old time standard in Newport, always considered an interesting part of town and not needing much enforcement," Sam Boyce said.

And local leaders preferred circumspect warnings rather than direct action. When complaints about the gambling were filed in 1953, a Jackson County grand jury requested that its investigative report be given "wide publicity so that any persons engaged in that activity may have sufficient notice to stop that unlawful procedure." Ever cautious of impugning Newport's moral character, the report suggested that public officials "try to prevent and stop any gambling, if any exists."[120]

When a club was padlocked, the public nuisance charges often stemmed from fighting and drinking. Similar to other towns, Newport's wealthy and powerful were subject to much gossip, but it was common people that often bore the brunt of enforcement.

On a Sunday morning in July 1951, a task force of ABC agents, state troopers, and county sheriff deputies raided Club 67, an establishment described in the newspaper as "a night club for negroes." The offi-

271

cers found a cache of iced-down beer being served by a waitress. The club's owner, charged with Sunday sales and sales without a license, was fined $150. About this same time, the state Revenue Commission granted a renewal of Bob Fortune's permit to sell liquor, citing insufficient evidence regarding allegations that he sold whiskey below the minimum price and sold to bootleggers.[121]

Charles Watson recalled encounters with the ABC when he leased the Silver Moon in the late 1950s. The agency had introduced arbitrary and unenforceable policies, he said, such as requiring whiskey bottles brought into clubs to be kept underneath the tables or allowing people to continue to drink their bottled beverages after beer sales ended at midnight. Owners of the clubs that violated these odd rules, Watson said, often received offers from local lawyers to help them avoid charges.

Summoned to an ABC hearing in Little Rock concerning allegations of Sunday beer sales, Watson said he was told to halt all beer sales for two weeks. "I think the ABC man was upset because my waitress wouldn't go out with him," Watson said. "They said, 'If you let us pull your license for two weeks, it would help us.' I agreed, but I got them to let me keep the beer inside, not have to sell it back to the distributor and then restock. After the meeting, an ABC man whispered to me, 'Don't sell too much beer when you're closed.'"

Watson suggested that a Newport alcohol distributor and power broker influenced the state and county-level enforcement by controlling local elections of sheriffs and constables. This was done by buying large amounts of poll tax, $1 each at the time, and bringing low-income voters, mostly black citizens, to the voting sites. As a result, Watson said, local deputies were uninvolved in pay offs and local police departments did not make uninvited appearances at the clubs.

One of Newport's most prominent attorneys at this time was Fred Pickens, a man whose courtroom skills earned him the nickname Fred "Pick 'em Clean" Pickens. Pickens' legal eloquence was admired by Doc Hawk, who related the story of Pickens gaining an acquittal for a man charged with stealing a hog. After the trial, Pickens asked the man if he did steal the animal. Hawk said the man answered, "Well, Mr. Fred, I thought I did, but after hearing you talk about it, I don't know."

Pickens came from a distinguished Arkansas family, and he served as chairman of the Board of Trustees at the University of Arkansas. But his wide involvement in Newport business and politics caused much speculation. John Harkey suggested that Pickens may have been motivated by an unsuccessful bid for Jackson County prosecuting attorney in 1946. "Fred was the golden boy, the chosen one, who might have been governor one day," Harkey said, "but losing that race to Millard Hardin, a country boy from Tupelo, might have given him the idea that he had to control all this."

Despite local and state enforcement, the perception remained in Newport that club owners who knew the right people could keep their businesses in operation. "If you wanted off of something, you called Fred," Elton Davenport said. "If something moved in this town, Pickens and Fortune wanted a piece of it."

Money on the Table

In the large, windowless room, men leaned over a pool table with dollars in their hands. A green cloth had been draped over the table, and loose piles of bills lay on the surface, $15,000 or more when the game was hot. The room had an odor of old beer and strong whiskey, and a haze of cigarette smoke hovered below the ceiling. Nights when a band was playing, the gamblers could hear the muffled music through the Silver Moon's stone walls. But they cared little for that when the green money lay out before them. Their eyes followed the dice thrown across the table as the shooter shouted his urgent commands to the numbers.

The "fader" watched with cool detachment. He matched the bets each man laid down, peeling the bills from the house bankroll and placing them on top of the gamblers' money. When a shooter "caught a point," the fader laid down a playing card with the elusive number to be hit on the next roll. Then more dollars were slapped onto the table, and the men called out their numbers as the dice were thrown.

The "stick man" used a long wooden tool to rake in the dice after each throw. It was bad luck, the players believed, if someone touched the dice between their rolls. There was a brief moment of stillness when all new bets had been placed, when the gamblers eyed the small field of cash and cards laid out on the table before them. For some who were farmers, the moment may have had a haunting similarity to their efforts in the fields, looking down a row of newly plowed and planted earth, the green spears of emerging cotton plants offering their own risky allure. Then the stick man pushed the small white cubes across the green cloth and the action resumed.

"It was all cash, no chips," Doc Hawk said. "We always paid in advance, and the money would just lay there. Mostly, we played with people we knew and had no trouble."

Hawk learned the fader's trade and the operation of Jackson County dice games in Swifton. His parents were field hands, even poorer than sharecroppers, he said. Their house had holes in the floor, and the windows lacked screens to keep out flies. Like others of his generation, Hawk moved away after high school. He worked at a steel mill in Michigan. Within a year, he was back in Arkansas. His older sister Evelyn married local club owner Bob King, who offered him a job. It was 1956, and Hawk was nineteen years old.

Two years later, Hawk was working at the Silver Moon, where Washam furnished the house money, usually a $10,000 bankroll, and where the games might continue without break from one afternoon until the evening of the next day. Not every game was a big play, Hawk said. Some rainy days, only a handful of local farmers might be passing the time with a low-dollar game.

Hawk knew half a dozen clubs in Jackson County where men shot dice. Some clubs also had poker tables. In addition, a few black clubs had backroom gambling where white players went after the Silver Moon closed. The "Y" was a black club in downtown Newport operated by Booker T. Washington. Dice games were played on a blanket and without a house bankroll. The men faded each other's bets, Hawk said.

"If I wanted to shoot $2, you would fade that with $2.20," he explained. "Booker would end up with all the change. He had a cigar box full of it."

Black gambling clubs used leather, funnel-shaped devices known as "horns." Dice were individually dropped into the small end of the horn, and they fell through a set of leather strings inside. When the

274

horn was lifted, the numbers shown on the dice were the gambler's roll. The horn kept gamblers from palming the dice, Hawk said, as some skilled players could hold two 1's together to avoid rolling craps or "snake eyes."

"Booker also made a little extra money by charging a dime if the dice fell out of the top of the horn," Hawk said. "He charged you a quarter if the dice fell to the floor."

The black colloquialism "Put it in the horn" came from this gambling device. White clubs did not use a horn, though at times a small "whip cup" was employed to keep players from palming the dice.

The gregarious Hawk left Jackson County's gaming tables in 1967 to open a restaurant in Louisiana, where he found a successful niche in the hospitality industry. He continued to operate a Newport catering business in 2007. Like the host of an expansive buffet, Hawk is a raconteur who serves a feast of memories and stories about the musicians, club owners, and gamblers from Newport's exuberant past.

"We didn't have a salary," Hawk said of his days at the dice table, "but we got a percentage of the winnings, sometimes twenty-five percent. And sometimes we'd go broke. We made a living, but it was fast money and we spent it all."

Nights at the Silver Moon

It got to be the thing to do, to go to the Silver Moon. In other words, it was the "in" thing back them. The Silver Moon was everything.
—Sonny Burgess

Stringy patches of weeds poke through the cracks of a broken concrete slab and the scattered gravel at the roadside site. In a drainage ditch alongside the hardscrabble clearing, entangled vines and weeds have woven a thick netting over a low strip of rubble. The concrete and stone remnants of the Silver Moon, bulldozed there nearly three decades ago, are slowly receding into the earth.

Vehicles on the highway sweep by with a droning hum of tires. The wind carries a faint metallic tang of diesel exhaust and asphalt. In the surrounding streets of north Newport, power poles maintain a tilted stance, many showing the effects of years of harsh weather, curved like a spine of aging bones.

Sonny walked among the debris and weeds on the familiar ground where the Silver Moon once stood, his white hair blowing in the breeze, dark glasses shielding his eyes from the bright spring sunlight. He stood on a patch of blue floor tile that once marked the club entrance and gestured across the site.

The Silver Moon in the 1950s. A roadside marque proclaimed it "Home of Famous Bands."

"The front of Silver Moon was here, close to the highway," Sonny said, sweeping his arm as he spoke. He pointed to the south side of the lot. "The original bandstand used to be there. You couldn't get but a couple hundred people in the original Moon, but when Don added on, you could get nearly a thousand in."

When Don Washam was ready to sell the club in the late 1960s, he first offered it to Sonny and Newport businessman James Free, Sonny's friend since childhood. A local farmer and gambler, Abe Jones, offered to back the men with $55,000, Washam's asking price.

"James wanted it, but I didn't," Sonny said. "I didn't want to be in the night club business and have to put up with the drunks."

A High-Class Honky Tonk

The club evolved much like Newport itself, rebounding from fires and changing economic fortunes. The original structure was a small, dark building on the open spaces north of town, a "trashy place," one older man said, offering little more than cold beer and a jukebox to local farmers. In the early 1940s, downtown Newport and the saloons along Front Street drew the nightlife business. But the huge airbase installation in east Newport and the explosive population growth that followed brought rapid change.

Don Washam planned a night club that could host orchestra-style performers such as Tommy Dorsey, Glenn Miller, and Louis Armstrong. His first addition was a small stage and dance area. By the mid-1950s, two additional expansions had transformed the squat cinderblock building into the largest club in the state, a 7,200-square-foot, rock-walled structure with an enormous dance hall. An unusual feature of the dancing area was its ceiling, where short strands of bare copper wire hung in evenly spaced rows. The non-electrified wires vibrated with music from the bandstand and served as a rudimentary device to carry the sound to the far rear of the room. The wires were likely installed by electrical wizard and early Silver Moon band leader Jimmy Davidson, Sonny said.

With its innovative sound system and a roadside sign proclaiming "Silver Moon, Home of Famous Bands" the club was no longer just a place for farm workers to drink beer and fight, Jim Dupree said. The Silver Moon had become a "high-class honky-tonk."

Martha Shoffner remembered the club's dance area as "a huge room with rock columns, lots of tables and starched white tablecloths, and a large hardwood dance floor that was always clean, at least until the end of the evening." Shoffner, born into a wealthy Jackson County family, was one of three Jackson County natives of Arkansas political prominence in 2006; Shoffner was elected state treasurer, Jim Wood was elected state auditor, and Mike Beebe became governor that year. (Shoffner was reelected in 2010, but she resigned from the office in 2013 after being indicted by a federal grand jury on charges of receipt of a bribe and extortion.)

The Pacers at the Silver Moon, with Jack Nance on drums. Note the ceiling wires, which were rows of bare copper wire, non-electrified, installed as a basic amplification enhancement.

Shoffner said she was raised with a social status that included charm school and a dress code of white gloves at Easter. "It was a very proper time," Shoffner said of her childhood. "We knew how to sit at the Silver Moon, with our knees together. As girls, we would slip into the Silver Moon on a summer's evening. You would feel the cold air as soon as you came in and smell the beer from the long bar. We'd go in the dance hall and get our hands stamped. We had to hide that mark on Sunday mornings when we went to church."

The Silver Moon's reputation as a rough place was affirmed by Johnny Ray Hubbard, who knew the site as an employee, a patron, and a performer. "It was daresome for a strange woman to come into that place," he said. "Somebody tried to get under that dress tail before she got out the door."

Phyllis Holmes recalled her first teenaged visit to the Silver Moon's dance hall when the large room featured tablecloths and candles.

Holmes said she was unaware the elegant club also was a venue for "ladies of the night" and that fights could break out at any time. "As a proper girl, there were things I wasn't to do—smoke, drink, or go to the Silver Moon," Holmes said. "I remember when the fights broke out; I climbed under the table thinking, 'My mother is going to kill me.'"

Betty Castleberry, the beauty pageant winner, recalled hearing about fights at the Silver Moon when she played bridge with her girl-friends. "It was kind of daring to go there, but it wouldn't ruin your reputation," Castleberry said. "You were labeled a 'bad girl' if you went to see Elvis, but not a prude. I remember my friends had been to see Elvis there, and we were all hanging on to the story when they told it."

Clever teenagers determined to enter the club used false identification cards whose printed birthdates were rarely scrutinized in the dim interior lighting. Dorsey Jackson, whose family was one of the largest landowners in the county, got inside the Silver Moon to see stars such as Conway Twitty and Jerry Lee Lewis. Sometimes he was accompanied by his high-spirited friend Doc Hawk for an evening of hilarity, such as the time they brought a drunken, miniature burro onto the dance floor, a prank the boys repeated at the B & I Club in Swifton.

"There were no photo cards then," Jackson said. "I used a card passed down from relatives. I was sixteen, and my ID said I was forty-six."

To raise the stature of his club, Washam hired local policeman Ben Lindsey for nightly security, and he instituted a punishment system that banned fighters for two weeks. Yet through it all, the Silver Moon remained a local bar to its loyal patrons—a place to shoot pool, to talk and flirt as you sat in a booth, to listen to the new music and watch the dancers.

Newport's young adults went to the Silver Moon hoping something good would happen, Steve Stephens said, perhaps meet a girl in the bar or take a date to the dark and seductive dance area in the back. "You felt like you were at the center of nighttime activity at the Silver Moon," Stephens said, confessing that he spent enough time in the club to declare rights to his own booth.

He was joined there by wealthy farmers and Razorback football players, middle-class store keepers and military veterans like himself home from Korea. Holiday shows were sold-out affairs—the Pacers on Christmas Eve, Ronnie Hawkins on New Year's night. The night before Thanksgiving, the club was filled for the annual Firemen's Ball, repeatedly drawing such overflow crowds that duplicate parties were held at Porky's Rooftop Drive In. Latecomers sent to Porky's likely felt slighted by that less-prestigious venue.

"Porky's got the rednecks and the toughs," Sonny said. "Don got the upper class at the Moon, the money people and those that wanted to be that way. He would close at midnight on Saturday because he didn't want the lower end of Front Street and Porky's coming there."

Despite the bouncers, and the prestige of the Silver Moon's big-name acts, the club never shed its local reputation as a place for wild partying. Harvey Haley said he often performed there as a teenager in the 1950s when his underage band worked for beer. He played there again in the 1960s when he worked as band director at Newport High School. Retired from an extensive career in music education, Haley still talked about his days on the bandstand at the Silver Moon, describing a near-feral scene of flying beer cans, screaming dancers, and a dark, crowded room where he believes more than dancing took place on the floor at the foot of the stage.

"There were always more legends about the Silver Moon than truth," Mike Beebe said. "There was a joke about parking your chainsaw at the door. And another about the club not admitting twelve year olds; you had to be thirteen to get in."

Newport's religious community made little effort to separate rumors from truth, according to Watson, who grew up in a local Baptist church. Watson said he was warned at an early age of the sinful club and told stories of murder and buried bodies at the site. "I was told that clubs like the Silver Moon were the worst places you could go," he said. "That talk came from people who had never been there. It never was as bad as I was told when in church."

When Watson's mother learned he had leased the club, she spoke her mind. They were attending church when she suggested that the people in the sanctuary and the moral atmosphere there were superior to the company her son found at the club. "I said, 'Mother, the people you see here, the deacons and secretaries, are the same people I see in the Silver Moon,'" Watson said. "She told me to shut up."

Stephens recalled a similar admonition from his mother. "She would tell me, 'Son, be careful at Silver Moon.' I said, 'Mother, I've been in the Marines four years. I can handle myself.'"

Managing the Moon

When a fire destroyed the building in 1987, the original Silver Moon had operated for more than forty-five years. There were intermittent periods in the 1960s when Newport public officials padlocked the club, and changes in ownership for a while renamed the business "The 21 Club." But peak years for the club came when Watson managed the site from 1959 to 1961, when the landmark institution commonly had its two-acre parking lot filled to overflowing.

"I tried to have a big-name act once a month," Watson said. "I knew people couldn't afford to come to every show, so I wanted them to have money to spend when I had the big ones."

Watson understood that people worked hard for money to enter the club. In the summer, many paid him with the dimes they earned picking strawberries at nearby Bald Knob. The door charge varied: $2 per person for stars such as Bob Wills or Jerry Lee Lewis; $1 per person for the Pacers or other popular acts with lesser national prestige. To publicize a show by Conway Twitty, Watson placed radio ads in Little Rock and Jonesboro. More than 500 table reservations were received before he could cancel the ads, Watson said. Never one to lose an opportunity, Watson then sold standing room admission. "We were packing them in," he said. "If Sonny was on Saturday night, we always had a full crowd."

"We'd open at 7 a.m. if it was raining," Watson continued. "Every farmer was there drinking beer. If the crowd got bigger, we'd open up the back gambling part. When those farmers hit a good rice harvest, they had big money."

Watson's lease of the Silver Moon gave him control of all aspects of the club, including the backroom gambling. "I ran my part of the club, and Don ran the gambling in his old house," Watson said. "It was mostly professional gamblers, not just common folks that would drop a few dollars."

Watson took the successful club to new levels. His affable personality and his experience in café management and restaurant equipment sales were a good fit. He took his eight-person staff to Memphis twice a year as a reward for their working on holidays. He maintained the building and cleared the large parking lot of empty beer cans every night. And he started a dress code that prohibited entry to men in overalls. In the dance area, women wore dresses and men wore coats and ties.

Watson's friendship with performers such as Sonny and Conway Twitty was rewarded by their repeated bookings at the club. The crowds were big, and money flowed. When the Silver Moon shut down at midnight, hundreds of people would head to the all-night restaurants that operated along Highway 67. Watson and his top employee Doc Hawk frequently went to Memphis.

"We'd close up the Silver Moon at midnight and be in West Memphis by 2 a.m.," Watson said. "Clubs like the Plantation Inn and Cotton Club were open all night."

Watson celebrated his success by buying a new Cadillac, despite advice from Washam about keeping a low profile. "Don told me if I bought that car, it would cost me," he said. "People were jealous."

Though he grew up in Newport and was familiar with the relationships that accompanied alcohol sales and gambling, Watson said he refused to make the payoffs that kept the system going. He believed he could avoid the practice because he operated the largest club in Arkansas, bought enormous quantities of beer from local distributors, and maintained his own security through a local constable inside the club.

On one occasion, Watson attempted to raise public awareness of the Silver Moon's positive impact on Newport's economy. From a Memphis bank, he obtained approximately 500 new silver dollar coins. He gave them to people as part of their change at the door of the club. Within an hour the Newport police chief arrived at the club to ask how he could get some of the popular coins. "Those silver dollars flooded the town," Watson said. "I was trying to show people how much money would come to Newport through the clubs."

Watson said he often went to Memphis on Sundays because people asked him to sell cases of beer that day. Through his clever discretion, Watson avoided potential allegations of illegal sales by people who meant him harm. The technique did not protect him from others who felt they were due some of his profits, however. "I didn't pay people off, and that got me in trouble," he said.

Two years at the Silver Moon were enough for Watson. Married in 1961, he moved to Tupelo, Mississippi, and joined his father-in-law in a business there. Still in Tupelo in 2014, he operates a large dance hall and is highly involved in promoting the town's musical heritage through its annual Elvis Presley Festival. Sonny and the Pacers have been regular performers at the festival and the Tupelo club. Not surprisingly, Watson's latest business venture, which features hundreds of photographs and memorabilia from the early years of rock and roll, is named the Silver Moon Club of Tupelo.

The Performers

You always wanted to play at the Silver Moon. It made you feel you could be part of something special.

—Johnny Scroggins

"The Moon used to get everybody that came through the area," Sonny recalled. Sun Records artists and other rock and rollers were among the most popular. Jerry Lee Lewis slammed the piano keys with "Great Balls of Fire," breaking the strings on the instrument. Carl Perkins tossed his blue suede shoes into the crowd of excited dancers. In October 1955, the Newport newspaper touted a Monday night show when local favorites, the Moonlighters, appeared with Elvis Presley, described as "the king of western bop…a 20-year old songster who has set the field of country music to talking with his unusual combination of folk music spiced with a 'rock and roll' beat."

The following summer, a newspaper ad proclaimed "the biggest Hill-Billy rock and roll show ever to hit this part of the country" would give two performances on July 17, 1956—the first, an outdoor concert at

Memorial Field, followed by "music for dancing" at the Silver Moon. Headliners at the shows were Johnny Cash, Roy Orbison, Warren Smith, and Eddie Bond. A week later, the Pacers' debut record was in Front Street stores, and "We Wanna Boogie" became the rallying cry of Silver Moon patrons eager to show their town pride through wild dancing.

Following the club's last remodeling in 1954, seating capacity of the spacious venue was reported in the newspaper as 600, though far larger numbers were recalled by performers and managers.[122] The overflow audiences may have stood along the walls or sat at long tables not part of the original floor plan. Given the attendance at other Newport musical events, the estimates seem plausible. The annual Farmers Day concert, conducted at the high school football field, frequently drew 7,000 to 8,000 attendees.

Ray Pearl and his Musical Gems Orchestra performed at the Silver Moon's 1954 reopening party and dance. The Chicago-based orchestra traveled widely and appeared in the "biggest hotels across the nation," a Newport newspaper ad for the event stated. At this time, the popularity of Pearl's big band and others like it was being challenged by smaller ensemble groups and the first individual rock and roll performers. But Don Washam planned on a traditional sound for his club's reopening with an orchestra whose style had been described in the Chicago press as "Play it sweet—play it smooth—play it dreamy."[123] In Newport, the newspaper ad encouraged people to "Get in on the fun. No be-bop, re-bop, or rag mop for the Musical Gems."

Local performers such as Punky Caldwell's group from Searcy and Newport's own big band, the Townsmen, continued to play at the club, but public taste was moving toward up-tempo rhythms and new dance styles. Bob Wills and His Texas Playboys frequently played their western swing music at the club in the late 1940s and early 1950s. The Memphis-based Snearly Ranch Boys was another band with a western or country sound very popular at the Silver Moon. And nationally popular groups, their music commonly called progressive or big band jazz, frequently played there. These included orchestras led by the Dorsey brothers, Jan Gardner, Freddy Martin, Stan Kenton, Paul Neighbors, Woody Herman, and others.

"The Pacers opened for Glenn Miller with Tex Beneke in early 1956," Sonny said. "'Red Headed Woman' just came out, and we were hot. In the last part of our show, several of Miller's musicians came on stage and played with us. They fit right in with what we were playing. People don't realize how good those guys were."

Prominent black musicians and groups began performing at the Silver Moon in the mid-1950s. Louis Armstrong appeared there in May 1954, the first black artist Sonny recalled playing at the club. He was followed by black musicians from Memphis: band leaders such as Willie Mitchell, Gene "Bowlegs" Miller, Wayne Jackson, Luther Steinberg, and others. These black artists were already popular with white audiences at the Plantation Inn in West Memphis, where white patrons danced to black music.

In the early 1960s, nationally famous black artists such as the Coasters and Fats Domino played at the Silver Moon. In the early years of the civil rights movement, black performers were accepted, but black patrons were not. That social contradiction was evident when Watson came to the Silver Moon one afternoon and found four black men waiting in the parking lot. They were the Coasters, on the bill to perform that night with Sonny and the Kings IV as back-up. Watson said the men were reluctant to enter the club on their own, knowing they would not be well received.

Dancers and Brawlers

Drinking and women starts more fights. Women still rule the world.
—Sonny Burgess

For girls from privileged homes, an evening of dancing at the Silver Moon was the perfect end to a summer's day. Both Martha Shoffner and Phyllis Holmes spoke of idyllic afternoons of boating parties on the White River, the predictable arrival of college boys with coolers of beer in their car trunks, and the girls' elusive promises of a nighttime rendezvous. Augusta High School cheerleader and homecoming queen Diane Siebert recalled bunking parties at her family's cabin on "The

Bay," a swimming area at that nearby White River town, and riding upriver for water festivals at Newport where her father, Augusta police chief Walter Jimerson, officiated at boat races.

The young women led the wholesome lives of small-town teenagers in the 1950s.

"Our after-school ritual was to go to the drugstore for Cokes and sit in a booth and talk, the same as our mothers had done that morning over coffee after they got us off to school," Siebert said. "On Saturday afternoons, our role was to be beautiful for whatever happened on Saturday night. Nothing ever did. But boys from Newport and Searcy would come to Augusta to find us."

The nights Siebert and her friends could not be found in Augusta, they were often driving to the Silver Moon. "With my girlfriends' help, I would sneak Daddy's car out of the garage and push it down the long driveway before turning on the motor," she said. "It was a forty-minute drive to Newport. There were fine, good-looking boys there."

Siebert had been taught the "Arkansas Push" in Augusta from a black teenager whose mother was the family's maid. She and her girl-friends practiced with each other, dancing to records of black music purchased, despite her mother's disapproval, when they shopped in Memphis. At the Silver Moon, Siebert and her friends found dancers who knew the current styles. They were often the "bad boys" who invited girls to the parking lot for necking, invitations never accepted by girls who cared about their reputations, Siebert said.

"One of us girls fell in love with the drummer in Sonny's band," Siebert said. "He was a hell of a dancer. He was fast; meaning, he was dangerous and fun."

In Jonesboro to the north, popular high school students John James and Susan Brown followed a similar pattern. John was well known in school because he had won a music program on *Pride of the Southland*, a Memphis television show. Susan had taken years of voice and tap lessons. She played basketball at Catholic High.

"Johnny had a car, a black and white 1955 Chevy," Susan said. "He was cute, tall and athletic, and he could dance. Mother said I couldn't date him because he had a bad reputation. But I did."

286

The two teenagers, married adults today, went to Swifton, Trumann, and Paragould for nights of dancing and fun. Susan remembered initially thinking of Newport as a "hick, one-horse town." Her opinion changed once they started going to the Silver Moon.

"It was exciting to get in," Susan said. "We didn't have fake IDs, but they didn't check us at the door. We were sixteen or so. Sometimes, we took bottles in. We stayed until it closed and got home by 2:00 a.m."

By ten o'clock on a typical weekend evening, Sonny and the Pacers would have the Silver Moon crowd enthusiastically dancing. The low stage gave musicians enough elevation to see when the dancing changed. "You could see across the Silver Moon and know when a fight was starting," Sonny said. "It was usually when we played something fast. So we'd change to a waltz and get into a slower tempo."

Doc Hawk recalled more than a dozen fights the night Fats Domino played at the club, the star's handlers pulling him from the stage each time a melee stopped the show and the club's bouncers moved people outside.

"There were tremendous fights, mostly fists, though once in a while a beer bottle was used," Kern Kennedy recalled. "But people didn't kill each other. The fights were just part of life, and then people would be friends again. That was the style. It was a certain code of honor you don't have today."

Susan James remembered a night when the band was on break and someone threw a beer bottle across the dance floor. "Both sides stood up like it was orchestrated and met in the middle of the room before the bouncers stepped in," she said. "It was a bunch of drunken rednecks whose attitude was 'I don't like your looks and I'm going to change them.'"

"I remember how barbaric it was," she added. "But that's what males did. Like hunting, it was part of the local culture."

The King of Clubs

What I've done all my life is run that club. It's my life. Fifty-five years behind a beer joint.

—Bob King

On a Saturday night in 1953, Sonny and some Newport friends drove up Highway 67 to Swifton. They were the Rocky Road Ramblers, the band Sonny had put together when he returned from the army earlier that year. Sonny had heard that a Swifton café, the B&I Club, was drawing lively crowds with a recently added dancing area and jukebox. He hoped to convince the owner Bob King that live music would be a good fit for the club.

As the musicians' car drove into the gravel parking lot, the screen door of the small white building slammed open and a cluster of three fighting men spilled out. In the midst of the brawlers, a smaller man was smacking the two fighters with a blackjack as he forced them outside. As the fighters broke apart and stumbled for safety, the man shouted at them and pointed to the parked cars. He stood in the doorway for a moment and looked about with authority, then pocketed the blackjack and reentered the building. As the stillness of the summer night returned, the boys in the car could hear the music of the jukebox from inside the club continuing its song of the honky tonk life.

"That really scared us when the screen door blew open and people came falling out, Bob in the middle of them with that blackjack in his hand," Sonny recalled. "We hadn't been hanging out at clubs and didn't know what to expect. We just went home."

Within a short time, however, Sonny's band was hired to play Friday nights at the Swifton club. King was aware of the increasing popularity of live music at the Silver Moon, and he recognized that his venue, though smaller and less glamorous, could also attract top performers. In the years that followed, King booked some of the nation's leading country and rock and roll musicians. Photos signed by the stars and newspaper articles about the club eventually covered a long "Wall of Fame" inside the B&I. The headline of one news story declared, "The

House That Rock Built. Arkansas Nightspot Is Legendary For Beer, Brawls And Barbecue."

In the 2000 article, King recounted an early incident when he expanded his original café with a dancing area: "I built a 20' x 20' area onto the front of the place. We had a curtain and you played the jukebox and people would go in there and dance. You didn't have no band then. Everybody called it 'dancing behind the curtain.' Then we built the club. It was 1953 when the club opened. I will never forget that. Somebody got into a fight and I tried to stop it and the guy hit me between the eyes with a beer bottle. Of course, the next day I had two black eyes."[124]

Similar to Newport, Swifton offered a choice of night spots. In addition to the B&I Club (named for Bob and Imogene, his first wife), Charley Bryant's 67 Club was well known for gambling. Another popular site was Mike's Place, a drinking, dancing, and backroom gambling site operated by Mike Hulen, a navy veteran like King who established a roadside business in his hometown.

"Bob got the country folks, which was great for us," Sonny recalled. "They'd come out of the farms, and they'd get drunk. They'd bring their babies in there, set them on the tables, and go dance. Mike got the more sophisticated town folks. He didn't want the rednecks."

At the B&I Club, music and dancing were in a dark, low-ceilinged room with chairs and tables to accommodate 250 people. In the mid-1950s, dancers packed the club: Friday nights for the Moonlighters and Saturday nights to hear the Searcy saxophonist Punky Caldwell. A large fan behind the stage tried to cool the overheated dancers but did little more than force musicians to constantly retune their instruments, Sonny recalled.

For Sonny, memories of the music and the crowds of bodies in the darkness of the dance floor are mixed with the blur of barroom antics: a midget who played the drums; a guy who fell through the ceiling; the time someone threw dynamite at the stage when the club was closed; and the Mexican burro drunk on tequila, brought onto the dance floor and then left in the back seat of King's 1951 Oldsmobile convertible.

Despite the nights of revelry and inebriation, King believed the country people who patronized his club had a personal dignity that has been lost in the modern age. "Back then, people that worked on the farm would come in and get to drinking and cutting up," King said, "and somebody would say they could or couldn't whup someone else. The next thing you know the two of them would go outside and fight. When they returned, they'd shake hands and that was the end of it. They'd often buy each other a beer. Sometimes, the winner would buy beer for the whole table."

Not all patrons were good-natured country folk eager for dancing and fun. King and other bar owners in small southern towns had customers who were mean-spirited, hardened men, volatile and dangerous, who drank too much after losing at the backroom dice table, who carried long, thin knives known as "pig stickers." King kept his blackjack handy. At times, a shotgun was kept under the bar. King also had an off-duty Arkansas State Trooper providing security.

The Swifton club owner could be as tough as necessary, but over many years King became known for his generosity and camaraderie. Watson called him "a big-hearted guy who would give you his last nickel, who gave away more than he took in." And a story is often told of King's lifetime friendship with Conway Twitty and the gambling money returned to the musician. King always credited his club's longevity and success to his second wife, Evelyn Hawk, a Swifton woman who worked as a waitress at Mike Hulen's club when she and King married. For more than fifty years, Evelyn kept the B&I books and kept the club solvent.

In the fall of 1955, King and Evelyn saw Elvis perform in Memphis. King contacted booking agent Bob Neal about bringing the young singer to Swifton. Elvis was paid $400 to play at the B&I. For an extra $50, King also arranged for Elvis and Johnny Cash, his opening act, to perform at a Swifton High School student fundraising event. One of the students was Evelyn's younger brother Doc Hawk, whose classmates were raising money for a senior class trip. King later gave Hawk his first job, cleaning up the B&I Club when it was closed on Sundays.

The night of December 9, 1955, remains a milestone in the musical heritage of Jackson County. Stories of the high school performance are still told by former students, at the time nearly hysterical girls screaming for their teen idol or curious boys who scoffed at the singer's impact on their girlfriends. Later that night, fans at the packed B&I Club were delighted as Elvis cavorted on stage with the Moonlighters and their talented guest, Punky Caldwell on clarinet. King, as well, has added to the legends of that night, retelling a conversation with Elvis. "Elvis asked me if I'd give Cash $10 to get him to sing a song," King said. "I told him no, I'd give him $20 to sing three songs."[125]

Like other memories from an earlier time, King's anecdote might be a mixture of fact and folklore. Since Cash had already been paid to perform at the club and the high school, King's bonus offer may have been little more than a playful exchange between the men.

Bob King died in 2008 at the age of 83. In 2010, a fire destroyed the roadhouse he opened in 1951 and operated through its final restructuring into two venues, the King's Capri and the King of Clubs. Evelyn passed away in 2012.

The memories remain. Swifton native Jim Harvey recalled carloads of girls arriving on Saturday nights from Arkansas State Teachers College two hours away in Conway. Newport teenager Phil McDonald recalled Elvis buying a condom from the B&I men's room machine, a girl from Tuckerman supposedly waiting for him in a truck outside.

Today, a gravel parking lot is the only relic at the site of Jackson County's last great roadhouse where a young and aspiring local musician got his first glimpse of the brawling, sensational life that lay ahead in the next sixty years.

Porky's Rooftop Drive In

If you called ahead, the girl who answered the phone would sometimes say, "Porky's Rough Top." You might hear others in the background laughing at her repeated joke.

Advance calls or reservations were not necessary at the notorious roadside restaurant. Cars drove in to the serving area and a waitress brought out barbeque sandwiches and bottles of cold beer. You could drive away with your food and drink or eat in your car. You could talk to people parked beside you as the jukebox selections played from small speakers on posts. Many evenings, you could hear the music from the open rooftop patio, mostly western waltzes with a fiddle and a steel guitar or an up-tempo hillbilly boogie played by local musicians.

"Porky loved Bob Wills, thought he hung the moon," Sonny said. "Porky had a big western swing band with some top session musicians. In Texas, they would have hit it."

"Free Dancing at Porky's Rooftop, Music by the Arkansas Playboys," newspaper ads commonly announced. Customers went through the restaurant and up the back stairs to find smiling Hershel "Porky" Sellers in a western hat and string tie leading his seven-member group. The small rooftop venue was crowded with couples dancing to the talented local band and, at times, big-name country acts such as Hank Thompson and Ernest Tubb.

As a young man, Sellers was well known in Newport as a dealer in used cars. His father ran the bowling alley at the airbase. In the fall of 1941, Sellers bought and began operating the Sunset Inn, perhaps hoping to book his musical idol Bob Wills at the club. During Christmas week that year, the twenty-three-year-old Sellers made a trip to Detroit, where he married Nan Belle Gangan, a recent divorcee. Perhaps the bombing of Pearl Harbor a few weeks earlier and the rapid mobilization of American military forces convinced Sellers that some extreme steps were necessary. On March 23, 1942, Sellers and his new bride, accompanied by two additional men, robbed the Bank of Tupelo in the south Jackson County farming town.

Hershel "Porky" Sellers operated the popular Porky's Rooftop, a Newport barbeque drive-in restaurant with a music venue on its upper level and gambling in the back room. Sellers' band, the Arkansas Playboys (also known as the White River Playboys), played western swing style music. From left: Johnny Duncan, guitar; Butch George, guitar; Bob Armstrong, piano; Charles Middlestat, drums; Sellers; Jimmy Helms, fiddle; Kinky King, fiddle; Gabby McCuen, steel guitar; 1955. (Photo courtesy of Jimmy Davidson.)

The robbery began just before midnight when Sellers' car pulled up to the Tupelo home of bank cashier H. C. Giles. Nan Belle rang the doorbell while the men waited in the car. When Giles came to the door, Nan delivered her cover speech, that she had been sent to the home from Mrs. Giles' mother in Marked Tree with news that a brother had been injured in the war. Giles brought her into their house, but he and his wife soon found themselves confronted by three men wearing masks and gloves. Two of the men forced Giles to accompany them to the bank and open the vault. After getting the money, they returned to the house and had Giles promise not to turn in an alarm for three hours. The new outlaws made their getaway with $1,162.

Giles kept his word and did not report the robbery until 4 a.m. FBI agents started on the case that afternoon, using the considerable information Mr. and Mrs. Giles gave them about the robbers. The girl, the FBI was told, was not masked. She was nervous and asked for a cigarette to settle her nerves.

Three days later, the four culprits were arrested in Detroit. They admitted to the robbery, and $898 of the stolen money was recovered. They were extradited to Arkansas, where in June 1942 the men were sentenced to three years in the federal penitentiary in El Reno, Oklahoma. Nan Belle's sentence is unknown, but she and Sellers were soon divorced. In later years, the Newport restaurant owner and musician told people he had little interest in a life of crime. Sellers claimed he robbed the bank simply to be excluded from military service during World War II.

By 1947, Sellers re-established himself in Newport with the opening of a drive-in restaurant in the downtown area, his youthful indiscretions of less interest than the lively dancing and tangy barbeque he provided. In October 1951, a grand opening was held for a second Porky's Drive In, this one located across an open field from the radio station KNBY on Highway 67 north of town. The drive-in originally had an open-air roof patio for dining and dancing.

"Porky's started outside in the summer," Jug Wallace recalled. "The mosquitoes would eat your ass off." By the time Elvis performed there in March 1955, walls and a roof had been built and a piano installed. Most of the early rock and roll musicians that performed at the Silver Moon and the B&I Club also played at Porky's, but the drive-in featured more country music acts than the other clubs.

Through the 1950s, ads in the daily newspaper identified the talent appearing at Porky's upstairs room:

- Dance Tuesday night featuring Chuck Harding's Colorado Cowhands (composer of "Honky Tonk Gal" and several other western numbers)—February 1955
- Dance tonight with music by the Arkansas Playboys, presenting Onnie Wheeler, recording and songwriter, featuring "Little Mamma" and "Run 'Em Off"—June 1955
- Bud Deckelman and his orchestra—July 1956
- Sammy Barnhart, followed by Tommy Trent, "hot fiddle man" now with Arkansas Playboys—September 1956

- Jimmy Haggett and his orchestra. Haggett was formerly with the Grand Ole Opry and now a radio announcer at KLCN Blytheville—April 1958
- Grand Ole Opry star Jimmy Newman ("Cry, Cry Darling") and Teddy Riedel of Heber Springs—June 1959

In addition to the music and dancing, Porky's was known for the other honky-tonk essentials: fighting and gambling. "Porky had the toughs from down on Front Street," Sonny said. "He throwed a few of them down the stairs. He could fight with them all."

Gambling was in a small back room with the dice table in a corner. Sonny recalled the attraction of the room to members of the Carl Perkins band. "Porky had a little gambling in the back, and he'd get Clayton, Jay, and Holland back there," Sonny said. "Carl didn't gamble. Porky would win all the money, then he'd turn around and give it back to Carl to give it to them later on."

Perkins' drummer W. S. Holland is the last surviving member of the group. "You meet so many people in your life, and Porky was one of a few you don't ever forget," Holland said. "I can see it now, Clayton throwing dice in a corner of the room. He would lose nearly all his money every time he played. Porky gave us back our money after the gambling. But I told Clayton there was something fixed about those dice."

Sellers died in 1998. The drive-in site is today occupied by an auto parts store. Across the still-empty adjacent field, the deserted KNBY radio building stands. Steve Stephens' career began as a radio announcer there.

"Porky's was a summer novelty, as open air club, often cool and pleasant on the upper level," Stephens said. "It didn't have the wicked aura that the Silver Moon had."

"Little Joints Everywhere"

There were so many clubs back then, little joints everywhere you could play. I played in just about every joint there was.

—Sonny Burgess

At many Arkansas clubs, musicians and customers alike found themselves in a world of wild music, hard drinking, and fighting.

In North Little Rock, the Pacers played at Club 70 and the Top Hat Club. Both clubs had chicken wire protecting their stages in the 1960s. And similar to clubs in Jackson County, both sites were notorious for their brawling, blue-collar patrons.

Rock 'n' Roll Highway (67)
Jackson County section

A - Mike's 67 Club
B - The B and I Club (aka Bob King's King of Clubs)
C - Charlie's Place
D - Swifton High School gymnasium
E - Hartsell's
F - Rainbow Tavern
G - Bloody Bucket
H - American Legion
I - Shamrock
J - Sunset Inn (Home of the beer drinking bear)
K - Silver Moon Club
L - VFW Club
M - Porky's Rooftop
N - KNBY Radio Station
O - Ricky and Ken's Club (Dinner Club and Zoo)
P - Woody's Club
Q - Jarvis' Bamboo Club
R - Newport Armory
S - GB's Place (Possum Grape)

Jackson
County
circa 1955

Jackson County clubs; 1950s. (Courtesy of Rock 'n' Roll Highway 67 Museum.)

The Pacers also played for more refined audiences at Ricky and Kens, a club built by Newport hotel owner Mose Brownstein to attract an elite country club and hunting crowd. And on summer nights in Pocahontas, the band stood on top of a sloping snack bar roof and played for families at the Skylark Drive-In Theater.

At all the sites, performers received an enthusiastic reception from young women. Yet even for Elvis, there were lessons in decorum. In 1955, he was told his performances were no longer welcome at Helena's Catholic Club. The venue was actually a social hall with a gym and stage built by St. Mary's Church. Elvis' third show that year at the site opened with Carl Perkins. Some 500 tickets had been sold out days in advance. After the show, the parish priest Father Keller discovered Elvis backstage signing an autograph on a girl's thigh.

The clubs listed below are among the dozens in northeast Arkansas where the Pacers played.

The **C&R Club** and **Cotton Club** at Trumann had the advantage of being in a wet township. The two clubs were located on opposite sides of Highway 63, which served as overflow parking area when top performers—Jerry Lee Lewis, Carl Perkins, Charlie Rich, Ace Cannon, Narvel Felts, and others—played there. Larry Donn told of Elvis being turned away by a Cotton Club manager who said, "You're never going to get anywhere acting like that on stage."[126]

Trumann was home to Arlen Vaden, who frequented the clubs. The Arkansas musicians he recorded on Vaden Records—Chuck Comer, Teddy Riedel, Bobby Crafford, and Bobby Brown—often played there. Brown, who had a brief stint as a Pacer when he toured with Sonny in 1958, had his first professional booking at the Cotton Club. That same night, Ronnie Hawkins and the Hawks showed up. The club owner convinced the bands to share the bill.

Gunshots and fighting were not uncommon. Riedel recalled the fatal shooting of a bartender at the C&R Club and bouncers carrying blackjacks to eject rowdy patrons. "A lot of the customers would fight just for the fun of it," Riedel said. "People laugh at me when I tell them I carried a gun under my front seat and a Bible in the glove box."

The **Delta Supper Club** at West Helena was located in a salvage yard on the edge of town. Helena native Ed Burks recalled junked cars pushed back for a parking area. In the 1940s, the club was a popular place for dinner and dancing, Burks said. By the 1950s, when local businessman Charlie Halbert was part owner, the club no longer served dinner. It had become a legendary night spot whose performers included country musicians from the Grand Ole Opry, Delta bluesmen, and the first rock bands of Levon Helm, Ronnie Hawkins, and Conway Twitty. The Pacers played there frequently as they traveled to Mississippi and other southern towns. Helm has written that the club's improvised air conditioning was a No. 3 galvanized washtub and a block of ice set in front of a window fan.[127] The club was also well known for its distinctive bar, which had been glued back together after an angry customer cut it in two with a chainsaw.

Jarvis' Club at Newport began when brothers Noble and Eugene Jarvis converted their family's appliance store to a tavern in 1951. The Beech Street club was near the south end of Front Street and Newport's historic red light district. The club was popular with salesmen that worked in northeast Arkansas. The Newport Police Department and jail were nearby.

The club was rebuilt following a 1962 fire, and a parquet dance floor was installed. Charles Jarvis, Noble's son, took over management and began booking live music. In the mid-1960s, Sonny and the Kings IV worked as the house band, playing four nights a week. The club attracted an upper-class and mixed crowd. There was no gambling, and fighting and drunks were rarely seen.

"Charles ran a good club, and we packed them in for seven years," Sonny said. "You had to get a seat before six o'clock, it was so packed."

Mike's Place at Swifton started in 1947, three years before Bob King opened his similar business. Mike Hulen was a U.S. Navy veteran who had earned ten battle stars in World War II as a gunner on the battleship *Missouri*. Opening a small club in his hometown and obtaining a beer license was not difficult for the confident, young entrepreneur. Hulen recalled having $30 in start-up capital at the time.

"I came home and worked for a rice mill at Tuckerman," Hulen said in a 2007 interview. "That was the first check I ever got that wasn't from the government. It was the last one also. I went into business for myself just past my 22nd birthday. I've had my beer license now sixty years."

To keep his business running smoothly, Hulen had to stand up to local toughs. "I did knock three or four of them on the head," he said. And he slept in his liquor store on some occasions. "Some folks thought I only parked my car outside and was not really in there," Hulen said. "One time I heard them banging on the door to get in. I fired through the window and scared them off."

Hulen said he maintained tight control over his club, advising bands on volume and prohibiting gambling. Mike's Place did attract a higher-class clientele than the B&I Club, but Hulen's memories of a gambling prohibition were not shared by all. Johnny James spoke of a continuous craps game in a small room in back of the club. James said he was outside one night, showing a girl his new car. "I turned on the alarm and the gamblers started bailing out of Mike's," he said.

OT's Club at Des Arc was in an old house. "We drove down one Friday, passing guys on tractors going there after dark," Sonny said. "I played in a room the size of a closet. They had sardine cans for ashtrays. But the kids from the college in Conway would come there and fight. There was a deputy sheriff who wore a big felt hat like Dick Tracy. They bloodied him up, and he never came back. One night, a guy shot a hole in ceiling. Another time, some guys were in a fight and the bouncer shot through the ceiling to quiet people down. It had hellacious crowds."

The **67 Club** at Swifton had a hole cut in the wall between the dance area and the bar. Drinks were passed through by owner Charley Bryant.

"It was one of the places where they'd fight every thirty minutes," Sonny said. "Charley had him a tear gas gun, and if a big fight started, he'd just shoot back in there. Everybody and the band had to leave."

The Spot at Des Arc was originally a hunting club. "The place was a dump, with cheap furniture, but it was always full when we played," Sonny said.

A Culture in Transition

Not far from Newport and the Silver Moon was the Plantation Inn at West Memphis, another large, popular Arkansas roadhouse. Both clubs benefited from the outpouring of talent from Memphis, but the Plantation Inn, being closer, could more easily employ the best of Memphis' black musicians. Historian Pete Daniel has written about the club offering teenagers a gateway experience to a southern culture in transition.

> All the patrons were white; all the musicians black. If transgressions occurred at the Plantation Inn, they comprise underage drinking, stimulating dancing, and the thrill of hearing an excellent black band. A high school girl would arrive from a prom with perfect hair and wearing a formal dress, a corsage and white gloves and according to Morris Berger's daughter-in-law, Bettye Berger, leave disheveled, barefoot, corsageless, perspired, and probably smooched.[128]

At the Plantation Inn and elsewhere, black musicians played for white audiences, and the lively dance music assisted in the gradual change in race relations. A few black clubs allowed white musicians to sit in, such as the White Swan and the Cricket Club at Brinkley where Louis Jordan once played. And Jackson County clubs accepted integrated bands. Punky Caldwell's group had two black musicians, and for a while, a black drummer from Newport, Willie Dupens, played with the Moonlighters.

While club owners allowed musicians a small degree of racial interaction, customers did not have the same privileges. Social custom allowed whites to attend black clubs, but black customers were not welcome at white clubs. Bobby Crafford recalled an incident when the Pacers played at the Trio Club in Pine Bluff. Black people wanted to enter, but the manager diverted them, saying the club was already filled to capacity. A week later, Crafford was contacted by FBI agents investigating the incident.

Like many musicians of his generation, Crafford had early exposure to black music. As a boy in Cotton Plant, he went to the tent shows of the traveling Rabbit Foot Minstrels. He also worked as a projectionist at the town movie theater, which offered late screenings of black films featuring Cab Calloway and Louis Jordan. Small-town movie theaters had black patrons sit in restricted balcony areas for general feature films. For the late shows that starred black artists, blacks were allowed open seating because no whites attended.

Arkansas towns used these and other functional compromises to avoid confrontation. But racial conflict was unavoidable, as Jimmy Ford experienced in Little Rock. "We had two black guys in the band, Arthur Grant on drums and Rudy Akins on piano, which caused a lot of problems back then," Ford said. "At white clubs, the blacks had to sit behind the jukebox. They couldn't walk across the room to get a Coke. At black clubs there were no problems until you walked outside. At a club on Little Rock's 9th street, the police threatened to arrest me or turn me over to the KKK. One pulled out his gun. Another slammed me against his car. It was rough. You had to watch your step."

Wine, Women, and Song

I don't care how ugly you are. If you can play music, there will be women.
—Kern Kennedy

The stories are told with a wink and a grin. They recount a time when late night indulgences were a measure of personal success, when young musicians responded to the relentless demands of the dancers, caught up in the momentum of the shows and the off-stage escapades. And when all their youthful energy and stamina were depleted, they would eventually collapse in a state of soggy exhaustion, slumped in the back seat of a car like fallen angels, riding a rural highway as the night sky showed the pale colors of dawn and the flat monotony of the Delta farm land lulled them to sleep.

Helena native and Rockabilly Hall of Fame guitarist C. W. Gatlin recalled his early days when the momentum of the music continued long past roadhouse closing time. When shows at the Silver Moon were over, Gatlin and his bandmates, too wound up to quit, drove to Brinkley and played at the Cricket Club and even later at a rough club on the shore of a nearby lake.

"We'd play the white clubs until they closed, then go to the black clubs," Gatlin said. "Some of the black clubs put Brown Mule tobacco in moonshine and sold it as whiskey. We'd hit that speed and whiskey and play all night long and all day Sunday until the next morning."

The behavior was more than simple thrill-seeking. The appeal of the music and the fulfillment of performance were powerful enticements. Saxophone legend Ace Cannon has known those feelings since he began playing with a popular Memphis band, the Snearly Ranch Boys, some sixty years ago. When Memphis clubs closed at midnight, Cannon and others crossed into Arkansas to sit in with West Memphis bands. On his wedding night in 1953, the musician and his new bride were driving to Hot Springs for their honeymoon when Cannon stopped off to play a gig at the Cotton Club. Bobby Crafford said he also played a show on his wedding night.

If the performers could not put aside the music on their wedding nights, the women who stayed after the shows could not help themselves either. These were the women who lined up on the hotel hallway couch, waiting their turn in a performer's room; women who passed their hotel keys across the bar during the band's break; women who went for long late-night drives; women who took you home, where you climbed out a rear window when a husband arrived.

Things occasionally got out of hand. On a West Coast tour, too much Thunderbird wine sent one of the Pacers falling backward off the stage, taking the drum set with him. Another night, some of the guys smoked cigarettes with ground-up aspirin added to the tobacco. The music was so bad, Sonny recalled, instruments were taken away and the inebriated guys sent home.

Band members hardly ever got involved in fights, though confrontations sometimes arose when a bar patron found a band member with his girl, Sonny said. But these situations were generally brief, he added. People did not get mad at the band. "Bands are kind of taboo, hands off," he said. "People want to talk to you, but they don't want to whip you."

A rockabilly musician's life on the road meant playing as loud as possible and driving as fast and far as possible. Packing up the equipment after an exhausting show could lead to error. At times, band equipment tumbled out of open car windows or fell from roof racks.

"People don't realize how it was to be traveling back then," Sonny said. "With four or five guys and instruments in one little car, you got to take a little drink of whiskey sometimes."

Getting Paid for a Night's Work

Maintaining a band is a bottom-line business with little cash reserve, and club owners sometimes took advantage of the young musicians. Getting paid for a night's work was challenging when a club manager or owner was not there at closing time.

Bobby Crafford had the Pacers in Tulsa when it happened to them. There was nothing to do but pack up and come back the next day. As they were loading the van, a Tulsa police car came by. Bobby told the officers that the club owner had run off without paying them. The cops informed Bobby that the guy was currently at the police station filling out papers about a stolen car. They gave Bobby a ride to the station, where he and the precinct staff confronted the owner. The man reluctantly pulled out his bankroll and paid the band's fee.

There were nights when club owners paid less than the band thought fair. Those conversations sometimes ended with tavern owners pulling out their handguns. And there were times when even a popular club, like the C&R in Trumann, seemed so empty and forlorn, so lacking in promise for the evening's work, that the band turned their vehicle around and drove back to Newport.

When Crafford managed the Pacers in the 1960s, he booked the band at the Cotton Plant American Legion Hut. Renting the building for $15, he hung a few posters in the area and had a full house of dancers buying the $2 tickets. But rarest of all were the nights of big money, the ones that justified all the frustration and sweat.

For Crafford, it took place at the popular 11/70 Club at Hazen. The Pacers were the opening-night band for the new club on Christmas Eve 1961. Bobby remembered the crowds and extra tables placed on the dance floor. A big payoff at the club was followed by a proud moment later that night for the young musician.

"The Pacers got seventy percent of the door, and I probably made $1,500 after I paid the band," Bobby said. "I had a pregnant wife at home. She'd been wanting a new car. I threw that money on the bed, and said, 'Here's your new car.'"

The End of the Road

On a tour in Canada, the Pacers found themselves in a familiar situation—sleeping two to a bed in a cheap hotel room, using band uniforms as extra bed sheets to keep warm. Kern Kennedy raked a fork across the room's ineffective radiator to get the hotel manager's attention and then shouted to the man some floors below, "We're freezing up here."

Johnny Ray Hubbard recalled the frozen roads and long drives with the window of the Cadillac stuck open. The cold weather and the cold personalities of northerners were far from the southern congeniality they had known. One time, a service station owner allowed them to defrost their ice-covered car, a gesture they thought friendly until "we went to thank him and he charged us $6," Hubbard said.

The Canadian clubs had work for the Americans and payment was dependable, but the jobs were like working anywhere. Band members made about $100 per week. They paid for their own hotel rooms and food, always alert to a possible free meal at the clubs. As he approached his 30th birthday, Sonny found the professional life he had eagerly sought some years earlier was wearing thin.

"There wasn't big money in Canada," Sonny said. "You're away from home a couple of weeks and playing clubs that are just another joint. You know there's no future in it."

Living on the road included episodes of late-night highway driving, brakes failing, tires slipping on wet roadways, and swerving off paved roadways to avoid herds of cattle crossing the open western highways. For a time in the early 1960s, the Pacers traveled in a renovated Greyhound bus outfitted with bunk beds and a wall urinal tube. That bus was set on fire one night because, Hubbard suggested, "someone might have found his girlfriend in there, or his wife."

The 1956 car crash of Carl Perkins' band was another reminder of the risks in every journey. Sonny remembered a moment in 1958 when the four band members traveled in his Mercury sedan. Another car, a similar model also with Arkansas license plates, went off the road at Flagstaff and killed all aboard.

"Everyone in Newport thought it was us," Bobby said. "I called the Silver Moon after a few days. I introduced myself and the fellow that answered could hardly talk. I said, 'Tell my wife I'm not dead.' He said they hadn't told her yet."

W. S. Holland, whose longevity in the music industry matches Sonny's, recalled the excitement of one of his first shows, when he and the Perkins brothers played at Helena in 1955. The outdoor show was at a ball field, Holland recalled, with Chet Atkins, Maxine Brown, and the Louvin Brothers also on the bill. Even after gassing up his 1948 Cadillac, Holland took home $17, an amount that far exceeded his wages at a Memphis air conditioning company.

"At the Helena show, three girls tried to get me to stay in Helena and party," Holland said. "I decided to play in a band the rest of my life."

But in time, the girls and the money slowed down, and life on the road seemed less attractive. Four years later, Holland was a changed man. He had played the shows, made the records, and appeared in a movie. Sun Records was no longer the vibrant center of his life. Holland decided to retire from music. "Sam Phillips made all the money he was going to make, and I'd spent all the money I made," Holland said. "I was three payments behind on my Cadillac when I met Joyce. She had a job and a car."

Holland quit the music business. He married and was working full time when Johnny Cash called him for a two-week tour. Holland went on the tour and then took Cash's next offer. He became a permanent member of the band, a relationship that lasted forty years.

Few musicians have that good fortune. Most face burnout in their late twenties and take their lives in other directions. A few who were successful in their early years were able to postpone the inevitable career change. Sonny and Bobby worked to keep the Pacers booked, but a time came for both to put away the music.

"I try to do this thing for fun," Sonny said. "You have a little fun and pick up a dollar or two, that's good. But when you start out not having any fun, just dreading playing, it's time to do something else."

Chapter 12.
A Vanished World

An Era Ends

Originally, the trees were everywhere. The forests of northeast Arkansas were thick with massive hardwoods, stands of virgin timber in the river-bottom wetlands and on the dry flat prairies, ready to be claimed by whoever got to them first. And when the seemingly endless woods were gone, only their names remained as signposts on the corners of downtown Newport streets—Beech and Walnut, Hazel and Pine.

Once, the White River teemed with mussels, fish, and waterfowl, its clear currents shaping the land, forming the wide sandy shoals thick with cattails and the narrow ox bow lakes shaded by lofty cypress tress, their knobby roots rising through the shallow waters. And when the river channel was dredged and the pearls harvested, only the shells remained to be drilled for button blanks and then crushed and mixed with gravel to pave a few downtown alleyways.

Once, the cotton fields were shaped by parallel rows that blossomed in a thick white blanket, the land worked by men and mules, share-cropper and tenant farmer families, Mexican field hands brought in by the truckload, all bent to their labor, their burlap sacks dragging behind them with increasing weight. And as the diesel smoke of the tractors and mechanical cultivators wafted across the land, the manually culti-vated cotton was replaced by less-labor-intensive crops, rice and soy-beans, and only the abandoned shacks and rural cemeteries remained of the vanished world of Delta agriculture.

For a time, Jackson County roadhouses and supper clubs radiated a vibrant energy, their stages blaring out a new, raw sound that gave voice to bold young men who strutted and posed, who shouted their autonomy in the infectious rhythms of rock and roll. And Newport itself, much like the young rockers it produced and the new music created, was overwhelmed in the celebration of its success.

Newport's repeated economic gains and then losses were the result of natural bounty depleted by rapid growth and the lack of sustainable policies. One seemingly unlimited resource after another was lost, the last being the rural labor force to support the arduous work. By the time of the most rapid change, 1960 and afterward, Newport was ablaze with its own wild celebration while also crumbling at the core.

When the wild child called rockabilly matured and softened into the calmer and more melodious rock and roll, Newport as well saw the end of its adolescent growth and its last windfall era. And as its character changed to match that of other Delta towns and Newport began to decline, only the gambling and clubbing remained.

In Newport, the rock and roll played on without interruption, seemingly more frenetic than ever. In the early 1960s, Sonny continued to perform with his new group, the Kings IV, and Bobby Crafford, recruiting new musicians and booking new gigs, kept the Pacers busy. The Silver Moon continued to host huge shows with Jerry Lee Lewis, Ronnie Hawkins, and other big name acts. Across the Delta in Memphis, however, Sam Phillips recognized it was time to change.

"I realized I couldn't do this any longer, couldn't do the type of experimentation I wanted. So I got out of the record business," Phillips said. "If you came through the Depression and didn't learn to be a good business person, you didn't learn much."

Newport's trade economy, like the music industry, was soon to change. And the tribute given the town in the 1954 economic analysis by the Federal Reserve Bank of St. Louis would soon ring hollow.

Saturday crowds at Newport's Front Street began to thin out. Cars no longer had to wait for choice parking spots. Newport's "shop at home" campaigns could not offset improvement of roads and the increasingly common drive to Jonesboro and other Delta towns where stores began providing more variety. The railroads as well, Kaneaster Hodges recalled, evidenced the outmigration.

"When I went to Princeton from 1956 through 1960, the trains were totally full of people leaving Arkansas," Hodges said. "Coming home they were empty."

Collapse of the Agricultural Pyramid, Changes at the Moon

Newport's demise can be represented in the collapse of the three-tiered agricultural pyramid—landowners on top, merchants in the center, and farm workers at the base—that once defined its economic and social structure.

The pyramid's collapse began with an elimination of the bottom tier. Mechanized agriculture and a shift to less-labor-intensive crops initiated the massive outmigration of the last generation of sharecroppers. Fewer farm families working the land resulted in dramatically reduced economic activity at the middle level. Small-town stores closed and businesses shut down. Empty storefronts, diminished municipal tax revenues, and a decreasing population became common.

The upper tier, however, experienced the least change. Still in possession of the land, wealthy families continued their large farm enterprises, often increasing through consolidation of smaller farms. The land continued to provide, whether farmed by locals or leased to external corporations. But a diminished quality of life in town influenced this wealthy group to shop and seek cultural fulfillment elsewhere.

Delta communities became towns of "haves" and "have-nots," an unforeseeable outcome amidst the opportunity and optimism of Newport in the 1950s. This changing economy was accompanied by increased activity at the Silver Moon and other clubs. As more drinking and gambling, more fights and more public nuisance problems became common, public tolerance decreased. The raft of problems was addressed by newly elected enforcement officials who had gained the support of Newport's conservative and religious communities. The first of these was Prosecuting Attorney John Harkey, a Silver Moon patron in his younger days, who responded to public concerns about gambling. Harkey acted on his election platform and rapidly introduced what he said were several previously unheard of measures, including padlocking the Silver Moon for months at a time. "People were very concerned about the gambling, and I had done everything but beg Don Washam to run it right," Harkey said.

The enforcement arm was Jackson County's sheriff Ralph Henderson, whom Harkey said was a "staunch Church of Christ member and very strict to stop all this." Reflective of Jackson County's previous era, Henderson's predecessor had been removed from office after being indicted for tax evasion, Harkey said.

An October 1961 raid on the Silver Moon was reported on the front page of the Newport newspaper, illustrated with photos of the gambling apparatus found in the club's back room. A temporary injunction was issued to suspend business at the club. When Silver Moon operators failed to appear at a hearing to contest the injunction, Circuit Court Judge Andrew Ponder issued a permanent closing order. The newspaper reported that Prosecuting Attorney Harkey had called thirty-two witnesses to testify in his prepared but unused case against the club.

That same month, Newport's Blue Room and two Swifton Clubs— the B&I and Charley Bryant's—had their beer permits suspended or canceled by the state ABC, the actions requested by Harkey. The enforcement crusade included another gambling raid and the arrest of five men in the Lawrence County town of Hoxie. Harkey stated that Jackson County gamblers had moved the game to the northern county to avoid the state investigators he was bringing in.

By the end of his term of office in 1964, Harkey had introduced another landmark action when his courtroom efforts resulted in the murder conviction of a white man sentenced for the killing of a black storekeeper during a robbery. That conviction, the first of its type in the modern South, Harkey said, reflected the racial equality he cultivated when he first ran for public office. "In 1960, I carried Jackson County, going door-to-door in the black community," Harkey said. "That was unheard of before me."

The previous laissez-faire attitude toward the gambling clubs returned when local attorney Sam Boyce replaced Harkey in the prosecutor's office for a two-year period, 1965–1967. A decade earlier, Boyce had frequented the Silver Moon. He performed a magician's act there, wearing a tuxedo and pulling rabbits from a top hat, at times opening for Sonny Burgess. He also arranged shows for the Pacers when he was a student at the University of Arkansas. The Silver Moon's gambling and drinking heritage had no onerous qualities for him, and few enforcement activities at the clubs were reported during his term in office.

But the atmosphere in Newport shifted again in 1967 with the election of Winthrop Rockefeller as Arkansas governor and his use of the Arkansas State Police to shut down gambling in Hot Springs. In Newport, the Hodges brothers, Kaneaster and David, were elected to positions of enforcement—David as Third District prosecuting attorney and Kaneaster as deputy prosecuting attorney and Newport city attorney. The brothers had grown up in Newport, and both had spent time as teenagers at the Silver Moon. Their father, Kaneaster Hodges Sr., was a respected lawyer in town, and the family was held in high esteem. David Hodges was a man of "impeccable ethics," according to Newport School Board president Jim Dupree, who announced he would shut down gambling if elected, including the slot machine at the country club. Kaneaster Hodges Jr. had an Ivy League education and was an ordained Methodist minister.

"From 1967 to 1969, we shut down the Silver Moon and the country club," Kaneaster Hodges, who continues his Newport law practice today, said. "We raided the country club for serving minors and serving alcohol on Sunday. And we found the craps tables at the Silver Moon were rigged. They had a hidden ledge under the table to switch to weighted dice so you would lose after you threw your point. We advertised that in the newspaper and made every effort to make it widely known."

The 1967 raid at the Silver Moon also made public news of the upstairs gambling room, and the ceiling entrance was nailed shut. In early 1968, David Hodges, elected chairman of the State Crime Commission, criticized the enforcement standards of the ABC.[129] Later that year, the agency stepped up its activities, and several Jackson County clubs had their permits suspended, including the Silver Moon again, which had recently changed ownership.[130]

In late 1967, Don Washam was ready for a change. He offered to sell the club to Sonny Burgess, who declined, despite having local backers willing to make the investment. Washam sold the Silver Moon to Jack Brinsfield, and for a time, the business name was changed to Jack's 21 Club. Brinsfield had owned a café and liquor store next door to the Silver Moon since 1948. The sign out front said "Eats…Jack's Place," and the business sold much of the whiskey that patrons brought into the club in paper sacks. Now Highway 67 was being widened and Brinsfield's small building, originally a service station, was to be demolished. The Silver Moon was set back far enough from the new highway to survive the change.

Washam did not have much time left, and the last two years of his life were marked by transition and loss. His son Don recalled that after the sale of the club, the family moved to Detroit, where his father worked in an automobile plant. They returned to Newport by the fall of 1968, renting a house in town until the family could return to its former home. Washam died of leukemia on July 18, 1969.

The Silver Moon continued, despite license suspensions and a diminishing prestige, as lesser artists replaced the headline acts that once performed at the club. And Newport reflected the larger change, evidenced through increased drinking and fighting in clubs and declining activity at Front Street stores.

"The retail businesses closed, but the liquor stores and clubs stayed around," David Stewart recalled. "Most of the prostitution was gone, but there was still a lot of drinking, fighting, and guns. I started on the police department in 1980, and the first five to six years here it was tough. We'd get numerous calls from women in Batesville, asking 'Is my husband in jail?' The word was if you were a policeman in Newport, you could get a job anywhere in state."

The original Silver Moon building was lost in a 1987 fire. Brinsfield replaced the structure with a metal building that sits on the far western edge of the site. Today, his son Grant owns the Silver Moon Banquet Hall and Hospitality House. A silhouette wolf howling at a full moon is painted on the exterior entrance wall of the alcohol- and tobacco-free dance club that caters to seniors. When he is not playing with the

Legendary Pacers, Sonny performs at the club with a local group called Jeannie and the Guys.

Some residents contend that overzealous individuals caused the end of the gambling era, as though Newport could have remained immune to the larger reformation that occurred statewide at the time. They link the economic decline of Newport to the actions of one or more elected officials who sought, they suggest with residual bitterness, to only make a name for themselves.

Beyond the rancor lies the essential paradox of subjective history, the passionate beliefs of people with similar experiences but widely divergent memories and interpretations. Among the elders of Newport, for example, are two men with extensive history at the Silver Moon. Both are intelligent and ethical; both are credible witnesses. One man spoke of entering the upstairs gambling room, and he described its interior layout in detail. The other denied such a room ever existed.

A third elder simply offered a melancholy reflection on his hometown's glory days. "When the gambling stopped, it slowed things down tremendously. The gamblers left. The Silver Moon closed. Don died. Sure it had some bad as well, but gambling did a lot for the community, and it ain't here now. I don't know who's right and who's wrong. Times change."

Minority Loss: Jews and Blacks

The complicated scenario of Newport's decline involves more than gambling and roadhouses. Changes experienced by two minority groups, the town's Jewish citizens and black citizens, are reflective of that history, as they are in many Delta towns.

Most early Jewish settlers in the Arkansas Delta were peddlers, attracted to towns where people were making a living. They found ample opportunity in Newport's thriving river-town economy of the late 1800s, becoming Front Street store owners and entrepreneurs. Jewish families, their names of Grossman, Lebovitch, Salenfriend, and Schneider more suggestive of turn-of-the-century New York City tenements than rural Arkansas, entered community life and helped build up the area. Leopold Thalheim had a general store in Newport and was on the board of the St. Louis and Iron Mountain Railway. Mercantile store owner and cotton buyer Sol Heinemann owned tugboats that hauled White River sand and gravel and harvested mussels for buttons. Businessman Lazar Hirsch served as city treasurer, recorder, deputy sheriff, and deputy clerk. And Sigmund Wolff and Isaac Goldman established a mercantile company that became one of the largest stores of its kind in the region. The two men became active promoters of Newport and accumulated diversified holdings in realty, clothing, banking, furniture, and farm supply. Noted architect Charles Thompson designed the Wolff-Goldman store in 1909, a Front Street edifice purchased in 1927 by P. K. Holmes Sr.[131]

"If something were to be done today for Newport," Marvin Thaxton suggested, only partially joking, "it would be to import another twenty Jewish families."

Mann Shoffner was a prominent man of Jewish heritage in Newport in the 1950s. The successful and widely respected mule trader was a grandson of pioneers Anias Ephraim Shoffner and Martha Shoffner, whose extensive farming operations gave rise to the southern Jackson County town with their family name.

Another was Mose Brownstein, one of the most socially active members of Newport's Jewish community. His involvements ranged from politics to gambling, cotton production, the salvage business, and hotel ownership, most notably the downtown Lavoy Hotel, which Brownstein bought and renamed the Shirley Hotel for his daughter. Arriving in Newport with few resources beyond his own business skills, Brownstein amassed several thousand acres of land near Amagon, where he established a hunting club and the nightclub Ricky and Ken's, the scene of many a lively evening when inebriated patrons would release the club's captive monkey from its cage.

"Mose Brownstein was a dreamer and a promoter," Thaxton said. "He would tell everyone in the coffee shop his business plans, tell you what he'd pay for things. He was a colorful character."

In a situation not uncommon in Newport's flush times, Brownstein had a lot of "unfortunate fires," Kaneaster Hodges added. Approached by an insurance salesman who tried to sell him a policy for tornado protection, Hodges said Brownstein replied, "How in the hell would you ever start a tornado?"

An early Jewish settlement in Jackson County included a disastrous agricultural enterprise in the hardwood bottomlands of the White River. Arriving in February 1883 as part of a resettlement movement known as Am Olam (The Eternal People), a group of nearly 200 European Jewish immigrants established a rural colony near Jacksonport. The intention was to produce and market barrel staves to a local lumber company. But the group made little profit, having poor understanding of the market value of their product and the production costs required.

More damaging, however, was the lack of preparation for the Delta heat and humidity, snakes and mosquitoes, malaria and yellow fever. By July, illness was epidemic and ten percent of the colonists had died. Starvation was a real threat. After a year of struggle, the group received financial help for relocation, and the Arkansas colony was abandoned.

The removal of this Jewish pioneer group prefigures the immense outmigration of other Delta agricultural communities in the mid-1900s. Similarly, the loss of Jewish families and businesses is reflective of the collapsed merchant middle class, the center of Newport's once-thriving economy.

Black Community Life

In contrast to the European Jewish settlers, Jackson County's black communities had no larger support group to rescue them from the mid-century's devastating changes. Though many farm families relocated, a larger portion of the black population simply bore the brunt of local change as they had always done and made the best of diminished opportunities. The community message to its young people, as it largely remains today for Delta blacks, was to look elsewhere for opportunity.

"More than anything, I recall the insistence that I do better than my parents," Charles Donaldson, a retired vice chancellor at the University of Arkansas at Little Rock and an inductee into the Newport Hall of Fame, said. Growing up in Newport in the 1950s and attending the segregated Branch High School, Donaldson recalled "a culture and village concept of sharing," a world where positive role models were preachers, teachers, and undertakers.

"Those were the professional careers I grew up around," Donaldson said. "Everyone worked, and we were taught an extreme diligence to a family belief to get an education, own your own home, and have a higher quality life."

Though his parents prohibited him from going to the lower end of Front Street on Saturday nights, Donaldson recalled car rides through the bustling activity, seeing people "elbow to elbow at the barber shops in the front of buildings and pool halls in back, liquor stores, and taxis and cafés." His childhood memories include a grandfather and his twin who bootlegged, bringing late night knocks on the door and the rustle of paper sacks.

"I wasn't sure what was going on," Donaldson said. "As a child, you have no real sense of right or wrong. Most of the older women were prim and very religious, but a lot of the men were gangbusters, out on Front Street, fun loving, drinking and gambling."

Donaldson recalled no overt racial problems at school or downtown. Community activist Doris Borders had a different experience. Encouraged by her college-educated father, Borders attended nursing school in Little Rock in the 1940s when black students were not accepted at the Newport training site. During her tenure on the Newport City Council in the 1970s, Borders said she endured racial slurs and opposition from council members who opposed her efforts to integrate the city swimming pool and obtain development assistance for the city. Her belief was that civil rights was a means of economic advancement for blacks, and, as blacks made up one-third of the population, this was a good thing for all of Newport.

"People thought all integration would bring was race mixing, but it was really for better jobs and education," Borders said. "If we really talk, you'll find out what you and I want in life is the same—a good home and good jobs for our children."

Joe Black is another of Newport's high achievers, appointed to the state Board of Education and president of Southern Bancorp Capital Partners, a Helena-based nonprofit organization that supports public education and economic development in the Delta. As a grandson of Pickens Black, his childhood in the progressive community of Blackville, as well as his family's insistence on education, shaped his understanding of key issues common to the Delta region.

"Careers were limited for educated blacks," he said. "The best and the brightest were teachers. Depending on your economic status, the youth counselors might direct you to be a tractor driver. At best, you had a future in semi- or low-skilled labor. Newport didn't diversify with education for all the population. This was not a way we could remain competitive."

Newport's decline was characteristic of the Delta, Black believes. As industrial development replaced agriculture, southern towns offered cheap land and cheap labor. But plants eventually moved farther south to find even cheaper land and labor.

"The economic decline was gradual," Black said. "First one store closed, then another. Then the movie theater wasn't there. Then the juke joints closed. People began to move away and we started seeing empty houses. It happens around you and you don't realize it. People were asleep at the wheel."

Failure to Thrive

It's a problem common to most Delta towns. We're old cotton country. When cotton went out, a lot of our economy went with it.
—Newport mayor David Stewart

The Delta is "a place where times were harder than anywhere else when times got hard," attendees at the 2011 Delta Regional Authority Conference at Little Rock were told. The speaker at the federal agency's annual meeting was Rodney Slater, a Marianna, Arkansas, native and former U.S. secretary of transportation. Like his black peers from Newport, Slater came of age in the post-King Cotton era of the Delta, when problems of limited education, poor health, and poverty became the standards of a disenfranchised population. And shrinking Delta towns had little to show other than abandoned manufacturing plants and rusting cotton gins to reflect the failure of industry's and agriculture's response to inherent problems.

"It's hard to be optimistic for small-town life," a former Swifton resident now living in Little Rock said. "People still farm, but that doesn't employ many. These small towns are good places to live if you don't mind the solitude and isolation."

Since the 1960s, Jackson County's agricultural economy has offered little opportunity to revitalize the region. Those resources remain controlled by a small group of wealthy families, their holdings engaged in large-scale farming, their fortunes less dependent on social welfare than on the economics of commodities and productivity.

"How to redistribute wealth in the Delta?" Jim Wood asked. "I don't know. It always ends up with one person getting all the money. It is like a Monopoly game."

And like a game in which properties are parceled out in separate units, some recalled Newport as a town divided into distinct areas: old families of wealth occupying the historic district downtown and newer middle-class families filling in neighborhoods to the east after the airbase opened up land for housing. Additional neighborhoods were associated with black residents, while others were populated by the most recent rural émigrés, lower-income white families relocated from their former farm homes.

The most critical observers view Newport's segregated areas and class systems as a breakdown of city planning. Town critics speak of missed opportunities, such as the town not accepting funds for the preservation of the downtown jail, another of Newport's bygone structures formerly on the National Register of Historic Places, the old building torn down in 2006. Further criticism cites a need for street cleanup, tighter restrictions on commercial trucks, and landscaping the central lake where a long-ago tourist park once garnered praise from 1950s travelers.

Voices of frustration and complaint can be found in many Delta towns once noted for their wealth and gentility. Yet nearby towns such as Searcy, Batesville, and Jonesboro seem to be flourishing. Newport was once larger and more prosperous, but today Searcy has a population three times the size of Newport's and a more diverse economy.

"Where did we go wrong?" Bill Fortune asked.

Answers across the community frequently identify long-established factions. The tension between agriculture and industry is often brought up. Newport's merchant class was eager to attract factories, while its farming leadership was less supportive of the strategy. Over time, the efforts to recruit industry narrowed to a smaller group, and interest declined.

Other historical divisions are mentioned, such as the competing services of the town's two banks and the town's two hospitals (which, for a time, denied medical privileges to doctors from the competing site), and the rivalry between the town's two powerful attorneys, both with strong personalities and both involved in local politics. The suggestion is that as Newport entered its period of greatest challenge, its wealth and leadership became concentrated in the hands of a few people with opposing views.

"People would say the power structure in Newport then, the landowners, wanted to keep it like it was," Jug Wallace said. "They were not bad people, but they wanted to have a say in the business aspects. Newport landowners simply didn't want a lot of industry for the fear of losing their farm labor. Some were in favor of Newport development. Others had an attitude of leave it like it is and see what happens."

The Road Ahead

> *Every town that hasn't prospered has a "one that got away" story. Every town thinks there is a small group that controls everything.*
> —Jon Chadwell, director,
> Newport Economic Development Commission

Newport's recruitment strategy in the 1950s was to attract big northern factories rather than grow on the small local level. The incentive was low productivity costs because of a low-wage work force. But southern developers chose not to cultivate the inherent skills and the strong work ethic of former agricultural workers. Eventually, the manufacturers went elsewhere for even lower production costs.

Consumers also looked elsewhere. Better roads across the Delta encouraged shopping in other towns. As competition shifted from across the street to across the region, Newport's merchant class began influencing their children to seek more professional jobs than those that remained in town. In wealthy agricultural families, younger generations could stay in town and run the farms. The children of the merchant class moved away.

Also in the 1960s, the civil rights movement had a huge impact on the Delta area. With southern racial attitudes in a national spotlight, some manufacturers became hesitant about investing in Newport and other Delta towns that were perceived as unstable.

In 2005, Newport's racial imbalance was noted by Warwick Sabin, at that time an editor at the *Arkansas Times* who wrote an article titled "The Road Ahead." Attending the Portfest Festival at Jacksonport, Sabin described families enjoying the summer event on the front lawn of the old courthouse, a site where some 6,000 Confederate soldiers surrendered in 1865. As country bands performed on the outdoor stage and vender booths sold food and southern merchandize, most notably a variety of Confederate flags, Sabin noted a complete lack of black citizens at the festival. Newport, like many Delta towns, was not only segregated socially and residentially, but economically as well. Blacks and whites, Sabin wrote, patronized separate stores, bars, and restaurants:

> The effect is that capital is not circulating, and Newport is not benefiting from the economic output that would be expected from a city its size. It might as well be two cities of 5,000 and 2,400. All of this affects the city's ability to attract new business, which will be necessary as manufacturing jobs continue to go overseas and the agriculture industry continues to consolidate. Communities with regressive social environments that can't retain their most talented young people are not likely to receive consideration from the new generation of companies that need well-educated, forward-thinking workers.[132]

Sabin (who was elected to the state legislature in 2013) suggests that Newport's long-term survival, similar to that of other Delta communities, depends as much on addressing quality-of-life considerations, including cultural amenities and community strength, as it does on addressing where the jobs are. Sabin believes the linkages between culture and economics are within the grasp of Newport leaders, and he suggested that a renovation of Newport's architecturally interesting downtown could unite and revitalize the community. Like others in Newport today, Sabin believes the old river town may once again have prosperous times ahead.

The Blue Bridge

Newport today still has that spark, the desire to be all it can be. The people have pride and a sense of hope. They can capitalize on that. They do need a little bit of luck and folks who are willing to work together and try new things.
—Governor Mike Beebe

A symbolic opportunity for Newport is the rusting highway bridge at the White River. The concrete and steel span, a local landmark since it was built in 1930, was placed on the National Register of Historic Places in 1990. The bridge's steel superstructure was painted blue in the 1970s when native son George Kell was on the state highway commission. Approximately 2,400 cars still cross it daily.

In 2011, the Arkansas Highway Department declared the bridge "structurally deficient" and announced plans to replace it. The department also stated that it would give Newport the amount that would be required to demolish the bridge, $1 million, if locals promise to maintain it. Mayor Stewart responded, "We'll do everything we can to keep it." Local leaders are exploring a plan that would divert traffic from the bridge to use it for recreational purposes. Many residents said they would like to see a walking trail over the bridge. Others suggested that a park or museum should be placed at the span's apex. With vehicles prohibited from the bridge, highway officials predict the structure would last another 100 years.

"This is like a home remodeling," Jon Chadwell said. "We're remodeling the town." Chadwell has engaged Union Pacific in an environmental clean up of its extensive rail yard. He is seeking to create green space and performance areas adjacent to the train depot and provide rent subsidies to attract businesses to the vacant commercial space along Front Street.

The development of a riverfront park with boardwalks and benches remains a formidable challenge. The White River frontage lies behind five-foot-high concrete flood-control walls. The concrete units can be lifted and repositioned with a crane, but the riverfront area remains undeveloped, and the mobile homes and trailers of squatters have occupied the area long enough to have property rights, Chadwell said.

Like a real estate agent showing off homes in a new subdivision, Chadwell takes visitors to Newport's industrial park, pointing out the rail, water, and power infrastructure in place. He speaks of the aluminum plant, the ambulance manufacturer, and the agricultural trailer company that occupy the site. His driving tour includes a steel mill, a food processing plant, and a boot manufacturing firm. He drives past the razor-wire-topped fencing of the two state prisons northeast of town where some 1,900 men and women are housed. The prisons, whose 550 employees have an average income in the mid-$40,000s, are the largest employers in town, Chadwell said.

A satellite campus of Arkansas State University now occupies the open space that was the Newport Air Base, and modern buildings are clustered in familiar campus-style arrangement. A small airport still functions on the site, but the former runways now feature a seemingly endless number of orange highway barrels, as eighteen-wheel tractors and trailers move among them as part of a driver training program provided by the school. Electrical poles lining one side of the field are scaled by trainees in a lineman training program.

Standing amidst the campus activity, Chadwell reflected on Newport's commercial prospects. "Newport now has more business licenses than it did in the 1950s," he said. "But those businesses are not concentrated on Front Street as they once were. So they are not as visible." He added, "Our path is not the same as it was fifty years ago. Some people have not seen the progress made, and they may believe that only problems remain. But progress is being made on many fronts. One challenge is to get this progress into the minds of those who saw the decline."

Through long years of experience, some disastrous, some to our great advantage, we have come to terms with the River. It has tempered our nature through the fire of many well-learned lessons and surprising rewards. As a result of this, one very distinct characteristic of Newport has been our optimism and our readiness to start all over again if need be. Taking one overflow after another, the Big Fire, the busted banks, and the Depression, we have nevertheless always had a feeling that we were living life fully and completely.[133]
—Lady Elizabeth Luker, *Newport Daily Independent*, 1958

Much has changed for a Delta river town over the lifetime of its most celebrated musical performer, Sonny Burgess. An Arkansas farmer's son has risen from rural obscurity to international recognition. Along the way, there have been profound sorrows and loss. Returning from a 2005 rockabilly festival in England, Sonny learned of the drowning death of his younger son Peyton, the news reaching him as he stepped off an airplane in Little Rock. Ever the professional, Sonny went on to the Pacers' performance, accepting the tragic news with a stoicism never revealed to the audience that July 4th evening.

Sonny has always lived in Newport, and his hometown loyalties are strong. Stan Perkins said his father Carl had the same qualities Sonny now displays. Both men stayed grounded within themselves and the communities where their hearts have always been.

"When you take away everyday living from people, the common things, when the only people around you are 'yes' people who are not really your friends, you've got a problem," Perkins said. "I think the world of Sonny and his connections with people. He can teach us all to lighten up and be ourselves."

Since 2006, Sonny has hosted *We Wanna Boogie*, a weekly show for the Arkansas State University radio station KASU. He answers questions phoned in by callers and jokes with co-host June Taylor. His on-air commentary, filled with stories of his long-ago peers and Sun package tours, is a treasure of rockabilly and American music history. And occasionally a story will be told about old Newport, the clubs, the shows, and the flush times of the 1950s. In Sonny's stories, there is no trace of the accusatory rancor that some townsfolk display when drawing up the old ghosts, refusing to balance that sadness with forgiveness or laughter.

During a 2012 radio show, when the sound of a ringing telephone interrupted an anecdote, Sonny responded with a journeyman performer's impeccable timing. "That's Elvis calling again," he said, laughing. "He wants me to play his songs."

Acknowledgements

Research for *We Wanna Boogie* was conducted at Arkansas public institutions in Newport, Helena, Little Rock, and North Little Rock. Organizations that significantly assisted the work include: the Arkansas History Commission, Central Arkansas Library System, Laman Library, Jackson County Historical Society, Jackson County Library, and Tri-County Genealogical Society.

Numerous individuals who generously shared their knowledge of music and Newport history are quoted throughout the book. Sonny Burgess and Bobby Crafford were exceptionally helpful. Many others with extensive awareness of music, Newport, and the Arkansas Delta are not identified in the chapters. They include Joel Anderson, Sue Ellen Burton, Bob Boyd, Roy Cost, Narvel Felts, Roland Janes, Phil McDonald, John Roberts, Bill Tucker, and Bubba Sullivan.

Research assistance, photographs, and materials were also provided by many individuals and institutions, including Henry Boyce, Rock 'n' Roll Highway 67 Museum; Mike Doyle, KASU Jonesboro; Halbert family of Helena; Ben Johnson, Southern Arkansas University; Ken King; George Lankford; Walter Lloyd; Shirlene Nance; Charles Snapp; Gene Sweat, Farmers Electric Co-op; and Martin Willis.

Editorial consultations and project support were received from Dr. Renie Bressinck; Don Castleberry; Michael Dregni; Phyllis and Douglas Holmes; Brad and Kelly Eichler; George Eldridge; Larry Golden; Preston Lauterbach; Mike Luster; Larry Malley; Jim McClelland; Doug Martin; Charley Sandage; Noel Strauss; Trip Strauss; and David Stricklin.

Many people who provided invaluable assistance and information have passed away during the seven years required to research and produce this book. Some were well-known performing artists; others were community figures whose extraordinary histories were known by very few others. I am deeply grateful and indebted to all.

Bibliography—Books

Altschuler, Glenn C. *All Shook Up: How Rock 'n' Roll Changed America*. New York: Oxford University Press, 2003.

Amburn, Ellis. *Dark Star: The Roy Orbison Story*. New York: A Lyle Stuart Book, Carol Publishing Group, 1990.

Aquila, Richard. *That Old Time Rock and Roll: A Chronicle of an Era*. New York: Schirmer, 1989.

Brown, Maxine. *Looking Back to See: A Country Music Memoir*. Fayetteville: University of Arkansas Press, 2005.

Burke, Ken, and Dan Griffin. *The Blue Moon Boys: The Story of Elvis Presley's Band*. Chicago: Chicago Review Press, 2006.

Clayson, Alan. *Only the Lonely: Roy Orbison's Life and Legacy*. New York: St. Martin's Press, 1989.

Cobb, James C. *The Most Southern Place on Earth: The Mississippi Delta and the Roots of Regional Identity*. Oxford: Oxford University Press, 1994.

Cochran, Robert. *Our Own Sweet Sounds*. 2nd ed. Fayetteville: University of Arkansas Press, 2005.

Cross, Wilbur, and Michael Kosser. *The Conway Twitty Story*. Toronto: Paperjacks, 1986.

Doggett, Peter. *Are You Ready for the Country*. New York: Penguin, 2000.

Daniel, Pete. *Lost Revolutions: The South in the 1950s*. Washington DC: Smithsonian Institution, 2000.

Daniel, Pete. *Standing at the Crossroads: Southern Life in the 20th Century*. New York: Hill and Wang, 1986.

Dattel, Gene. *Cotton and Race in the Making of America*. Lanham, MD: Rowman and Littlefield, 2009.

Dougan, Michael. *Arkansas Odyssey: The Saga of Arkansas from Prehistoric Times to Present*. Little Rock, AR: Rose Publishing Co., 1995.

Dregni, Michael, ed. *Rockabilly: The Twang Heard 'Round the World: The Illustrated History*. Minneapolis: Voyageur Press, 2011.

Escott, Colin. *Good Rocking Tonight: Sun Records and the Birth of Rock and Roll*. New York: St. Martin's Press, 1991.

———. *Lost Highway: The True Story of Country Music*. Washington DC: Smithsonian Institution, 2003.

———. *Roadkill on the Three-Chord Highway: Art and Trash in American Popular Music*. New York: Routledge, 2002.

Escott, Colin, with Martin Hawkins. *Sun Records: The Brief History of the Legendary Label*. Cape Town, South Africa: Quick Fox, 1980.

Guralnick, Peter. *Feel Like Going Home*. New York: Outerbridge and Dienstfrey, 1971.

Halberstam, David. *The Fifties*. New York: Villard, 1993.

Hanley, Ray. *Images of America, A Journey through Arkansas, Historic Highway 67*. Mount Pleasant, SC: Arcadia, Tempus Publishing, 1999.

Hawkins, Ronnie, with Peter Goddards. *Ronnie Hawkins: The Last of the Good Ole Boys*. Ontario: Stoddart, 1989.

Helm, Levon, with Stephen Davis. *This Wheel's on Fire: Levon Helm and the Story of the Band*. New York: William Morrow and Co., 1993.

Homer, Sheree. *Catch that Rockabilly Fever: Personal Stories of Life on the Road and in the Studio*. Jefferson, NC: McFarland & Company, 2010.

Johnson, Ben. *John Barleycorn Must Die: The War against Drink in Arkansas*. Fayetteville: University of Arkansas Press, 2005.

Lauterbach, Preston. *The Chitlin' Circuit and the Road to Rock 'n' Roll*. New York: W. W. Norton & Co., 2011.

LeMaster, Carolyn Gray. *A Corner of the Tapestry: A History of the Jewish Experience in Arkansas, 1820s–1990s*. Fayetteville: University of Arkansas Press, 1994.

Lindsey, Michael. *The Big Hat Law: The Arkansas State Police 1935–2000*. Little Rock: Butler Center Books, 2008.

Louvin, Charlie, with Benjamin Whitmer. *Satan is Real: The Ballad of the Louvin Brothers*. New York: Itbooks, Harper Collins, 2012.

Marcus, Greil. *Mystery Train: Images of America in Rock 'n' Roll Music*. New York: Plume, 1997.

McNutt, Randy. *We Wanna Boogie: An Illustrated History of theAmerican Rockabilly Movement*. Hamilton, Ontario: HHP Books, 1988.

Moore, Scotty, with James Dickerson. *Scotty & Elvis: Aboard the Mystery Train*. Jackson: University of Mississippi Press, 2013.

———. *That's Alright, Elvis*. New York: Schirmer Books, 1997.

Morrison, Craig. *Go Cat Go: Rockabilly Music and Its Makers*. Champaign: University of Illinois Press, 1998.

Naylor, Jerry, and Steve Halliday. *The Rockabilly Legends: They Called It Rockabilly Long before They Called It Rock and Roll*. Milwaukee: Hal Leonard Corporation, 2007.

Palmer, Robert. *Deep Blues*. New York: Penguin, 1981.

———. *A Tale of Two Cities: Memphis Rock and New Orleans Roll*. Brooklyn: Institute for Studies in American Music, 1979.

Perkins, Carl, and David McGee. *Go, Cat, Go: The Life and Times of Carl Perkins, The King of Rockabilly*. New York: Hyperion, 1996.

Trimble, Vance. *Sam Walton: The Inside Story of America's Richest Man*. New York: Penguin, 1990.

Tosches, Nick. *Country: The Twisted Roots of Rock and Roll*. Cambridge, MA: Da Capo Press, 1996.

———. *Hellfire: The Jerry Lee Lewis Story*. New York: Grove Press, 1998.

———. *Unsung Heroes of Rock and Roll: The Birth of Rock in the Wild Years before Elvis*. New York: Charles Scribner's Sons, 1984.

Wald, Gayle. *Shout, Sister, Shout: The Untold Story of a Rock and Roll Trailblazer, Sister Rosetta Tharpe*. Boston: Beacon Press, 2007.

Walton, Sam, with John Huey. *Sam Walton: Made in America*. New York: Doubleday, 1992.

Whayne, Jeannie, and Willard B. Gatewood, eds. *Arkansas Delta: Land of Paradox*. Fayetteville: University of Arkansas Press, 1993.

Appendix

Internet Resources

Official website for Sonny Burgess and the Legendary Pacers:
www.legendarypacers.com

Discography, 1956–2010:
http://sonnyburgess.voila.net/homepage.html

Extensive details on Sun Records sessions, as well as all nine episodes
of "The Rock 'N' Roll Highway" video produced by the Arkansas
Department of Parks and Tourism:
http://www.706unionavenue.nl

Listings of singles, albums, EPs, compilations, and Razorback
recordings: http://koti.mbnet.fi/wdd/sonnyburgess.htm

Information on Sonny Burgess and other Sun artists:
www.sunrecords.com

Sonny Burgess discography: www.allmusic.com

List of French re-issues of Sonny Burgess' and others' Sun recordings:
sun600.voila.net/homepage.htm

Biographical and recording information:
http://www.encyclopedia.com/doc/1G2-3496000017.html

Entries on Sonny Burgess, Newport, Jackson County, Rockabilly,
Rock and Roll Highway 67: www.encyclopediaofarkansas.net

Pacers' Achievements

Awards:
Induction, International Rockabilly Hall of Fame, *Now Dig This* magazine 1991
Induction, U.S. Rockabilly Hall of Fame, Jackson, TN 1999
Induction, U.S. Rockabilly Hall of Fame, Nashville, TN 2002
Rockabilly's Finest Award, Sun Records 2002
Arkansas Traveler, Arkansas Governor's Office 2002
Arkansas Walk of Fame, Hot Springs 2007
Arkansas Entertainers Hall of Fame 2007

Museum Exhibits:
Theo's Rock 'n' Roll Museum, Clarksdale, MS
Rock and Soul Museum, Memphis, TN

Appearances:
Kennedy Center
Library of Congress
National Folk Festival (multiple states)
Elvis Festival, Tupelo, MS
National Rockabilly Festival, Jackson, TN
Southern Folklore Festival, Memphis, TN
Memphis in May
Clearlake Festival, IA
Viva Las Vegas
Dukes of Hazzard Festival, TN
European Rockabilly Festivals:
    Hemsby
    Rockabilly Rave
    Wildest Cats in Town
    High Rockabilly
    Screaming Summer
    Blue Monday
    Rhythm Riot
    Rockabilly Bombardment
    Rockin' Race Jamboree

Pacers' Band Members

The Drifting Cowboys, Rocky Road Ramblers, and Moonlighters:

Sonny Burgess
Russ Smith
Johnny Ray Hubbard
Gerald Jackson
Bobby Stoner
Paul Whaley
Kern Kennedy
Russell Smith
Al Wilson
Bob Armstrong
Forest Miller
Charles Middlestat
Paul Buskert
Eddie Hill
Davy Hooks

The Pacers:

Sonny Burgess
Kern Kennedy
Bobby Crafford
Joe Lewis
Jack Nance
Bobby Crafford
J. C. Caughron
Johnny Ray Hubbard
Russell Smith

The Pacers (1960s):

Bobby Crafford
Kern Kennedy
Jim Aldridge
Fred Douglas
J. C. Caughron
Joe Cyr
Jerry Kattawar
Fred Johnson
Glen Kennedy
Joe Shelnut
Johnny Ray Hubbard
Jimmy Ray Paulman

Kings IV & V:

Sonny Burgess
Skeeter Grady
Tommy Tims
Doug Greeno
Gene Grant
Bob Nelson
Buck Odie

The Legendary Pacers:

Sonny Burgess
Kern Kennedy
Bobby Crafford
Jim Aldridge
Fred Douglas
Charles Watson II

Songs Composed by Sonny Burgess

Ain't Got a Thing
    (with Jack Clement)
Always Will
Bamboo
Cotton Pickin' Mind
Daddy Blues
Down at Big Mary's House
    (with Bobby Brown)
Farmers' Blues
Find My Baby for Me
Gone
Gotta Find My Baby
Hangin' Round My Gal
Hootchy Kootchy
Itchy (with Billy Lee Riley
    and Jack Clement)
Jesus My Savior Divine
K. K.'s Boogie
    (with Kern Kennedy)
A Kiss Goodnight
Little Town Baby
Meet Me Anywhere
Mr. Blues
My Little Town Baby
Oh Mama
One Broken Heart
Red Headed Woman
Rock 'n' Roll Daddy
Rockin' in England
    (with Larry Cheshier)
Sadie's Back in Town
So Soon
Still Rockin'
Stoned in Love with You
Stuck Up (with Larry Cheshier)

Sunrock Boogie
Thunderbird (with Billy Lee
    Riley and Jack Clement)
Today I've Nothing But Love
    (subtitle: Today, Tomorrow,
    and Forever)
Tomorrow Night
Truckin' Down the Avenue
We Wanna Boogie
Whatever Happened to the Girls
    I Knew
You

Sun Sessions that Produced Singles

Catalog #: Sun 247
Sun Single: Red Headed Woman / We Wanna Boogie
Recorded: May 2, 1956
Released: July 25, 1956
Musicians:
    Sonny Burgess
    Joe Lewis
    Johnny Ray Hubbard
    Russell Smith
    Kern Kennedy
    Jack Nance
Other Titles Recorded at Same Session:
    Wings of an Angel
    The Prisoner's Song
    All Night Long
    Life's Too Short To Live

Catalog #: Sun 263
Sun Single: Ain't Got a Thing / Restless
Recorded: Late 1956
Released: January 24, 1957
Musicians:
    Sonny Burgess
    Johnny Ray Hubbard
    Russell Smith
    Kern Kennedy
    Jack Nance

Catalog #: Sun 285
Sun Single: Bucket's Got a Hole in It / Sweet Misery
Recorded: August 14, 1957
Released: December 1957
Musicians:
    Sonny Burgess
    Johnny Ray Hubbard
    Kern Kennedy

Jack Nance
Jack Clement, guitar overdub
Addition of women's choir, Gene Lowry singers, some time after.
Singers included: Stan Kesler, Dianne Stephens, Carolyn Gray,
Don Carter, Lee Holt, Bill Abbott, Asa Wilkerson
Other Titles Recorded at Same Session:
All My Sins
Daddy Blues
My Babe
Whatcha' Gonna Do

Catalog #: Sun 304
Sun Single: Thunderbird / Itchy
Recorded: August 10 or 30, 1958
Musicians:
Sonny Burgess
J. C. Caughron,
Bobby Crafford
Johnny Ray Hubbard
Charlie Rich, piano
Billy Lee Riley, harmonica

Additional Recordings with Unknown Date (1957/58), Possibly
This Session:
Tomorrow Night
Tomorrow Never Comes
Skinny Ginny
So Soon
Mama Loochie

Catalog #: Phillips 3551
Sun Single: Sadie's Back In Town / A Kiss Goodnight
Recorded: 1959
Released: January 1960 Also European release as: London CTS 9064
and London MSY 4189
Musicians:
Sonny Burgess
J. C. Caughron
Frankie Suddeth, bass

Raymond Thompson (drums/voice of Woody Woodpecker, laughter by Sonny)

Backup by Cliff Thomas group (piano player unknown)

Other Titles Recorded at Same Session:

A Kiss Goodnight

All My Sins Are Taken Away (Hand Me Down My Walking Cane)

Goin' Home (Ain't Gonna Do It—Fats Domino)

Smoochin' Jill

End Notes

Introduction by Sonny Burgess

1. The Swift Jewel Cowboys were an eight-member western and hillbilly swing group sponsored by the Swift Shortening and Oil Company. The band was widely heard on radio broadcasts from Memphis in the 1930s. Beginning in 1939, they performed across the mid-South, often at rodeos and grocery stores, where a Jewel-packet top was a free ticket to the show.

Slim Rhodes (1913–1966, born Ethmer Cletus Rhodes in Pocahontas, Arkansas) and the Mother's Best Mountaineers were a popular Memphis-based band during the 1940s and '50s that often performed in Newport and were heard daily on WMCT-AM in Memphis, Tennessee, sponsored by Mother's Best Flour. By 1953, they also had a 30-minute live show on KATV-TV in Pine Bluff, Arkansas. The Rhodes family band included brothers Gilbert and Hilburn and sister Bea and originally performed as the Log Cabin Mountaineers.

Gene Ridgeway and Jimmy Davidson were Jackson County musicians and bandleaders popular in the 1940s.

The Wilburn Brothers, Teddy (1931–2003) and Doyle (1930–1982), were from Hardy, Arkansas. Their extensive and successful careers began when they were child performers in the late 1930s; this is when Sonny likely saw them in Newport. They were discovered by Roy Acuff, who brought them to the Grand Ole Opry in 1940, but child labor laws prohibited their professional work for a decade. They were members of the Grand Ole Opry from the 1950s to the 1980s, the period when their recording and music publishing success was achieved.

Chapter 2. High Water Marks

2. *Newport Daily Independent*, December 5, 1958.

Chapter 3. Ramblers and Moonlighters

3. Burgess' birth year is frequently listed as 1931, which is incorrect; he was born in 1929.

4. The federal Rural Electrification Act of 1935 created the REA (Rural Electric Administration). As late as 1948, initial installations were still being made in rural Arkansas Delta counties

5. *Blue Suede News*, 51 and 52, 2000.

6. Harold Franklin Hawkins (December 22, 1921–March 5, 1963), better known as Hawkshaw Hawkins, was an American country music singer popular from the 1950s into the early '60s, known for his rich, smooth vocals and music drawn from blues, boogie woogie, and honky tonk. At 6'5" tall, he had an imposing stage presence, and

he dressed more conservatively than some other male country singers. Hawkins died in the 1963 plane crash that also killed country stars Patsy Cline and Cowboy Copas. He was a member of the Grand Ole Opry and was married to country star Jean Shepard.

7. Paul Whaley obituary: http://www.legacy.com/obituaries/timesheraldonline/obituary.aspx?n=paul-whaley&pid=154720239

Chapter 4. Rockabilly and Razorbacks

8. Michael Dregni, ed., *Rockabilly: The Twang Heard 'Round the World: The Illustrated History* (Minneapolis: Voyageur Press, 2011).

9. Colin Escott, *Roadkill on the Three-Chord Highway: Art and Trash in American Popular Music* (New York: Routledge, 2002).

10. Escott, *Roadkill*.

11. "The Sun Recordings, in His Own Words," *Now Dig This* 102 (September 1991).

12. Sandra Hubbard, *Steve's Show*. Documentary film. Little Rock: Morning Star Studio, 2003.

13. Cyrus Whitfield "Johnny" Bond (1915–1978), born in Enville, Oklahoma. Best known for his 1947 hit "Divorce Me C.O.D.," one of his seven Top Ten hits on the Billboard country charts.

14. Winford Lindsey "Wynn" Stewart (1934–1985), born in Morrisville, Missouri. Best known for his 1956 hit "Waltz of the Angels."

15. Enos William "Skeets" McDonald (1915–1968), born in Greenway, Arkansas. Best known for the Slim Willet-penned song "Don't Let the Stars Get in Your Eyes."

16. Crafford's reference is to Kern Kennedy's work with Chuck Comer, recording Comer's "Little More Lovin'" at the KLCN radio studio in Blytheville for Vaden Records.

17. "Good Rockin' Tonight: The Legacy of Sun Records, American Masters," WNET Channel 13. New York, 2001.

18. Ken Burke and Dan Griffin, *The Blue Moon Boys: The Story of Elvis Presley's Band* (Chicago: Chicago Review Press, 2006).

19. "Sonny Burgess," Cub Koda, http://www.allmusic.com/album/sonny-burgess-mw0000187997

Chapter 6. Portraits of the Pacers

20. Pete Daniel, *Lost Revolutions: The South in the 1950s* (Chapel Hill: University of North Carolina Press), 300, 305.

21. Daniel, *Lost Revolutions*, 93.

22. *Batesville Daily Guard*, May 2012.

23. *Newport Daily Independent*, October 21, 1955.

24. Preston Lauterbach, *The Chitlin' Circuit and the Road to Rock 'n' Roll* (New York: W. W. Norton & Co., 2011).

25. Nick Tosches, *Unsung Heroes of Rock and Roll: The Birth of Rock in the Wild Years before Elvis* (New York: Charles Scribner's Sons, 1984), 25.

26. Tosches, *Unsung Heroes of Rock and Roll*, 36.

27. "Good Rockin' Tonight."

28. Glenn C. Altschuler, *All Shook Up: How Rock 'n' Roll Changed America* (New York: Oxford University Press, 2003).

29. Jeannie Whayne, "Interview with Billy Lee Riley," *Arkansas Historical Quarterly* 55 (Autumn 1996).

30. Peter Daniel, "Rhythm of the Land," *Agricultural History* 68 (Fall 1994).

31. "Good Rockin' Tonight."

32. Greil Marcus, *Mystery Train: Images of America in Rock 'n' Roll Music* (New York: Plume, 1997).

33. Hank Williams interview with Alexander City, AL, disc jockey Bob McKinnon, March 1950, http://www.youtube.com/watch?v=eZodYUpu1VI&feature =related

34. Sheree Homer, *Catch that Rockabilly Fever: Personal Stories of Life on the Road and in the Studio* (Jefferson, NC: McFarland & Company, Inc., 2010).

35. "Sun Records," http://en.wikipedia.org/wiki/Sun_Records_(other_companies) and http://en.wikipedia.org/wiki/Sun_Records

36. Robert Palmer, *Deep Blues* (New York: Penguin, 1981), 222.

37. J. M. Van Eaton, Oral history, National Association of Music Merchants, http://www.namm.org/library/oral-history/jm-vaneaton

38. "Good Rockin' Tonight."

39. "Good Rockin' Tonight."

40. Daniel, *Lost Revolutions*, 131.

41. Elvis' Jackson County shows in 1955 included: March 2 at Newport Armory and Porky's Rooftop; July 21 at Silver Moon; October 24 at Silver Moon (with Moonlighters); and December 9 at Swifton High School and B&I Club (with Moonlighters).

42. *Newport Daily Independent*, March 1, 1955.

43. The Tennessee Two was Marshall Grant and Luther Perkins. In 1960, drummer W. S. Holland was added, and the band changed its name to the Tennessee Three.

44. *Newport Daily Independent*, April 1, 1957.

45. Dregni, *Rockabilly: The Twang Heard 'Round the World*, 48.

46. Jerry Naylor and Steve Halliday, *The Rockabilly Legends: They Called It Rockabilly Long before They Called It Rock and Roll* (Milwaukee: Hal Leonard Cooperation, 2007), 131.

47. Stan Perkins' comments are recorded at the Guitar Plaza in Walnut Ridge on Arkansas' state-designated "Rock 'n' Roll Highway 67."

48. Randy McNutt, *We Wanna Boogie: An Illustrated History of the American Rockabilly Movement* (Ontario: HHP Books, 1988), 91.

49. "Moon Mullican," http://en.wikipedia.org/wiki/Moon_Mullican

50. Craig Morrison, *Go Cat Go: Rockabilly Music and Its Makers* (Champaign: University of Illinois Press, 1996).

51. Van Eaton, Oral history, National Association of Music Merchants.

52. Cost's website contains an encyclopedic listing of the musicians who played in the Shadows. The roster, a "Who's Who" of central Arkansas talent, reveals a continuing legacy. In addition to Nance, Shadows members have included Jimmy Ford; Johnny Scroggins; Tommy "Pork Chop" Markham; saxophone player Warren Crow, who continues to coordinate an annual Club 70 musicians' reunion; and Ron Hughes, current leader of the Greasy Greens, a twelve-member rock band with more than thirty years of Arkansas performance history.

53. Arlen Vaden (1930–2003) was a radio disc jockey and gospel singer whose Vaden Records label operated from 1958 to 1961. Vaden utilized recording studios in

various locations, including radio station KLCN in Blytheville. Arkansas artists who recorded for Vaden include Bobby Crafford, Bobby Brown, Joyce Green, Larry Donn, Teddy Riedel, and Chuck Comer.

54. Levon Helm, with Stephen Davis. *This Wheel's on Fire: Levon Helm and the Story of the Band* (New York: William Morrow & Co., 1993), 24.

55. John Hughey (1933–2007) began his career as a member of his elementary schoolmate Conway Twitty's first band, the Phillips County Ramblers. Hughey played steel guitar with fellow Arkansan Slim Rhodes and as a member of Conway Twitty's country group from 1968 to 1988. He recorded with various other acts, including Loretta Lynn and Vince Gill. Known for a distinctive playing style called "crying steel," which focused primarily on the higher range of the guitar, Hughey was inducted into the Steel Guitar Hall of Fame in 1996.

56. Interview with Ronnie Hawkins by Bob Cochran, *Arkansas Historical Quarterly* 65 (Summer 2006).

57. Interview with Ronnie Hawkins by Bob Cochran.

58. Original Rockhousers members were Bill Harris, bass (replaced by Jimmy Evans); Jimmy Ray Paulman, guitar; Billy Weir, drums; and Lou Houston, steel guitar.

59. Levon Helm, *This Wheel's on Fire*.

60. *Batesville Daily Guard*, December 4, 2009, 1B.

61. *Jenkins v. Commissioner*, T.C. Memo 1983-667 (U.S. Tax Court Memos 1983).

62. Peter Guralnick, *Feel Like Going Home* (New York: Outerbridge and Dienstfrey, 1971), 203–8.

63. "Good Rockin' Tonight."

64. *Batesville Daily Guard*, September 3, 2009.

65. Scotty Moore, with James Dickerson, *Scotty & Elvis: Aboard the Mystery Train* (Jackson: University of Mississippi Press, 2013), 253.

66. Wilbur Cross and Michael Kosser, *The Conway Twitty Story* (Toronto: Paperjacks, 1986), 131.

67. *Newport Daily Independent*, December 4, 1958.

Chapter 7. Keep on Rocking

68. "*Gijon Stomp!*" http://www.allmusic.com/album/gijon-stomp%21-mw0001385654

69. *Montreal Gazette*, September 3, 2011.

Chapter 8. Arkansas Rock 'n' Roll Highway 67

70. Act 497 of 2009. http://www.arkleg.state.ar.us/assembly/2009/R/Acts/Act497.pdf

71. Bobby Lee Trammell (1934–2008) was a rockabilly singer who recorded for several West Coast record labels and Arkansas' Vaden Records. "Arkansas Twist" was released in 1962, the first imprint of the Jonesboro label, Alley Records. Trammell served in the Arkansas House of Representatives from 1997 to 2002.

72. Wilbur Steven "Bill" Rice of Datto, Arkansas, is a Grammy Award-nominated country music singer and songwriter. Rice charted six singles between 1971 and 1978, including the Top 40 hit "Travelin' Minstrel Man." Better known for his songwriting, Rice has received seventy-three awards from the American Society of Composers, Authors and Publishers (ASCAP), the most by any songwriter. In 1974, Rice had eleven songs on the country music charts at the same time.

73. Jimmy Driftwood (1907–1998) was a Grammy Award-winning singer-songwriter who wrote more than 6,000 songs. Driftwood began composing songs to augment the state history lessons he taught at a one-room schoolhouse at Timbo, Arkansas, in the 1930s. He gained national fame in 1959 when Johnny Horton recorded his song "The Battle of New Orleans."

74. Charley Sandage is an Arkansas educator, film producer, and musician whose "Arkansas Stories" project, from which "Up on Highway 67" is taken, includes a collection of original songs about people and events in Arkansas history, a K-6 Arkansas history curriculum, and a teacher's guide.

Chapter 9. Newport Origins

75. Ray Hanley, *Images of America, A Journey through Arkansas, Historic Highway 67* (Mount Pleasant, SC: Arcadia, 1999).

76. *Stream of History*, October 1964.

77. Ben Johnson, *John Barleycorn Must Die: The War against Drink in Arkansas* (Fayetteville: University of Arkansas Press, 2005), 47–49.

78. *Stream of History*, July 1975.

79. Jeannie Whayne and Willard B. Gatewood, eds. *Arkansas Delta: Land of Paradox* (Fayetteville: University of Arkansas Press, 1993), 232.

80. Whayne and Gatewood, *Arkansas Delta*, 230–31.

81. Whayne and Gatewood, *Arkansas Delta*, 218–19.

82. Whayne and Gatewood, *Arkansas Delta*, 11.

83. *New York Times*, December 18, 1882.

84. *Wichita Daily Times*, Wichita Falls, TX, August 24, 1915.

85. *Stream of History*, August 1983.

86. "Cowboy Jack Clement—Newport Arkansas," by Bresh Digital TV, 2006

87. "Aunt Caroline Dye," *Encyclopedia of Arkansas History & Culture*.

88. During the army years, the planes may have included training aircraft: B13, AT6, PT22, or PT25.

89. Vance Trimble, *Sam Walton: The Inside Story of America's Richest Man* (New York: Penguin, 1990).

Chapter 10. Newport in the 1950s

90. Hayden Thompson, born in 1938, is a Mississippi native and veteran rockabilly singer who performed on Sun Records package tours with Sonny Burgess and Billy Lee Riley in the 1950s. He recorded only one song, "Love My Baby," at Sun Studios, released in 1957 on Phillips International.

91. United Harmonizers members—vocals: Theopolis Henderson, Tom Watson, Ted Hatchett, Gus Hatchett, Norris Stephenson; piano: Minnie Bell Stephens.

92. *Newport Daily Independent*, September 18, 1958.

93. *Newport Daily Independent*, January 12 1950.

94. *Newport Daily Independent*, July 12–19, 1954.

95. *Newport Daily Independent*, June 17, 1955.

96. *Newport Daily Independent*, January 16, 1959.

97. *Newport Daily Independent*, January 10, 1956.

98. *Newport Daily Independent*, July 10, 1957.

99. *Arkansas Democrat*, August 16, 1959.

100. *Newport Daily Independent*, November 2, 1959.

101. *Newport Daily Independent*, September 10, 1959.

102. Daniel, "Rhythm of the Land."

103. "Josephine Graham," *Encyclopedia of Arkansas History & Culture*.

104. *Newport Daily Independent*, July 19, 1958.

105. *Newport Daily Independent*, January 31, 1951, "You Can Survive the Atom Bomb."

106. *Newport Daily Independent*, May 28, 1954.

107. *Arkansas Democrat*, October 10, 1958.

108. *Newport Daily Independent*, May 10, 1957.

109. *Newport Daily Independent*, November 21, 1958.

110. Whayne, "Interview with Billy Lee Riley."

111. *Arkansas Democrat-Gazette*, September 1, 2008.

112. *Newport Daily Independent*, January 23, 1959.

113. *Newport Daily Independent*, January 4, 1955.

114. *Newport Daily Independent*, June 29, 1959.

115. Hal Erickson and Mark Deming, "Jailhouse Rock-Synopsis/Jailhouse Rock—Review." *Allrovi*. Rovi Corporation. http://www.allrovi.com/movies/movie/jailhouse-rock-v25765

116. *Newport Daily Independent*, October 16, 1959.

117. *Newport Daily Independent*, December 28, 1967.

Chapter 11. Roadhouses and Rednecks

118. *Arkansas Democrat-Gazette*, August 3, 1997.

119. *Arkansas Democrat-Gazette*, August 3, 1997.

120. *Newport Daily Independent*, February 6, 1953.

121. *Newport Daily Independent*, July 13, 1950, and July 7, 1951.

122. *Newport Daily Independent*, December 9, 1954.

123. *Chicago Tribune News*, February 28, 1997.

124. *Memphis Commercial Appeal*, October 15, 2000.

125. *Batesville Daily Guard*, December 14, 2010.

126. *Trumann Democrat Tribune*, September 24, 2009.

127. Helm, *This Wheel's on Fire*.

128. Daniel, *Lost Revolutions*, 128.

129. *Newport Daily Independent*, January 15, 1968.

Chapter 12. A Vanished World

130. *Newport Daily Independent*, April 18, 1968.

131. Carolyn Gray LeMaster, A Corner of the Tapestry: A History of the Jewish Experience in Arkansas, 1820s–1900s (Fayetteville: University of Arkansas Press, 1994).

132. Warwick Sabin, "The Road Ahead," *Arkansas Times*, June 6, 2005.

133. *Newport Daily Independent*, December 5, 1958

Index

About the Author

A New York native and an Arkansan by choice, **Marvin Schwartz** is a professional writer whose work focuses on state culture and heritage. *We Wanna Boogie* is his eighth book of Arkansas history. After earning an MFA in poetry from the University of Arkansas, he found a place in his adopted state as a journalist, speech and grants writer, educator, and director of nonprofit organizations. His diverse professional experiences include chronicling the efforts of state farmers and rural communities and teaching creative writing in public schools. He has directed programs to bring Holocaust education to Arkansas students and generated support for museums, health initiatives, youth programs, and housing. He is also a national champion masters swimmer and an avid mandolin player.

CPSIA information can be obtained
at www.ICGtesting.com
Printed in the USA
BVHW081956130721
611303BV00001B/2